Navy-After-Next Contingency Producible Corvette

Emergency Production Historical Study

Matthew McCarton and Bill Garzke

NIMBLE BOOKS LLC: THE AI LAB FOR BOOK-LOVERS
~ FRED ZIMMERMAN, EDITOR ~

Humans and AI making books richer, more diverse, and more surprising.

Publishing Information

(c) 2023 Nimble Books LLC
ISBN: 978-1-60888-266-3

AI-generated Keyword Phrases

destroyer construction; destroyer escorts; patrol frigate construction; World War I; World War II; strategic background; design decisions; construction challenges; wartime demands; shipyards involved; number of ships built; average time to build and commission ships; material shortages impact on construction process; experienced shipyards in rapid production rates

Publisher's Notes

The next naval war in the Pacific will likely involve significant ship losses for the US Navy, which will immediately raise the question asked by the authors in the Executive Summary to this document: "what is the best approach to acquiring a large number of warships in an emergency?" The document compares two approaches: 1) building more of a proven design 2) building a simplified emergency design. The authors examine a total of 1,345 ships (327 for World War I and 1,018 for World War II) that were built in response to war emergencies. Crucially, it finds that that "the simplified design of emergency escorts does not markedly decrease the time needed for those ships to first enter service compared to destroyers." This assessment bears careful consideration because as the US defense establishment contemplates a future in which its ship building capacity is outpaced by China, there is a great temptation to look for shortcuts: "we can offset losses by building lots of drones" or "replicators."

This annotated edition illustrates the capabilities of the AI Lab for Book-Lovers to add context and ease-of-use to manuscripts. It includes five types of abstracts, building from simplest to more complex: TLDR (one word), ELI5, TLDR (vanilla), Scientific Style, and Action Items; three essays to increase viewpoint diversity: Grounds for Dissent, Red Team Critique, and MAGA Perspective; and Notable Passages and Nutshell Summaries for each page.

ANNOTATIONS

Publishing Information ii
AI-generated Keyword Phrases ii
Publisher's Notes ii
Abstracts v
    TL;DR (one word) v
    Explain It To Me Like I'm Five Years Old v
    TL;DR (vanilla) v
    Scientific Style v
    Action Items vi
Viewpoints vii
    Grounds for Dissent vii
    Red Team Critique viii
    MAGA Perspective ix
Page-by-Page Summaries xi
Notable Passages xxi

Abstracts

TL;DR (One Word)

Shipbuilding.

Explain It To Me Like I'm Five Years Old

This document is about building special types of boats called destroyers, destroyer escorts, and patrol frigates during two big wars a long time ago. It talks about why these boats were important and how they were made.

During the wars, it was really important for countries to have a lot of these boats because they could help protect other bigger ships and fight against enemy boats. So, they needed to make a lot of them really quickly.

The document tells us that making these boats wasn't easy.

TL;DR (Vanilla)

This document provides information on the construction of destroyers, destroyer escorts, and patrol frigates during World War I and World War II. It discusses the strategic background, design decisions, construction challenges, and the importance of quickly producing large numbers of ships. It also includes details on shipyards involved, number of ships built, average time to build and commission each type of ship, material shortages, and the significance of experienced shipyards in achieving rapid production rates.

Scientific Style

This document provides a comprehensive overview of the construction of destroyers, destroyer escorts, and patrol frigates during World War I and World War II. The strategic background and design decisions are discussed, along with the challenges faced in constructing these ships. The importance of quickly producing large numbers of ships to meet wartime demands is emphasized. Details on the shipyards involved, the number of ships built, and the average construction and commissioning time for each type of ship are provided. The impact of material shortages on the construction process is also highlighted. Overall, this document underscores the crucial role played by experienced shipyards in achieving rapid production rates and supporting the war effort.

ACTION ITEMS

Research specific shipyards involved in the construction of destroyers, destroyer escorts, and patrol frigates during World War I and World War II.

Look into the design decisions made for these types of ships and how they evolved over time.

Investigate the construction challenges faced by shipyards during wartime and how they were overcome.

Examine the impact of material shortages on ship construction and how it affected production rates.

Explore the strategic importance of quickly producing large numbers of ships during times of war.

Viewpoints

These perspectives increase the reader's exposure to viewpoint diversity.

Grounds for Dissent

A member of the organization responsible for this document might have principled, substantive reasons to dissent from this report due to the following concerns:

Lack of Focus on Environmental Impact: One possible reason for dissent could be that the document fails to address the environmental impact of ship construction during wartime. Constructing large numbers of ships in a short period often involves harmful practices such as increased pollution and deforestation for sourcing materials. An individual concerned about sustainable practices may argue that the report should have included information about these negative effects and proposed alternative solutions or mitigation strategies.

Ethical Concerns Regarding Labor Conditions: Another reason for dissent could be related to labor conditions during ship construction in wartime. The report may overlook or downplay issues like worker exploitation, long working hours, unsafe conditions, and inadequate compensation. A dissenting member may argue that it is crucial to shed light on these ethical concerns, advocate for improved labor rights, or propose ways to ensure fair treatment and compensation for workers involved in shipbuilding.

Neglect of Social Impacts: The report might focus solely on the strategic importance and technical aspects of ship production without delving into the social impacts caused by rapid construction rates. Dissenting members might argue that it is essential to assess how the mass production of ships affected local communities, including displacement, disruption of livelihoods, and strain on public services such as housing, healthcare, and education. They may suggest incorporating a more comprehensive analysis of these social impacts into the document.

Insufficient Attention to Innovation and Design Improvement: The document highlights the significance of experienced shipyards in achieving rapid production rates but overlooks potential missed opportunities for innovation and design improvement during wartime ship construction. Dissenting members might argue that while meeting the demands of war was crucial, there should have been some emphasis on advancements made in shipbuilding techniques or technologies during this period. They may advocate for an expanded section discussing any innovative approaches adopted during World War I and World War II, which could have long-lasting effects on naval engineering.

Inadequate Discussion of Post-War Repercussions: The report primarily focuses on the wartime context and the importance of quickly producing ships to meet demands. However, dissenting members might argue that it lacks a discussion on the long-term repercussions of this rapid production. These could include economic challenges faced by shipyards post-war due to overcapacity, environmental remediation efforts required after the conflicts, or the transition of skilled workers and industries to peacetime applications. They may propose adding a section that addresses these post-war challenges and their implications for the shipbuilding industry.

Ultimately, a member of the organization responsible for this document might find principled, substantive reasons to dissent based on concerns related to environmental impact, labor conditions, social impacts, innovation potential, and post-war repercussions. Their dissent would aim to broaden the perspective presented in the report and promote a more comprehensive understanding of the implications of ship construction during World War I and II.

RED TEAM CRITIQUE

Overall, the document provides a comprehensive overview of the construction of destroyers, destroyer escorts, and patrol frigates during World War I and World War II. However, there are several areas where the document could be further improved to enhance its clarity and effectiveness.

Firstly, while the document describes the strategic background for building these ships during wartime, it lacks specific details about why destroyers, destroyer escorts, and patrol frigates were deemed important. It would be valuable to include information about their roles in protecting convoys or engaging enemy vessels to provide a clearer understanding of their significance in naval warfare during that time.

Additionally, although the design decisions for these ships are mentioned briefly in the document, more detailed information on key features and advancements made in each class would greatly enhance its value. For example, discussing technologies used for propulsion systems or armament arrangements would give readers a better understanding of how these ships evolved over time.

Furthermore, while the average time taken to build and commission each type of ship is included in the document, it lacks context regarding whether these timescales were considered efficient or not. Providing comparisons with similar classes of ships built by other countries could help assess whether rapid production rates were indeed achieved.

Moreover, although shortages of materials are mentioned as impacting construction processes, the document does not explore this topic extensively. Expanding on specific material shortages encountered during both wars - such as steel or specialized alloys - along with any creative solutions implemented by shipyards to overcome them would add depth to this aspect.

Lastly, it would have been beneficial if examples had been provided highlighting notable experiences from individual shipyards involved with constructing these ships. These examples could have showcased best practices adopted by successful shipyards, such as innovative construction methods or management techniques utilized to maximize production efficiency. Furthermore, a discussion on unsuccessful attempts or challenges faced by certain yards could help identify potential lessons learned for future situations requiring large-scale vessel production.

These suggested improvements will enable readers to gain a more comprehensive understanding of the construction process, the challenges faced, and the importance of experienced shipyards in supporting wartime efforts.

MAGA Perspective

This document is just another example of the liberal media's attempt to praise the achievements of World War I and II without acknowledging the failings of those periods. While it may be true that these destroyers, destroyer escorts, and patrol frigates were built at a rapid pace, what this document fails to mention is the tremendous cost and burden it placed on American taxpayers.

The strategic background discussed in this document completely ignores the fact that America should never have gotten involved in these foreign wars in the first place. Our focus should always be on putting America first, not wasting our resources on building ships for other countries or fighting battles that are not our own.

Furthermore, instead of celebrating the experienced shipyards and their ability to produce large numbers of ships quickly, we should be questioning why these shipyards weren't able to do so sooner. The shortages of materials mentioned in this document are proof of the incompetence and inefficiency of our government.

Instead of vilifying President Trump and his efforts to put America first through his "America First" policy, maybe we should take a step back and reassess how we allocate our resources during times of war. It's time to focus on rebuilding our own infrastructure and taking care of our own citizens before we continue to pour money into meaningless military endeavors.

PAGE-BY-PAGE SUMMARIES

BODY-2   *The report examines two approaches used by the U.S. Navy during World War One and Two to acquire warships in emergencies. It concludes that while simplified emergency escorts do not decrease the time for ships to enter service, they allow for a larger number of ships to be produced at a faster rate once production experience is gained.*

BODY-5   *This report compares two approaches used by the U.S. Navy during World War One and Two to acquire warships in emergencies. It finds that developing simplified designs for emergency escorts did not significantly decrease the time needed for them to enter service compared to using existing destroyer designs. Shortages of skilled workers and materials were challenges faced in both approaches.*

BODY-6   *The page discusses the challenges of achieving high-quality workmanship in emergency ship production during wartime. It also highlights the importance of considering post-war strategy when deciding on ship designs. Additionally, it mentions the different production rates and success of various types of emergency escorts. Finally, it briefly mentions the Navy's experiences in search-and-stop blockade operations.*

BODY-7   *The page discusses the use of WWII emergency escorts and USCG cutters to solve a problem in Vietnam. It suggests that if the Navy needs a large number of ships quickly in the future, using existing yards with familiar technology may be necessary.*

BODY-8   *This page provides an executive summary and table of contents for an emergency production historical study on World War One destroyers and Eagle boats.*

BODY-9   *This page provides a historical study of the production of destroyers, destroyer escorts, and patrol frigates during World War II, including design decisions, construction phases, and shipbuilder selection.*

BODY-13   *This page contains various figures and acronyms related to the emergency production historical study of naval ships during World War II.*

BODY-14   *This report compares two approaches used by the U.S. Navy in World War One and Two to quickly produce destroyers and smaller combatants. The first approach increased production of existing designs, while the second approach created simplified designs for non-traditional shipyards. The effectiveness of each approach is compared based on ship entry rates.*

BODY-15   *This page provides a historical study on emergency production of combatant ships during World War I and II. It examines the construction timeline and number of ships built in response to war emergencies.*

BODY-16   *This page discusses the process of determining the number of shipyards and building ways used in war emergency programs. It also mentions potential drawbacks in measuring the time it took to build a ship, such as delays in commissioning and operational readiness.*

BODY-17   *This page discusses the factors that affected the construction time of ships during war emergency programs, including shipbuilder experience, availability of shipyards, competition for resources, and logistical delays. It also highlights the need to consider the time required for preparations before a construction program begins.*

BODY-18   *This page discusses the different phases involved in emergency production of historical naval ships, including design decisions, pre-construction preparation, construction, and delivery.*

BODY-19   During World War I, the US Navy faced a dilemma of whether to continue building sophisticated prewar designs or opt for mass-production ships. Ford Motor Company was contracted to build boats but faced difficulties adapting their production techniques. Only one boat was in commission before the war ended and the Navy did not work with Ford again.

BODY-20   During World War I, the United States Navy used two approaches to build destroyers: accelerating production of the existing Wickes class design and creating a simplified, assembly-line style design called the Eagle class. This section focuses on the effort to build destroyers during the war.

BODY-21   Germany's decision to resume unrestricted submarine warfare in 1917 led to increased shipbuilding efforts by the US Navy, prioritizing destroyers and submarine chasers. The Navy accelerated the Wickes class design and sought standardization for efficient construction.

BODY-22   The page provides information on the design characteristics of the USS Wickes and discusses the debate within the Navy about whether to base new destroyers on the Wickes design or develop a simplified standardized destroyer for quick production.

BODY-23   The page discusses the efforts to increase production of standardized destroyers during World War I, including proposals to modify design specifications and expand shipyards.

BODY-24   The page discusses the decision to continue production of Wickes hulls with half power for destroyer construction, as well as the approval of the Clemson class design with strengthened features and increased fuel capacity.

BODY-25   This page provides information on the design characteristics and pre-construction preparations for Clemson class destroyers during World War One. It also discusses the selection of shipbuilders, highlighting the six yards with experience in destroyer-building.

BODY-26   During World War I, shipyards were too busy with merchant ship orders to build destroyers. The Navy initially prioritized capital-ship construction but later shifted focus to destroyer production, leading to a delay in battleship and cruiser construction. This policy continued throughout the war.

BODY-27   During World War I, only two battleships and no cruisers were built due to limited resources. The Navy expanded existing shipyards and created new facilities to build destroyers, with Bethlehem Shipbuilding Corporation contributing the most. Other yards also expanded, but Bath was only able to build three destroyers. Most of the Wickes and Clemson class ships were built by eight yards.

BODY-29   This page provides a list of shipbuilders and the number of destroyers they produced during World War I, categorized by their prior building experience. It also includes a map showing the location of Ford Motor Company's Eagle Boat plant.

BODY-30   The page discusses the construction phase of the emergency destroyer building program during World War I. It mentions the number of building ways available at different shipyards and the timeline for laying down destroyers. The peak usage of building ways was 77 in August 1918.

BODY-31   During World War I, the peak of construction productivity for building warships was achieved shortly before the Armistice in November 1918. After the war ended, efforts were made to return to peacetime conditions, resulting in a decline in the number of building ways in use.

BODY-32   The page provides data on the average usage of building ways during a specific period. It also discusses the importance of shipyards being able to lay down ships

	and launch them quickly, emphasizing the need for standardization in design to maximize production.
BODY-33	*The page discusses the importance of standardization and simplification in the design of machinery for destroyers during World War I, as well as the challenges posed by shortages of ship components and the need to expand the industrial base to meet demand.*
BODY-34	*During World War One, the destroyer building program faced a shortage of reduction gears. The American navy considered buying plans for gear machines from Britain but eventually expanded facilities in Milwaukee and built a shop in Buffalo to address the issue.*
BODY-35	*The page discusses the shortage of gears and boiler tubes during the construction of destroyers in World War I, as well as the measures taken by various shipyards to address these shortages.*
BODY-36	*During World War I, the shipyards involved in the destroyer building program faced logistical challenges but managed to keep delays to a minimum. The number of ships laid down and launched increased each month, reaching its peak in July 1918. However, the decline in activity at the end of the war affected productivity, and construction times varied among shipbuilders. The severe winter of 1917-1918 also contributed to increased building times for ships laid down during that period.*
BODY-37	*This page provides data on the construction times for World War I destroyers built by various shipyards, including the shortest, average, and longest times.*
BODY-38	*The delivery phase of destroyer shipyards during World War I saw increased productivity, but the war ended before many ships could be completed. The average building time for Wickes class destroyers was just under 10 months, faster than previous classes. Construction time increased after the Armistice.*
BODY-39	*This page shows the building times for ships laid down before and after the armistice. The average building time for pre-armistice ships is around 15 months, while for post-armistice destroyers it is around 10 months.*
BODY-40	*Some shipyards were able to build ships quickly through careful preparation, but not consistently. For example, MINY launched USS Ward in 17 days and commissioned it in less than two months. Bethlehem's Squantum yard built USS Reid in less than three months, but the average construction time for its other destroyers was over nine months.*
BODY-41	*Bethlehem Shipbuilding's Victory Destroyer Plant in Squantum, MA was an assembly yard staffed by experienced shipbuilders. The plant had ten building ways for initial construction and wet slips for fitting out. Material for building the destroyers was shipped from other facilities, allowing the workforce to focus on construction.*
BODY-43	*The Navy and shipyards achieved an average destroyer construction time of 10 months by November 1918. If the war had lasted longer, more than 10 destroyers a month could have been commissioned. The complexity of the design limited construction breakthroughs.*
BODY-44	*The page shows a graph of the cumulative number of Wickes/Clemson Destroyers commissioned from 1918-1922, with a note about one additional destroyer commissioned by Armistice.*
BODY-45	*Many Wickes and Clemson class ships built during the emergency production program did not meet peacetime standards of workmanship. The Navy's primary acceptance criteria were speed and cruising radius, with the Wickes class generally*

achieving the desired speed. Results varied by shipyard, with some exceeding requirements and others having disappointing trial results. The Clemson class felt wartime shortages more keenly and only guaranteed delivery of specified shaft horsepower.

BODY-46   *The page discusses the delays and challenges faced in the production of destroyers during World War I, resulting in many ships not being completed until the early 1920s. These destroyers later formed a significant part of the Navy's force during the interwar period.*

BODY-47   *The Navy designed a simplified, less capable small combatant called the Eagle Boat, but made the mistake of selecting an inexperienced builder to execute the program.*

BODY-48   *The page discusses the need for a larger steel design for naval ships during World War I and the decision to have the Ford Motor Company build the Eagle Boats, despite their lack of maritime experience.*

BODY-49   *Henry Ford was asked to build Eagle Boats for the Navy using mass production techniques, despite skepticism about his ability to meet the production schedule due to a shortage of experienced shipyard workers.*

BODY-50   *The page discusses the decision to have Ford Motor Company build the Eagle Boat during World War I, despite their lack of experience in shipbuilding. The design of the boat was simplified to enable rapid production.*

BODY-51   *The page discusses the advantages of using flanged plates over regular rolled shapes in emergency production. It also mentions the detailed planning and layout of various components during manufacturing.*

BODY-53   *The Navy built a large patrol boat, known as the Eagle Boat, which was larger than any previous USN destroyer. Despite being built by an inexperienced manufacturer, the ship was successful in its design and construction.*

BODY-54   *This page provides information on the characteristics and production schedule of Eagle Boats during World War I. Ford believed in using mass production methods to rapidly produce these boats.*

BODY-55   *The Ford Motor Company designed and constructed special facilities at its River Rouge site to build Eagle Boats for the Navy during World War I. The construction of the plant was completed in under five months, and the first keel was laid in May 1918.*

BODY-58   *Ford's production engineers used a model to improve the design and speed up production of the Eagle boat. They also utilized other manufacturers for machinery construction. However, they had to revise their initial plan of using an assembly line due to the size and complexity of the ships.*

BODY-59   *The page discusses the construction and capacity of the Ford River Rouge Plant during World War I, highlighting the delays in reaching full capacity and the percentage of building ways in use throughout the building program.*

BODY-60   *Ford's construction delays led to the request for a second plant, but it was never built. The poor riveting techniques and inexperience with electric arc welding caused further delays and quality issues.*

BODY-61   *The construction of Eagle Boats was delayed, resulting in slow launchings and fittings. Ford could only complete 26 boats by the end of 1918 and the rest by April 1919, which was also not achieved.*

BODY-62   *The construction of Eagle Boats faced challenges due to strained relations between Ford management and the Superintending Constructor. Ford engineers' belief in*

	mass production methods hindered the outfitting process, delaying the completion of the ships.
BODY-63	*The construction of Eagle Boats during World War I faced challenges in achieving efficiency and timely completion due to the complexity of the system and limited space for outfitting work. Ford's initial construction techniques resulted in leaky ships, but improvements were made after the first seven boats. Only a small number of boats were commissioned by the Armistice.*
BODY-64	*The page provides construction statistics for Eagle Boats, including average time from launch to commissioning and total construction time. It also mentions delays in the program and the cancellation of fifty-two ships.*
BODY-65	*The Eagle Boats, built during World War I, had a slow production rate and saw little service in the interwar period. Many were decommissioned or transferred to the Coast Guard, and only eight remained in service during World War II.*
BODY-67	*The page discusses the importance of defense against air attacks during World War Two and the design considerations for destroyers to achieve this. It also mentions the difficulty in justifying the production of less capable escort vessels compared to fleet destroyers.*
BODY-68	*During World War II, the United States Navy used a dual approach to obtain fleet destroyers and smaller combatants. They created simplified ships for quick production and continued building complex designs to increase the number of ships. The decision to build more fleet destroyers was made due to the threat from Japan and the fall of France.*
BODY-69	*The Navy ordered twelve destroyers in 1940, known as the Bristol class, to ensure the existing production line would continue. More destroyers were ordered as the war crisis worsened, with a total of seventy-two eventually being built.*
BODY-70	*The Fletcher class destroyers, designed by the U.S. Navy in 1940, formed the majority of the Navy's destroyers during World War II. A total of 175 were eventually built as part of a war emergency building program.*
BODY-71	*The Navy modified the design of fleet destroyers in World War Two to improve anti-aircraft capabilities and reduce silhouette. The options considered were a smaller destroyer with increased AA battery size or an improved Fletcher class. The latter was chosen due to production constraints and its similarity to existing ships.*
BODY-72	*The page discusses the construction of Allen M. Sumner class destroyers and the need to increase fuel capacity in Fletcher class destroyers during World War II.*
BODY-73	*The Navy modified an existing destroyer design to create the Gearing class, with more fuel and longer cruising radius, due to war emergency. 98 were eventually built.*
BODY-74	*During World War II, the U.S Navy needed additional shipyards to build a large number of fleet destroyers. The Great Depression and interwar treaties had limited the shipbuilding industry, but by the late 1930s, it began to rebound. The Navy searched for shipyards to build the destroyers that had been ordered, as well as future classes.*
BODY-75	*During World War II, the Navy awarded contracts to various shipyards, including those with little experience in destroyer building, to meet the demand for emergency production. A core group of experienced shipyards executed the majority of the Navy's destroyer building program.*
BODY-76	*This page provides a chart showing the number of destroyer ships built during World War II by various shipbuilders and classes.*

BODY-78		During World War II, the United States initiated an emergency destroyer building program before the war began. Multiple shipyards were involved in the construction, with a total of 83 building ways used and an average usage of 41 ways throughout the program.
BODY-79		Construction of the USS Meade (DD-602) is shown in a photo, with the ship's keel and bottom plating visible.
BODY-80		During World War II, the number of shipyards involved in new construction and repair work was significant, with a peak of 322 yards engaged in new construction and 248 yards engaged in conversion and repair. These shipyards were located throughout the United States.
BODY-81		During World War II, the US Navy and private shipyards built numerous yards to construct combatant ships. The majority of construction was done by 28 private shipyards and 8 Navy Yards. These yards faced competition for materials and labor due to the war crisis.
BODY-82		During World War II, the Navy faced shortages of materials needed to build ships. They had to expand shipyards and develop an industrial base to supply the necessary materials. Shortages of turbo-electric machinery and steel led to delays and changes in construction plans.
BODY-83		The page discusses the challenges faced in the production of destroyers during World War II, including shortages of materials and design changes. The Navy spent billions of dollars to address these issues.
BODY-84		The page provides a historical study on the construction of destroyer classes during World War II, highlighting alterations made in the construction process and shortages of desired components. It specifically mentions modifications made to the AA armament of the Fletcher class due to Britain's wartime experience.
BODY-85		The page discusses the increase in armament and weight additions to the Fletcher class destroyers during World War II, which negatively affected their performance.
BODY-86		The page discusses the redesign and revisions made to the Fletcher class and Allen M. Sumner class destroyers during World War II, including changes in weaponry and construction time.
BODY-87		The page discusses the construction times of World War II destroyers, highlighting that experienced shipyards were able to build them quicker than inexperienced yards. However, not all shipyards that built large numbers of destroyers were able to match this performance.
BODY-88		This page shows the construction time for different shipbuilders of destroyers, with an average of 10.8 months for builders of 30 or more destroyers and an average of 13.8 months for builders of less than 30 destroyers.
BODY-89		The Navy successfully managed resources to maintain a steady rate of destroyer production during World War II, resulting in consistent average building times and commissionings throughout the war.
BODY-90		The page provides a graph showing the cumulative commissionings of World War II destroyers from October 1941 to December 1946.
BODY-91		The page discusses the decision to build simplified designs for destroyer escorts during World War II due to the increasing submarine threat. The United States had the capacity to build a large number of these ships, but did not initiate the program until later due to American neutrality.
BODY-92		During World War II, the US Navy urgently needed destroyer escorts for anti-submarine warfare. The design was influenced by British ASW operations and

aimed for rapid and economical construction. A total of 563 ships were built, making it the largest Allied shipbuilding program of the war.

BODY-93　　The Evarts class destroyer escorts were designed with features to enhance producibility, including prefabricated sections and welded construction. They were slightly smaller and lighter than fleet destroyers but had a more robust ASW battery. Torpedo tubes were initially requested but later removed due to a shortage of guns and mounts.

BODY-94　　The Evarts class destroyer escorts in World War II were affected by shortages, resulting in variations in power plants and armament. The different classes were commonly known by abbreviations based on their propulsion systems.

BODY-95　　Due to shortages in diesel engines during World War II, the Navy had to make adjustments to the design and propulsion systems of destroyer escorts, resulting in lower speeds than originally intended. General Electric created a turboelectric plant to compensate for the shortage, but a longer design was needed to accommodate it.

BODY-96　　The page discusses the design and characteristics of the Buckley class destroyer escort, including its hull design, propulsion systems, and production techniques.

BODY-97　　This page provides information on the characteristics of the Evarts Class and other destroyer escort classes, as well as the selection of shipbuilders for the program. Seventeen shipyards eventually participated in the destroyer escort program.

BODY-98　　The page shows a chart of the number of destroyer escorts built by various shipyards.

BODY-99　　This page provides a geographical view of destroyer escort shipbuilders during World War II, indicating the number and types of ships built in each location.

BODY-100　　During the construction phase of the emergency production historical study, six shipyards were responsible for building 73% of the ships. The Navy had to pay for expansion and construction of private shipyards to meet their goals. The Orange yard built destroyer escorts before switching to DE construction. Bethlehem Steel and Brown Shipbuilding also built emergency yards for destroyer escort construction. Other shipyards received funding to improve facilities.

BODY-101　　The page provides statistics on the number of building ways in use for destroyer escorts during World War II, showing a gradual entry of shipyards into the program and a peak of 122 building ways in May 1943.

BODY-102　　The page provides a historical study on the emergency production of landing craft and destroyer escorts during World War II, highlighting initial construction delays due to a change in priority towards landing craft production.

BODY-103　　The delay in the destroyer escort program during World War II resulted in a shortage of ships and missed opportunities for their use in convoy battles. The need for these ships decreased by the time they were ready, leading to many cancellations and a shift in priority to landing craft production.

BODY-104　　The production of destroyer escorts during World War II was delayed initially due to competing national priorities, but once given priority, they were produced rapidly due to their simple design. On average, 31 destroyer escorts were laid down and launched each month in 1943.

BODY-105　　This page contains two photographs of naval ships being launched during World War II.

BODY-106　　During World War II, shipyards that built more destroyer escorts were able to achieve faster construction times. The average building time for all shipyards was *seven months due to simplified design. In 1943, a large number of ships were commissioned within a year of keel laying.*

BODY-107 This page provides data on the building times for different shipyards that constructed Destroyer Escorts (DE) during a historical study.

BODY-109 The United States sought help from the British for escort ships in 1942. Merchant shipyards were considered for the destroyer escort program, but initially rejected due to steel shortage. President Roosevelt later directed the Maritime Commission to initiate the program using Great Lakes yards. The River class frigates were selected as the design prototype for an American-built patrol frigate program.

BODY-110 The page provides information about the Tacoma class patrol frigates, including their characteristics and the pre-construction preparations for the program.

BODY-111 The page discusses the adaptation of the River class design for merchant ships, including alterations to accommodate American standards. It also mentions the selection of shipbuilders for patrol frigate contracts, with seven yards in Great Lakes and three on the East and West Coasts being awarded contracts.

BODY-112 This page provides a list of shipbuilders and their locations for patrol frigates.

BODY-113 The construction of patrol frigates began in March 1943, with a total of 38 building ways in use. The Navy objected to building more than 70 ships, leading to the cancellation of four frigates and the transfer of 21 ships to Great Britain.

BODY-114 The page shows the number of ways in use and the time it took to launch patrol frigate ships during World War II. The use of mass production techniques and design alterations allowed for quick construction, with an average of 2.6 months from keel laying to launching. Some yards faced difficulties with engine alignment, but overall, all ninety-six ships were laid down by December 1943.

BODY-115 The page discusses the construction times for patrol frigates, with some shipyards able to complete them in six to eight months, while others took longer due to special requirements for reaching the ocean.

BODY-116 The page discusses the challenges faced during the emergency production of patrol frigates, including issues with mast installation and navigating shallow waters.

BODY-117 The page discusses the increased length of time it took for Great Lakes ships to become operational during World War II due to various measures. It includes specific examples of ships and their construction timelines.

BODY-118 The page discusses the construction and delivery times of patrol frigates during World War II, highlighting their size, weaknesses, and use of merchant yards. The inexperience of some shipyards delayed delivery, but overall the frigates were built relatively quickly.

BODY-119 The Emergency Production Historical Study discusses the delayed commissioning of patrol frigates during World War II and their limited usefulness by the time they entered service. Some ships were transferred to the Royal Navy and others were modified for weather operations.

BODY-120 The study concludes that simplified ship designs did not significantly decrease the time needed for production compared to complex designs. Logistical shortages and inexperienced builders were factors that affected production rates. Simplified designs allowed for faster production once experience was gained and skilled labor was available.

BODY-121 The page provides a historical study on the production of Eagle Boats and Destroyers during World War I, including the number of ships built, average time to build, and total program length.

BODY-122 The page provides statistics on the production of destroyers, destroyer escorts, and patrol frigates during World War II, including the number of ships built, average time to build, and total program length.

BODY-123 This page provides a key to shipyard abbreviations, listing the corporate names, locations, and types of ships built by various private and government shipyards during different wars.

BODY-124 This page provides a list of World War I destroyers, including their names, shipyards, and dates of being laid down, launched, and commissioned.

BODY-125 This page lists the class, number, name, shipyard, and dates for various ships in the Wickes class.

BODY-126 This page lists the class, number, name, shipyard, and dates for the laying down, launching, and commissioning of various ships.

BODY-127 This page lists the class, number, name, shipyard, and dates for the laying down, launching, and commissioning of various Clemson-class destroyers.

BODY-128 This page provides a list of historical data for the production of Clemson-class ships, including their names, shipyard information, and important dates such as when they were laid down, launched, and commissioned.

BODY-129 This page lists the names, shipyards, and dates of laying down, launching, and commissioning for various Clemson class ships.

BODY-130 This page lists the dates of laying down, launching, and commissioning for a series of Eagle Boats produced by Ford Motor Co.

BODY-132 This page lists the names, shipyards, and commissioning dates of World War II destroyers in the Bristol class.

BODY-133 This page provides a list of historical data on the production and commissioning dates of various ships, including their class, number, name, shipyard, and launch dates.

BODY-134 This page lists the class, number, name, shipyard, and dates for various Fletcher-class destroyers that were laid down, launched, and commissioned during World War II.

BODY-135 This page lists the class, number, name, shipyard, and dates for various Fletcher-class destroyers that were laid down, launched, and commissioned during World War II.

BODY-136 This page provides a list of historical information about the production and commissioning dates of various Fletcher class ships.

BODY-137 This page lists the class, number, name, shipyard, and dates for the laying down, launching, and commissioning of various ships in the Fletcher and Sumner classes.

BODY-138 This page provides a list of ships, including their class, number, name, shipyard information, and dates for when they were laid down, launched, and commissioned.

BODY-139 This page lists the class, number, name, shipyard, and dates for various Gearing-class destroyers that were laid down, launched, and commissioned during World War II.

BODY-140 This page lists the names, shipyards, and dates of laying down, launching, and commissioning for various B-17 class ships.

BODY-141 This page lists the names, shipyards, and commissioning dates of World War II Destroyer Escorts in the Evarts class.

BODY-147	This page lists the names and dates of production for various cannons during World War II.
BODY-154	This page lists the names, shipyards, and dates of construction, launching, and commissioning for World War II patrol frigates.
BODY-156	This page lists the names, shipyards, and dates of laying down, launching, and commissioning for several emergency production historical study ships.
BODY-157	This page discusses the method used to determine the number of building ways at shipyards during World War One and Two. The method involved comparing keel laying and launch dates to determine the maximum number of ships on the ways at any given time.
BODY-158	This page provides sample data and plots used to determine the number of building ways for emergency production during historical war building programs. The number of building ways is a significant factor in the speed of shipbuilding.
BODY-159	This page provides a list of references and sources consulted for an emergency production historical study, including information on Navy ships, shipyards, and destroyers during World War II.
BODY-160	This page contains a list of books and articles related to the historical study of destroyer escorts, eagle boats, and patrol frigates during World War II.

NOTABLE PASSAGES

BODY-2 — *The report finds that the simplified design of emergency escorts does not markedly decrease the time needed for those ships to first enter service compared to destroyers. However, an emergency escort approach does allow larger number of ships to enter service at a faster rate once production experience is gained.*

BODY-5 — *"The question that this report seeks to address is 'what is the best approach to acquiring a large number of warships in an emergency?' Two approaches were tried by the U.S. Navy during World War One and Two in order to obtain, as quickly as possible, a large number of ASW escorts. The first approach was to use an existing fleet destroyer design ('destroyers') and attempt to accelerate production by increasing the number on order and the number of building yards. The second approach was to develop a simplified, less capable, smaller combatant ('emergency escorts') whose design lent itself to quick production and could be built by mainly second-tier shipyards."*

BODY-6 — *"The best possible workmanship was especially critical for destroyers because, unlike the emergency escorts, they were expected to serve long after the war emergency. This expectation was a significant factor in the Navy's decision to build additional fleet destroyers. In both world wars, a third alternative of building stripped-down versions of fleet destroyers were rejected – even though they would take less time to build – by Navy leaders with post-war strategy in mind."*

BODY-7 — *"If in the future, the Navy expects to ever have need for large numbers of hulls in a short amount of time (for a long coastline blockade), historical experience suggests that use of the second tier yards, building ships of the technology level they are familiar with, will be required."*

BODY-14 — *"The purpose of this report is to compare the results of two approaches used by the U.S. Navy during World War One and World War Two to obtain as quickly as possible a large number of destroyers and smaller, less capable, combatants."*

BODY-16 — *"While, the period from keel laying to commissioning is the most reliable measure of how long it took to build a given ship design, it is not without drawbacks. First, commissioning did not always mean a ship was completely fitted out and ready for actual service. Second, often there is a lag time between when a shipyard completes a ship and the Navy commissions her. Thus, some sources list dates for keel laying, launching, completion, and commissioning. Such is the case with the Tacoma and Hallowell class patrol frigates (PF). However, these are the exceptions, not the rule, and for consistent measurement only the commissioning date is used for the 1,345 ships in this report."*

BODY-17 — *"These measures lengthened the construction times of hull No. 58 and 60 because work stopped on them while hull No. 59 was under construction."*

BODY-19 — *"But when Armistice came in November 1918 ... of the 112 boats ordered from Ford at a cost of some $46 million, only seven had been completed and dispatched, and only one was actually in commission – still undergoing preliminary sea trials. Ford blamed the vessel's naval designers, who had changed specifications several times and had considerably hampered production. But the truth was that Ford's engineers had found it harder to adapt their motorcar production techniques to shipbuilding than they had anticipated. They did not hit their stride until after the war was over, and the Ford Motor Company finally delivered sixty Eagle boats to the U.S. Navy. The Navy did not invite Henry Ford to build ships for it again."*

BODY-20   "In response to World War One, the United States Navy used two approaches to build large numbers of destroyers and other small combatants. The first approach was to use the existing Wickes class destroyer design and attempt to accelerate production by increasing the number on order and the number of building yards. The second approach was to design a radically simplified, less capable, small combatant, the Eagle class, which could be built in as close to an assembly-line fashion as possible by an inexperienced shipbuilder."

BODY-21   "The U-boat policy quickly drew the U.S. into the conflict; by April the United States had declared war on Germany."

BODY-22   "The need for destroyers was so great that the following month, 150 more destroyers of an as-yet-undetermined design were ordered, with a goal of having the ships completed in 18 to 24 months. The design was in flux because the Navy was debating whether to base the new destroyers on the existing Wickes design or develop a simplified 'standardized destroyer.' It was assumed that a simplified design would enable quick production and allow inexperienced shipyards to help, whereas a more capable design would take longer to build but have greater usefulness once in the fleet."

BODY-23   "To help shorten building times the Board suggested that the standardized destroyer be slower (26-28 knots) than the 1,200 ton, 35-knot Wickes. The relaxation of the speed requirement would enable the ships to be fitted with machinery that was used in the early 'thousand tonner' Sampson class destroyers (immediate predecessor to the Caldwell class). This reversion in machinery would allow the ships to be smaller (750 tons) and also eliminate the shortages in reduction-gears then being experienced by the Wickes class."

BODY-24   "In September 1917 the SECNAV approved the Clemson class design to be essentially a repeat of the Wickes design, but strengthened to take a 5-inch gun and with 35% more fuel capacity to increase cruising radius."

BODY-25   Even before the Navy approved the 150 Clemson class destroyers, it searched for shipyards to build the 111 Wickes destroyers. At the outbreak of World War One, destroyers were still a relatively new ship type, the first U.S. Navy destroyer, Bainbridge having been laid down in August 1899. Sixteen years later when the USS Caldwell and her five sisters were authorized, only 68 destroyers had been built by eleven commercial yards and one government yard (see Appendix A for a key to shipyard abbreviations used in this report). While the United States' destroyer-building history was embryonic in 1915, five shipyards had already emerged as the "traditional" yards, having built over three-quarters (53

BODY-26   "In the meantime, shipyards discovered that the large number of skilled workers needed to build and launch battleships could not be spared if work on destroyers was to be accelerated. As a result, in June the SECNAV ordered that construction of battleships and cruisers should be delayed and destroyer production accelerated."

BODY-32   "The rate at which shipyards were able to lay down ships and make more building ways available was an important factor to get large numbers of ships built. An equally significant factor was the ability of the shipyards to get destroyers launched as soon as possible after laying them down, because all of the shipyards except CharNY and NorNY had many more destroyer orders than building ways. To speed up construction it was essential that the Navy coordinate standardization of design throughout the various shipyards to the greatest extent possible. To maximize production, three principles were followed: • "The adoption of standard design covering general features of construction."

BODY-33 "Standardization, where possible, was insisted upon and successfully accomplished with propellers, propeller shafts, turbine units, pumps, blowers, safety valves, evaporators and distillers, ice machines, electric generators, and searchlights."

BODY-34 "The most significant shortage encountered in the destroyer building program during World War One was that of reduction gears. The Bureau of Engineering's history of its war efforts states that 'probably no other part of the machinery equipment of the entire DD program gave cause for more concern.'"

BODY-36 "For those 99 ships, the shipyards were able to launch them approximately five months on average after they had been laid down. This average grew to almost 7 months after the Armistice because of the work slowdown."

BODY-40 "For instance, MINY was able to launch USS Ward only 17 days after keel-laying and commissioned the ship less than two months later by pre-assembling material and maximizing the use of prefabrication."

BODY-43 "The ability of the Navy and the shipyards to achieve an average destroyer construction time of 10 months by November 1918 was a significant achievement. Had the war lasted until into 1919, as was generally assumed, more than 10 destroyers a month could have been commissioned."

BODY-45 "'leaky seams and loose rivets were the rule; boiler tubes had to be re-rolled wholesale; and a bushel basket-ful of nuts and bolts was collected from inside steam and water lines during shakedown.'"

BODY-47 "In contrast to the decision to continue the current design of fleet destroyers, the Navy opted to design a radically simplified, less capable, small combatant and selected an inexperienced builder to execute the program."

BODY-48 "While a notional ASW ship was desired quickly, by late 1917 the nation's shipyards were filled to capacity with combatant and merchant ship construction. As such, developing a complex design that would require experienced builders and significant construction time was not a viable option. Only small maritime firms and/or inexperience builders were available, necessitating a radically simplified design for the Eagle Boats."

BODY-49 "In 1917, Ford was one of the most famous and respected men in American and his company's capacity for mass production was a matter of national pride. The previous year, Ford Motor Company produced almost 600,000 Model T automobiles by using the principals of mass production."

BODY-50 "The Eagle Boat program went forward with Ford Motor Company as the sole builder, largely because of the SECNAV's personal enthusiasm for Ford. Resigned to the decision, all that the General Board could do in December 1917 was 'place on record its view that both the subchaser and the new patrol boat were emergency designs, neither of which would have been acceptable in a less urgent situation.'"

BODY-51 "The strakes, angles, frames and gussets were drawn up and the positions of all rivet holes were laid out. No detail was omitted that would hamper manufacturing if left to be laid out in the shop."

BODY-53 "In fact, the Eagle Boats were larger than any USN destroyer built before 1903."

BODY-54 Believing that his company could rapidly produce Eagle Boats using mass production methods and the assembly line, Ford set an ambitious building schedule. He promised to deliver the first Eagle Boat no later than mid-July 1918. The schedule called for ten the following month, 20 in September, and 25 each month thereafter. Thus, in January 1918 Ford promised that he could deliver at least 56 Eagle boats by

BODY-55	"The most impressive accomplishment was the construction of the 350 x 1,700 ft. main assembly building (B-Building). More than half a mile long 'with steel-framed, hundred foot tall walls which were nothing but undisturbed expanses of glass' the B-Building accommodated three parallel assembly lines, each with seven stations, and two large outfitting buildings."
BODY-58	"Initially, they believed that each Eagle boat could be built on a moving assembly line like the Model T. However, the size of the ships and the sheer number of different construction steps made this impossible."
BODY-60	"The first seven Eagle Boats had inferior riveting because Ford's workforce found the task more difficult than anticipated because of their pre-riveting preparations. Workers would stand on ladders and try to bolt steel plates together using short-handled wrenches. However, their technique did not bring the plates together in a sufficiently tight manner. As a result, metal shavings worked in between the plates and prevented the rivets from pulling the plates together to form a strong enough seal (see Figure 29). As a result, the Superintending Constructor's team of inspectors found that the first Eagle Boats were not water-tight or oil-tight because of poor riveting techniques."
BODY-62	"The root of the problems arose from the Ford engineers' confidence that mass production methods could be applied to shipbuilding. While the quality of riveting and welding improved with time and more building stations were used as more workers were hired, Ford's promise to rapidly build 100 Eagle Boats was defeated by the time required to complete outfitting of the ships."
BODY-63	"However, the Eagle Boats were a vastly more complex system. Ford was eventually able to standardize the construction of the Eagle hulls and devote large number of workers to the task. But the final outfitting tasks, such as installing turbines, boilers, piping, wiring, armament, and other equipment required more time on average than the construction of the hulls."
BODY-64	"After the Armistice the Navy's need for Eagle Boats ceased and a reappraisal of the program led to the cancellation of fifty-two ships.67 At the same time Ford sought to generate positive publicity after enduring severe congressional criticism of the program."
BODY-67	"For American planners, the chief obstacle to embarking on an austere escort vessel program had been the difficulty of justifying the manufacture of ships that were similar in size and cost to the 1,630-ton (Benson-class) fleet destroyers already on the ways, but that were designed purposely to be less capable (e.g., slower, with fewer guns) in order to facilitate multiple production."
BODY-68	"For smaller combatants the Navy created simplified ships, whose designs lent themselves to quick production at inexperienced or purpose-built shipyards. For fleet destroyers, the Navy opted to continue building complex designs and get more ships by increasing the number on order and the number of building yards."
BODY-71	"The Navy's primary design goal was an improvement to the anti-aircraft battery and a reduction of the silhouette."
BODY-73	"The resulting Gearing class destroyers had 168 tons more fuel and 30% longer cruising radius than the Allen M. Sumner class."
BODY-75	"As in World War I, a core group of experienced shipyards executed the Navy's destroyer building program. Eighty-five percent of all 415 destroyers were built by just seven private yards."
BODY-81	"In peacetime, when materials, facilities and labor were abundant, the Navy and the Bureau could decentralized detailed shipbuilding and component scheduling to

contractors and manufacturers. Under war conditions neither contractors nor the Navy had full control of the planning and scheduling of ship programs. There programs competed with Army, aircraft, Maritime, Lend Lease, civilian, and other needs for materials, machines and men, there not being enough to go around. The problem faced by the Bureau therefore was new, both in magnitude and in complexity."

BODY-82 "BuShips assessed that 'its greatest headache centered on the problem of upland facilities capable of manufacturing the components and materials necessary to keep the shipyards supplied. It is not unreasonable to state that the Bureau devoted as much effort to the increase of production capacity in supporting industries as to the increase of the shipbuilding facilities.'"

BODY-83 "The effort to get large numbers of destroyers into commission as rapidly as possible was complicated by the numerous mid-war alterations to the destroyer's design. America's involvement in World War II was over twice as long as that of the First World War (46 versus 20 months). With almost four years of direct wartime experience, plus two more observing as a neutral, many shortcomings in the designs of the destroyers were discovered and improvements were implemented."

BODY-84 "Regardless of when alterations were made in the construction process, they could only be implemented if there were no shortages of the desired component. For instance, by the end of 1941 the AA armament of the Fletcher class was modified because of Britain's wartime experience. The quadruple 1.1-inch cannon initially intended for the Fletcher class was replaced by one twin 40-mm Bofors gun and the original four single 0.5 inch machine guns were replaced by single 20-mm mountings."

BODY-85 All of these weight additions, coupled with the hurried construction of the war emergency building program, negatively affected the performance of the Fletcher class. For instance, the first Fletcher class destroyer to commission, USS Nicholas (DD-449), displaced 2,589 tons and could make only 37 knots versus a desired 38 knots. Furthermore, trials revealed that the ships could reach a maximum continuous sea speed of about 32-33 knots, which only equaled the Benson class destroyers.92 Because

BODY-86 "As discussed earlier, shortages of material did lead to delays in construction in the early part of the war. However, once these initial delays were overcome, the construction time of destroyers was steady. Because modifications to designs were implemented first to destroyers under construction and then later backfitted when possible to those already built, the building ways were continuously turned over and the shipyards were able, on average, to steadily produce destroyers. As in World War I, the complex design of the fleet destroyer precluded large numbers of ships being constructed in a short amount of time. The average construction time for all 415 destroyers was slightly under one year."

BODY-89 "The Navy's goal was to get large numbers of destroyers into service as rapidly as possible. As such, while the faster construction times at certain yards was encouraging, their finite number of building ways meant that they could only build so many destroyers in a given period. And, because the complex design of the fleet destroyers was not conducive to rapid production, of more import to the Navy was the proper management of resources to enable experienced, inexperienced and purpose-built shipyards to construct as many destroyers as possible at a steady rate. In this they were successful."

BODY-91 "For the nine months before France's defeat the average monthly loss of shipping to U-boats was 62 ships (194,500 tons). However, when Germany gained Atlantic ports with the fall of France in mid-1940, the naval strategy of the United States and Great Britain was considerably altered. In the nine months after the fall of France, U-boats sank a monthly average of 100 ships (413,351 tons). For the British, the protection of convoys, and thus the construction of destroyer escorts, became of the highest national priority."

BODY-92   "The attack on Pearl Harbor the following month quickly altered the United States' strategic outlook. The U.S. Navy itself now required a large number of destroyer escorts. Within the next year 1,005 destroyer escorts were ordered."

BODY-93   "The resulting Evarts class destroyer escorts were 290 feet long and displaced almost 1,200 tons -- only 60 feet shorter and about 400 tons lighter than the Bristol class fleet destroyers then being laid down. However, they were 14 knots slower and had fewer guns than the Bristol class. This relatively slight difference in size but significant difference in offensive capabilities created some misgivings about embarking on the destroyer escort program for Great Britain."

BODY-94   "Perhaps no other ship type's design was affected more by shortages in World War II."

BODY-95   "The first shortage appeared during the detailed design of the Evarts class in late 1941. Around that time the Navy selected General Motors V12 diesel engines in tandem with electric drive for the Evarts class (97 ships) in order to avoid the need for reduction gears, which were experiencing a bottleneck in production. However, diesel engines were also in short supply. As a result, while the original Evarts design called for eight diesel engines, they received only four. This reduced shp 12,000 to 6,000 and lower the design speed of the class from 24 to 19 knots."

BODY-100   "As in World War I, the Navy found that it was necessary to pay for expansion and/or construction of private shipyards to achieve its goal of getting large numbers of ships constructed."

BODY-101   This staggered entry of shipyards in the destroyer escort program was reflected in the number of building ways in use. By May 1943 all 17 yards had building ways in use for destroyer escorts and it was in this month that the peak of 122 building ways were in use simultaneously (see Figure 52). However, over the course of the 31 months that DE were on the building ways, only half that number were average ever in use because of the gradual entry of the different shipyards into the program and the tapering off of the program beginning in late 1943.

BODY-102   "The buildup in 1942 of the number of building ways dedicated to DE construction was also affected by landing craft construction. In 1942 President Roosevelt issued an executive order that assigned a higher priority to landing craft construction than destroyer escorts because it was hoped that an amphibious assault on Western Europe could be launched in September 1942. The building ways at Philadelphia and Boston Navy Yards were directly affected by this change in priority because both were assigned orders for LST construction. As a result, both ceased laying down destroyer escorts after April 1942 and switched over to LST production. DE keel layings did not resume until September 1942 at Boston and January 1943 at Philadelphia - a delay of six and nine months, respectively

BODY-104   "The delayed entry of large numbers of destroyer escorts were the result of competing national priorities and were not a negative reflection of the producibility of the destroyer escort design. While the ships laid down before November 1942 took almost 11 months on average to build, once priority was given to the destroyer escort program in November 1942 and all shipyards began to reach full capacity, the ship were able to be produced rapidly because of their simple design."

BODY-106 "The rapid building time and the large number of shipyards and building ways dedicated to the program in 1943 produced a substantial number of ships in a relatively short time. While the first ships were not commissioned until the twelfth month after the first keel laying, only a year later in January 1944 more than 300 were commissioned (see Figure 58). Two hundred more were commissioned by the following January (the 36th month from the first keel laying)."

BODY-109 "In June 1942, the Maritime Commission proposed that merchant shipyards could be put to better use if they built escort craft based upon a British corvette design. It was reasoned that more escort craft in service would lead to more U-boat sinkings, which would reduce merchant ship losses and, thus, the need for merchant shipbuilders."

BODY-113 "In December 1943, four patrol frigates were canceled (PF 95-98) and twenty-one ships (PF 72-92) were transferred to Great Britain as the Colony class."

BODY-114 "On average the ninety-six ships were launched only 2.6 months after they were laid down."

BODY-115 "The entire program averaged slightly less than eleven months total construction time. However, the average for each shipyard varied considerably (see Table 18). Kaiser and Consolidated Shipbuilding, both in California, and Walsh-Kaiser in Rhode Island were able to achieve total building times on average of six to eight months because there were able to quickly fit out and complete the ships after they were launched."

BODY-118 "The first PF from these yards were commissioned six months after the construction program began. However, the inexperience of many of the Great Lakes yards, which built 47% of the ships, coupled with the special needs of getting the ships to the sea, delayed delivery for a significant part of the program."

BODY-119 By the time the ships began to enter service in late 1943 the Battle of the Atlantic had shifted decisively in favor of the Allies and their usefulness had largely passed. Of the ninety-six ships built, twenty-one were transferred to the Royal Navy. The remaining seventy-five ships were manned by Coast Guard crews. Twenty-four of the patrol frigates were modified to operate as weather ships. The 3-inch/50 gun was replaced by a balloon hangar and five of the 20mm guns were removed. In the summer of 1945 twenty eight of the ships that had were not operating as weather ships were loaned to the Soviet Union for Operation Olympic, the planned invasion of Japan.

BODY-120 "While the limited capability ship programs required more initial preparations, once in production their simplified design generally lent themselves to rapid production. As a result, a simplified design does allow larger number of ships to enter service at a faster rate once production experience is gained and the labor force becomes trained."

NAVY-AFTER-NEXT
CONTINGENCY-PRODUCIBLE CORVETTE (CPC)
EMERGENCY PRODUCTION HISTORICAL STUDY

FEBRUARY 2004
S&FAC REPORT NO. 9070-03-C5
NAVSEA 05D -134 - DTD NOV 19, 2004

Distribution Statement A: Approved for Public Release; Distribution is unlimited

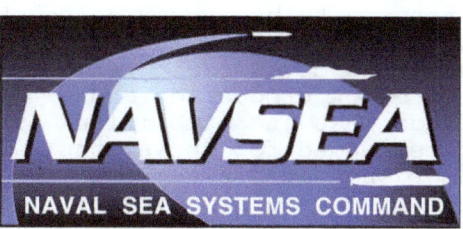

FUTURE CONCEPTS AND SUFACE SHIP DESIGN GROUP (05D)
NAVAL SEA SYSTEMS COMMAND
1333 ISAAC HULL AVENUE S.E.
WASHINGTON NAVY YARD, D.C. 20376

REPORT DOCUMENTATION PAGE

Form Approved
OMB No. 0704-0188

Public reporting burden for this collection of information is estimated to average 1 hour per response, including the time for reviewing instructions, searching existing data sources, gathering and maintaining the data needed, and completing and reviewing this collection of information. Send comments regarding this burden estimate or any other aspect of this collection of information, including suggestions for reducing this burden to Department of Defense, Washington Headquarters Services, Directorate for Information Operations and Reports (0704-0188), 1215 Jefferson Davis Highway, Suite 1204, Arlington, VA 22202-4302. Respondents should be aware that notwithstanding any other provision of law, no person shall be subject to any penalty for failing to comply with a collection of information if it does not display a currently valid OMB control number. **PLEASE DO NOT RETURN YOUR FORM TO THE ABOVE ADDRESS.**

1. REPORT DATE (DD-MM-YYYY) SEA 05D - dtd nov 04	2. REPORT TYPE Historical Study	3. DATES COVERED (From - To) Dec 03 - Nov 04
4. TITLE AND SUBTITLE Navy-After-Next Contingency Producible Corvette: Emergency Production Historical Study		5a. CONTRACT NUMBER
		5b. GRANT NUMBER
		5c. PROGRAM ELEMENT NUMBER
6. AUTHOR(S) Matthew McCarton and Bill Garzke		5d. PROJECT NUMBER
		5e. TASK NUMBER
		5f. WORK UNIT NUMBER
7. PERFORMING ORGANIZATION NAME(S) AND ADDRESS(ES) Computer Sciences Corporation Maritime Plaza #1 Washington DC 2003		8. PERFORMING ORGANIZATION REPORT
9. SPONSORING / MONITORING AGENCY NAME(S) AND ADDRESS(ES) NAVSEA 05D1 1333 Isaac Hull Ave SE Washington Navy Yard DC 20376-5060		10. SPONSOR/MONITOR'S ACRONYM(S)
		11. SPONSOR/MONITOR'S REPORT NUMBER(S)

12. DISTRIBUTION / AVAILABILITY STATEMENT
Distribution Statement A: Approved for Public Release; Distribution is unlimited

13. SUPPLEMENTARY NOTES

14. ABSTRACT
The question that this report seeks to address is "what is the best approach to acquiring a large number of warships in an emergency?" Two approaches were tried by the U.S. Navy during World War One and Two. The first approach was to use an existing fleet destroyer design and attempt to accelerate production by increasing the number on order and the number of building yards. The second approach was to develop simpler and less capable emergency escort designs which lent themselves to quick production and could be built by mainly second-tier shipyards. The report finds that the simplified design of emergency escorts does not markedly decrease the time needed for those ships to first enter service compared to destroyers. However, an emergency escort approach does allow larger number of ships to enter service at a faster rate once production experience is gained.

15. SUBJECT TERMS
mass production ships, ASW Escorts, World War I, World War II, force levels

16. SECURITY CLASSIFICATION OF:			17. LIMITATION OF ABSTRACT	18. NUMBER	19a. NAME OF RESPONSIBLE PERSON
a. REPORT Unclassified	b. ABSTRACT Unclassified	c. THIS PAGE Unclassified	UL	163	19b. TELEPHONE NUMBER (include area code) (202) 781-4347

Standard Form 298 (Rev. 8-98)
Prescribed by ANSI Std. Z39.18

Navy-After-Next
Contingency Producible Corvette (CPC)
Emergency Production Historical Study

February 2004

SFAC REPORT NO. 9070-03-C5

Signature Page

_____
Author

_____
SFAC Task Leader

_____
SFAC Program Manager

_____
NAVSEA 05D1

_____ for HOWARD FIREMAN
NAVSEA 05D

NAVY-AFTER-NEXT
CONTINGENCY-PRODUCIBLE CORVETTE (CPC)

EMERGENCY PRODUCTION HISTORICAL REPORT

February 2004
FINAL REPORT

Researched and Written By: Matthew McCarton (CSC)

Reviewed By: Bill Garzke (CSC)

Approved By: Philip Sims (NAVSEA 05D)

Cover Photograph: "USS *Meade* (DD-602) afloat immediately after her launching, at the Bethlehem Steel Company shipyard, Staten Island, New York, 15 February 1942. Note that the keel of USS *Brownson* (DD-518) is being laid on the slipway just vacated by *Meade*." Naval Historical Center Photographic Section, photo # 19-N-30805.

EXECUTIVE SUMMARY

The question that this report seeks to address is "what is the best approach to acquiring a large number of warships in an emergency?" Two approaches were tried by the U.S. Navy during World War One and Two in order to obtain, as quickly as possible, a large number of ASW escorts. The first approach was to use an existing fleet destroyer design ("destroyers") and attempt to accelerate production by increasing the number on order and the number of building yards. The second approach was to develop a simplified, less capable, smaller combatant ("emergency escorts") whose design lent itself to quick production and could be built by mainly second-tier shipyards. This historical study was undertaken in conjunction with the development of the Contingency-Producible Corvette (CPC) ship concept (Ref. 1) as modern design suitable for rapidly increasing the number of USN ships.

This report examines a total of 1,345 ships (327 for World War I and 1,018 for World War II) that were built in response to war emergencies. It finds that the simplified design of emergency escorts does not markedly decrease the time needed for those ships to first enter service compared to destroyers. This is because significant time was first required to develop the simplified designs, and then select, equip, and train second-tier shipbuilders to construct the ships. The time needed to get destroyers into service compares favorably with the emergency escorts because the destroyers were already in production and the shipyards had an experienced workforce and a network of existing supporting firms to build components such as machinery. Materials and component shortages were generally not the controlling factor for the length of time needed to build destroyers or emergency escorts. Short-term materials and component shortages required several restructurings of the emergency escort program and delivery some ships with reduced horsepower prolusion plants. Long-term materials and component shortages were avoided in both wars through an enormous industrial expansion that was only possible because of the magnitude of the war emergency. However, for both ship types shortages of skilled, experienced laborers and available in-yard manufacturing machinery, coupled with the urgencies of the building program, led to instances of workmanship that did not meet peacetime standards. The best possible workmanship was especially critical for destroyers because, unlike the emergency escorts, they were expected to serve long after the war emergency. This expectation was a significant factor in the Navy's decision to build additional fleet destroyers. In both world wars, a third alternative of building stripped-down versions of fleet destroyers were rejected – even though they would take less time to build – by Navy leaders with post-war strategy in mind. This forward-thinking was fortuitous. The post-war (WWI and WWII) Congresses were not willing to fund new ships, but the more capable ships in the Navy's inventory were better starting points for the conversion and upgrades, which the Congresses were willing to fund, than the alternative austere versions.

While the emergency escort programs required more initial preparations, once in production, their simplified design generally lent themselves to rapid production. As a result, an emergency escort approach does allow larger number of ships to enter service at a faster rate once production experience is gained. However, to achieve this faster rate of production experienced second-tier shipyards must form the core of the building program, as was the case with the primary emergency escorts (Destroyer Escorts (DE)) in World War Two. The very austere emergency escorts, the *Eagle* boat (WWI) and Patrol Frigates (WWII), did not achieve a rapid production rate because of the use of inexperienced builders to execute the entire the *Eagle* boat production (in a from-the-ground-up new yard) and half of the patrol frigate program.

For the last two decades, the Navy's experience in search-and-stop blockade has been in the exceptionally blockade-suitable Persian Gulf and Red Sea region with its narrow entrances and the target of interest were large merchant ships. Conventional frigates and destroyers successfully served in this role. However, before that, the Navy's role in Vietnam required stopping and searching a multitude of small ships along 100s of miles of open coast. That blockade situation required a large number of ships but only a simple combat system was needed for such duty. The number of ship problem in Vietnam was solved by use of residual WWII emergency escorts (DEs) and USCG cutters. The former ship type no longer exists in the reserve fleet and homeland security duties will prevent diversion of today's USCG assets. If in the future, the Navy expects to ever have need for large numbers of hulls in a short amount of time (for a long coastline blockade), historical experience suggests that use of the second tier yards, building ships of the technology level they are familiar with, will be required. Attempts to create brand-new yards have historically not been successful for rapidly increasing the numbers of warships.

Table of Contents

EXECUTIVE SUMMARY v
1. INTRODUCTION 1
    1.1   Purpose 1
    1.2   Ship Classes Examined 1
    1.3   Methodology 2

PART I: WORLD WAR ONE 6
2. WORLD WAR I DESTROYERS 7
    2.1   Design Debate Phase 7
        2.1.1   Strategic Background 7
        2.1.2   Acceleration of Existing *Wickes* Design 8
        2.1.3   *Clemson* Debate: Complex or Simplified Design? 9
    2.2   Pre-Construction Preparations Phase 12
        2.2.1   Selection of Shipbuilders 12
        2.2.2   Competing Building Priorities 13
        2.2.3   Expansion and Creation of Shipyards 14
    2.3   Construction Phase 17
        2.3.1   Number of Building Ways 17
        2.3.2   Shortages and Industrial Expansion 19
    2.4   Delivery Phase 25
3. EAGLE BOATS 34
    3.1   Design Decision Phase 34
        3.1.1   Strategic Background 34
        3.1.2   Simple Design for Rapid Construction 35
    3.2   Pre-Construction Preparations Phase 35
        3.2.1   Selection of Ford Motor Company 35
        3.2.2   *Eagle* Boat Design 37
        3.2.3   Development of the River Rouge Plant 41
    3.3   Construction Phase 45
        3.3.1   Production Problems 45

	3.4	Delivery Phase	51

PART II: WORLD WAR TWO 54

4. WORLD WAR II DESTROYERS 55

    4.1 Design Decision Phase 55

        4.1.1 *Bristol* Class: Continuation of Existing Production Line 55

        4.1.2 *Fletcher* Class: Backbone of the War Emergency Program 57

        4.1.3 *Allen M. Sumner*: Design Modification Due to War Experience 58

        4.1.4 *Gearing* Class 59

    4.2 Pre-Construction Preparations Phase 61

        4.2.1 Selection of Shipbuilders 61

    4.3 Construction Phase 65

        4.3.1 Number of Building Ways 65

        4.3.2 National Shipbuilding Effort in World War II 67

        4.3.3 Shortages and Industrial Expansion 69

        4.3.4 Mid-War Design Changes 70

        4.3.5 Total Construction Time 73

5. DESTROYER ESCORTS 78

    5.1 Design Decision Phase 78

        5.1.1 Strategic Background 78

        5.1.2 Simple Design for Rapid Construction 79

        5.1.3 Design Variations 81

    5.2 Pre-Construction Preparation Phase 84

        5.2.1 Selection of Shipbuilders 84

    5.3 Construction Phase 87

        5.3.1 Number of Building Ways 88

        5.3.2 Initial Construction Delays 89

6. PATROL FRIGATES 96

    6.1 Design Decision Phase 96

    6.2 Pre-Construction Preparations 97

        6.2.1 Selection of Shipbuilders 98

6.3	Construction Phase	100
6.4	Delivery Phase	105
7.	CONCLUSION	107
APPENDIX A	KEY TO SHIPYARD ABBREVIATIONS	A-1
APPENDIX B	SHIP DATA	B-1
APPENDIX C	METHOD FOR DETERMINING NUMBER OF BUILDING WAYS	C-1
APPENDIX D	REFERENCES AND SOURCES CONSULTED BY TOPIC	D-1
APPENDIX E	ENDNOTES	E-1

LIST OF TABLES

Table 1: War Emergency Ships Examined in this Report	2
Table 2: Design Characteristics, *Wickes* Class Destroyers	9
Table 3: Design Characteristics, *Clemson* Class Destroyers	12
Table 4: Building Way Statistics, WW I Destroyer Shipbuilders, by Start Date	17
Table 5: Construction Times for WW I Destroyer Builders, By Number Built	24
Table 6: *Eagle* Boat Characteristics	41
Table 7: Percentage Days Ways in Use, *Eagle* Boats	46
Table 8: Construction Statistics, *Eagle* Boats	51
Table 9: World War II Destroyer Class Characteristics	61
Table 10: Building Way Statistics, WW II Destroyer Shipbuilders, By Start Date	65
Table 11: Construction Times for WW II Destroyers, By Average Per Yard	74
Table 12: DE Class Hull and Propulsion Differences	82
Table 13: *Evarts* Class Characteristics	84
Table 14: Building Way Statistics, DE Shipbuilders, By Start Date	88
Table 15: Construction Times for DE, By Shipyard	93
Table 16: *Tacoma/Hallowell* Class Characteristics	97
Table 17: Building Way Statistics, PF Shipbuilders, By Start Date	100
Table 18: Construction Times for PF, By Shipyard	102

LIST OF FIGURES

Figure 1: USS *Wickes* (DD-75) 9

Figure 2: USS *Broome* (DD-210), *Clemson* Class Destroyer 11

Figure 3: WW I Destroyer Shipbuilders, By Class/Number Built................................ 15

Figure 4: World War I Destroyer Shipbuilders, Geographic View............................... 16

Figure 5: USS *Colhoun* and *Stevens* on the building ways, BethQ, October 1917 18

Figure 6: Number of Ways in Use, JUN 1917 – OCT 1921, All Destroyer Shipbuilders.. 19

Figure 7: Boilers under construction at Norfolk Navy Yard, May 1917 21

Figure 8: USS *Zane* (DD-337) launching at MINY, AUG 1919.................................... 24

Figure 9: Building Times for Ships Laid Down Before Armistice 26

Figure 10: Building Times for Destroyers Laid Down After Armistice 26

Figure 11: USS *Ward* (DD-139) Under Construction, Mare Island, May 1918............. 27

Figure 12: Bethlehem Shipbuilding's Victory Destroyer Plant, Squantum, MA 28

Figure 13: Unidentified destroyer launching at BethSQ 28

Figure 14: Interior View of (Dry) Building Ways, BethSQ.. 29

Figure 15: Interior View of Wet Slips, BethSQ... 29

Figure 16: Monthly Commissionings of Wickes/Clemson Destroyers, 1918-1922 30

Figure 17: Cumulative number of Wickes/Clemson Destroyers in Commission, 1918-1922.. 31

Figure 18: Destroyers fitting out at BethSF in 1920.. 33

Figure 19: *Eagle* Boat Under Construction, View 1 38

Figure 20: *Eagle* Boat Under Construction, View 2 39

Figure 21 *Eagle* Boat Under Construction, View 3 39

Figure 22: *Eagle* Boat Under Construction, View 4 40

Figure 23: *Eagle* Boat No. 2 on Trials 41

Figure 24: Main *Eagle* Boat Assembly Building ("Bldg. B"), River Rouge Plant 43

Figure 25: Transfer Table, River Rouge Plant 43

Figure 26: *Eagle* Boat No. 60 Launching, View 1 44

Figure 27: *Eagle* No. 60 Launching, View 2 44

Figure 28: Number of Stations in Use, Ford River Rouge Plant, MAY 1918 – AUG 1919 46

Figure 29: Hull Construction on *Eagle* Boats 48

Figure 30: Monthly *Eagle* Boat Keel Layings and Launchings, MAY 1918-AUG 1919 49

Figure 31: *Eagle* Boat fitting out 50

Figure 32: Length of Construct Milestones, *Eagle* Boats 51

Figure 33: Cumulative Commissionings of *Eagle*s Boats, 1918-1919 53

Figure 34: USS *Laffey* (DD-459), *Bristol* Class Destroyer 56

Figure 35: USS *Fletcher* (DD-445) 57

Figure 36: USS *Soley* (DD-707), *Allen M. Sumner* Class Destroyer 59

Figure 37: USS *Benner* (DD-807), *Gearing* Class Destroyer 60

Figure 38: WW II Destroyer Shipbuilders, By Class / Number Built 63

Figure 39: WW II Destroyer Shipbuilders, Geographical View 64

Figure 40: Construction of USS *Meade* (DD-602), *Bristol* Class, BethSI, JUN 1941 66

Figure 41: Number of Ways in Use for DD Construction, All Shipyards 67

Figure 42: Construction Spans of Destroyer Classes during World War II 71

Figure 43: USS *Fletcher* (DD-445) at MINY, AUG 1943 showing recent alterations 72

Figure 44: Construction Time, Builders of 30 or more Destroyers 75

Figure 45: Construction Time, Builders of Less than 30 Destroyers 75

Figure 46: Construction Time for World War II Destroyers, By Quarter 76

Figure 47: Cumulative Commissionings of World War II Destroyers 77

Figure 48: USS *Canfield* (DE 262), *Evarts* Class Destroyer 81

Figure 49: USS *Darby* (DE 218), *Buckley* Class Destroyer 83

Figure 50: Destroyer Escort Builders, By Number Built 85

Figure 51: Destroyer Escort Shipbuilders, Geographical View 86

Figure 52: Number of Ways in Use for DE Construction, All Shipyards 89

Figure 53: Monthly Keel Layings and Launchings of DE, FEB 1942-DEC 1944 91

Figure 54: USS *Swasey* (DE-248) launching at Brown Shipbuilding, MAR 1943 92

Figure 55: USS Leopold (DE-319) launching at Orange, TX, JUN 1943 92

Figure 56: Building Times for Shipyards that built more than 30 DE 94

Figure 57: Building Times for Shipyards that built less than 30 DE 94

Figure 58: Cumulative Number of Destroyer Escorts in Commission, 1943-1945 95

Figure 59: USS *Tacoma* (PF-3) 97

Figure 60: Number of Patrol Frigates Built, By Shipbuilder 98

Figure 61: Patrol Frigate Shipbuilders, Geographical View 99

Figure 62: Number of Ways in Use, Patrol Frigate Shipbuilders 101

Figure 63: USS *Lorain* (PF 93) Launching at ASB-L, March 18, 1944 103

Figure 64: USS *Grand Forks* (PF 11) Just Launched 103

Figure 65: Construction Times, East and West Coast Builders 104

Figure 66: Construction Times, Great Lakes Builders 105

Figure 67: Cumulative Commissionings of Patrol Frigates 106

Figure 68: Rate of Commissioning of War Emergency Ships in World War I 108

Figure 69: Rate of Commissioning of War Emergency Ships in World War II 109

LIST OF ACRONYMS

CNO	Chief of Naval Operations
CPC	Contingency-Producible Corvette
DD	Destroyer
DE	Destroyer Escort
PF	Patrol Frigate
PE	*Eagle* Boat
BuShips	Bureau of Ships
BuC&R	Bureau of Construction and Repair
BuEng	Bureau of Engineering
dcp	depth charge projectors
dct	depth charge tracks
nm	Nautical Mile
SECNAV	Secretary of the Navy
shp	shaft horse power
tt	torpedo tubes

1. INTRODUCTION

1.1 Purpose

The purpose of this report is to compare the results of two approaches used by the U.S. Navy during World War One and World War Two to obtain as quickly as possible a large number of destroyers and smaller, less capable, combatants. The first approach was to select an existing fleet destroyer design and attempt to accelerate production by increasing the number on order and the number of building yards. The assumed benefits of this approach were that (1) existing destroyer builders already had the experienced workforce, tooling, and facilities to build the existing or mod-repeat design, and (2) there would be no break in production because the selected design was already under construction. The second approach was to create a simplified ship design that lent itself to quick production and select mainly second-tier shipyards to build them. The assumed benefits of this approach were that (1) the simplified design would greatly decrease construction time and (2) allow shipyards with little or no experience in combatant construction to build many or all of the ships, thus, avoiding the need for traditional destroyer builders to take on the work, and (3) allow non-traditionally-Navy industrial resources to be used. This approach assumed that the simplicity of the design would off-set the inexperience of the selected non-traditional yards and the time necessary to create the design and prepare the shipyards. To determine the effectiveness of the two approaches, this report compares the rate at which ships entered service for each of the war emergency building programs.

1.2 Ship Classes Examined

The examination of the Navy's two approaches to obtaining large numbers of destroyers and smaller combatants was undertaken in conjunction with the design of the Contingency-Producible Corvette (CPC) ship concept (Ref. 1), whose construction would be accomplished by present-day second-tier shipyards. As such, this report examines similarly sized combatants built in response to war emergencies. A total of 1,345 ships (327 for World War I and 1,018 for World War II) were examined for this report (see Table 1).

Table 1: War Emergency Ships Examined in this Report

	Type	Class -- Number Built
World War I	Destroyer (DD)	*Wickes* – 111
		Clemson – 156
	Patrol Escort (PE)	*Eagle* Boat – 60
World War II	Destroyer (DD)	*Bristol* – 72
		Fletcher – 175
		Allen M. Sumner – 70
		Gearing – 98
	Destroyer Escorts (DE)	*Evarts* – 97
		Buckley – 148
		Edsall – 85
		Cannon – 72
		Rudderow – 22
		John C. Butler – 83
	Patrol Frigates (PF)	*Tacoma* – 96

1.3 Methodology

The most straightforward method of comparing the results of the two approaches used by the Navy during the two world wars is to determine the construction timeline of the 1,345 ships examined in this report. For purposes of this report, three major construction milestones of a ship were established:

- Date that the ship's keel was laid down on the building way
- Date that the ship was launched from that building way
- Date that the ship was commissioned

These three dates, along with other data, are listed for each of the 1,345 ships in Appendix B. They provide the essential benchmarks for each ship's construction. The number of days from the keel laying of a ship to its commissioning is used to determine the length of time it took to construct each ship. The rate at which ships were commissioned and entered service can then be plotted based upon the start date of the building program – measured, in this instance, as the date that the first keel was laid down. However, this plot must be examined in conjunction with the resources made available to each program. Each of the war emergency programs differed in the number of ships built and the number of shipyards involved, or more precisely, the number of building ways at each shipyard. Determining the number of shipyards used in a building program was a matter of examining various official Navy publications (see Appendix A, Sources Consulted). Determining the number of building ways at each shipyard that were actually used for the respective building programs was accomplished by comparing each ship's keel laying and launch dates. For a more detailed explanation of how the number of ways was determined see Appendix C.

While, the period from keel laying to commissioning is the most reliable measure of how long it took to build a given ship design, it is not without drawbacks. First, commissioning did not always mean a ship was completely fitted out and ready for actual service. An example of this is the *Fletcher* class destroyers (see Section 4.1.2). When the ships began to be commissioned in the summer of 1942 the Navy was experiencing a shortage of MK 51 directors for the Bofors gun. As a result, the first *Fletchers* did not receive their MK 51 directors immediately and because of this their arrival in the Pacific theater was delayed until the fall of that year. When examples of logistical shortages causing a lag between commissioning and operational readiness have been found, they are noted in the report. Second, often there is a lag time between when a shipyard completes a ship and the Navy commissions her. Thus, some sources list dates for keel laying, launching, *completion*, and commissioning. Such is the case with the *Tacoma* and *Hallowell* class patrol frigates (PF). However, these are the exceptions, not the rule, and for consistent measurement only the commissioning date is used for the 1,345 ships in this report. This decision may result in assigning longer building times to some ships but it is assumed that this period is negligible because the Navy commissioned ships as quickly as possible after they were completed due to the needs of war.

A second caution with the data is that some ships were constructed in extremely short periods because building materials were prepositioned or there was a concentration of the shipyard's work force on a single ship. These examples often received much publicity, especially during wartime when propaganda and morale are important. As a result, they often give a false impression of the time necessary to build a <u>large number</u> of ships in a consistent manner over a period of time. For example, *Eagle* Boat No. 59 was laid down and launched in only twelve days. Ford Motor Company touted this as a representative example of its productivity, glossing over the fact that this feat was accomplished because the entire workforce of Ford's *Eagle* Boat plant was concentrated on hull No. 59 and materials were carefully prepositioned.* These measures lengthened the construction times of hull No. 58 and 60 because work stopped on them while hull No. 59 was under construction. When explanations for instances of very short or very the long building times are found, they are noted to dispel false impressions. In any case, these instances are few and the report's emphasis on average building times for the 1,345 ships negates their effect.

The caveats mentioned above point to the fact that the war emergency programs were subject to both internal and external pressures. As a result, each shipbuilding program is examined in context with the myriad factors that affected construction time, including:

- Shipbuilder experience
- Number of shipyards (building ways) available
- Competition for building ways and/or material from other ship programs
- Logistical delays and/or shortages of material

In addition, to truly measure how long it took to get large numbers of ships into service an examination of the period before the shipbuilder became involved is necessary. As mentioned above, one method to determine producibility is to measure the rate that ships were commissioned once the first keel was laid down. However, this measurement does not reflect the often significant time necessary to undertake a construction program. Preparations include the time needed to debate the selection of a

---

* Henry Ford ordered this effort to offset the negative publicity surrounding his inability to deliver <u>large numbers</u> of *Eagles* on schedule.

complex fleet destroyer or simplified design, the development of preliminary and detailed design, the search for and negotiations with shipbuilders, and the upgrading or building of ship facilities to execute the program. All of these other factors need to be discussed to gain a true understanding of the effort necessary and potential pitfalls for the U.S. Navy to get large numbers of ships designed, built and put into commission.

As a result, each war emergency building program will be examined through four phases:

- Design Decision Phase, which includes examination of the internal Navy design decision process and the strategic environment in which they were made.

- Pre-Construction Preparation Phase, which includes the selection of shipbuilders, and the expansion or creation of shipyards.

- Construction Phase, which discusses the rate at which building ways were made available, any logistical shortages that occurred, and the average length of time for hull construction, fitting out, and total construction times.

- Delivery Phase, which summarizes all of the previous phases and shows the rate that the ships were commissioned.

PART I: WORLD WAR ONE

"World War I introduced an entirely new feature to American destroyer design, a sudden need for very large numbers of ships. The problem is a recurrent one, and the dilemma is always the same: should the Navy continue to build the sophisticated prewar designs, or should it choose instead a specialized (and necessarily austere) mass-production ("mobilization") type?"
   ~Norman Friedman – U.S. Destroyers, An Illustrated Design History~

"But when Armistice came in November 1918 ... of the 112 boats ordered from Ford at a cost of some $46 million, only seven had been completed and dispatched, and only one was actually in commission – still undergoing preliminary sea trials. Ford blamed the vessel's naval designers, who had changed specifications several times and had considerably hampered production. But the truth was that Ford's engineers had found it harder to adapt their motorcar production techniques to shipbuilding than they had anticipated. They did not hit their stride until after the war was over, and the Ford Motor Company finally delivered sixty Eagle boats to the U.S. Navy. The Navy did not invite Henry Ford to build ships for it again."
   ~Robert Lacey – Ford: The Men and the Machine~

2. WORLD WAR I DESTROYERS

In response to World War One, the United States Navy used two approaches to build large numbers of destroyers and other small combatants. The first approach was to use the existing *Wickes* class destroyer design and attempt to accelerate production by increasing the number on order and the number of building yards. The second approach was to design a radically simplified, less capable, small combatant, the *Eagle* class, which could be built in as close to an assembly-line fashion as possible by an inexperienced shipbuilder. This section examines the effort to build destroyers in World War One, while Section 3 examines the *Eagle* class.

2.1 Design Debate Phase

2.1.1 Strategic Background

The United States maintained official neutrality for almost three years after the outbreak of World War One in August 1914 and an effort was made to keep the nation on a peacetime footing.* This effort was reflected in the limited scope of the Navy's destroyer construction programs. In March 1915, congressional authorization was given to the six-ship *Caldwell* class, which were of a new design from previous U.S. Navy destroyers. Each of the six ships incorporated many experimental features and they were considered prototypes.[1] As the *Caldwell* class destroyers began to be laid down in August 1916, the Fiscal Year 1916 destroyers were developed. The resulting *Wickes* class destroyers closely matched the *Caldwell* design, but with a modified hull form for greater efficiency and much more power to achieve 35 knots. In August 1916, Congress authorized construction of twenty *Wickes* (DD-75 through 94), and the Navy let contracts for their construction in December. However, events were rapidly unfolding in Europe that would alter the Navy's strategic outlook and drastically

---

* President Wilson had been reelected in 1916 by emphasizing his having "kept us out of war."

change its shipbuilding strategy. On January 31, 1917, Germany announced its intention to resume a policy of unrestricted submarine warfare. This decision was quickly felt at sea. In February and March over 1.1 million gross tons of merchant shipping was sunk by German U-boats (although the extent of the losses were kept secret by the British Admiralty). The U-boat policy quickly drew the U.S. into the conflict; by April the United States had declared war on Germany. Once the war began, the Navy "determined to concentrate construction upon such types as were most necessary, taking into consideration the time required to construct such vessels" (*emphasis added*).[2] Priority for emergency construction was given as (1) Destroyers, (2) Submarine chasers, and (3) Small destroyers (what would become *Eagle* Boats).[*,3]

2.1.2 Acceleration of Existing *Wickes* Design

The Navy's approach to getting large numbers of fleet destroyers into service in response to the war was threefold. First, it increased the number on order of the *Wickes* class design (see Figure 1 and Table 2), which existed on paper but had yet to be laid down. An additional 91 *Wickes* class destroyers (DD-95 to 185) were authorized in March 1917. Second, it attempted to increase the number of shipyards that build destroyers. And, finally, the Navy sought the maximum possible standardization and simplification of design because of the need for a large number of shipbuilders to be involved in the program. The first of the 111 *Wickes* class destroyers began to be laid down in June 1917.

---

[*] The order of priority continued with cargo vessels, submarines, conversion of troop ships, conversion of repair ships, mine sweepers, seagoing tugs and harbor tugs.

Figure 1: USS *Wickes* (DD-75)[4]

Table 2: Design Characteristics, *Wickes* Class Destroyers[5]

Design Displacement	1,247 tons
Length on Waterline	310' 0"
Beam	30' 11 ½ "
Draft (mean)	9' 0"
Speed	36 knots
Crew	100
Armament	4 x 4" 2 x 37mm 12 x 21" torpedo tubes (tt) 2 x depth charge track (dct.)

2.1.3 *Clemson* Debate: Complex or Simplified Design?

The need for destroyers was so great that the following month, 150 more destroyers of an as-yet-undetermined design were ordered, with a goal of having the ships completed in 18 to 24 months.[6] The design was in flux because the Navy was debating whether to base the new destroyers on the existing *Wickes* design or develop a simplified "standardized destroyer." It was assumed that a simplified design would enable quick production and allow inexperienced shipyards to help, whereas a more capable design would take longer to build but have greater usefulness once in the fleet. A special Navy Board on Devices and Plans Connected with Submarine Warfare recommended that a standardized destroyer should be designed, to "enable all auxiliary machinery and equipment to be procured in lots of identical units and thus secure the benefits of quantity production."[7] To help shorten building times the Board suggested that the standardized destroyer be slower (26-28 knots) than the 1,200 ton, 35-knot *Wickes*. The relaxation of the speed requirement would enable the ships to be fitted with machinery that was used in the early "thousand tonner" *Sampson* class destroyers (immediate predecessor to the *Caldwell* class). This reversion in machinery would allow the ships to be smaller (750 tons) and also eliminate the shortages in reduction-gears then being experienced by the *Wickes* class.[8] If all of these measures to enhance producibility were implemented the Board argued that 200 standardized destroyers could be built "relatively quickly."[9] At first, this plan was approved by the SECNAV but was later reversed due to objections from the Navy's two primary ship design organizations, the Bureau of Construction and Repair (BuC&R) and the Bureau of Steam Engineering (BuEng). The two bureaus argued that the Board's plan would not result in destroyers entering the fleet quickly. They estimated that two and a half years would be necessary to complete the 200 standardized destroyers. As proof, they pointed out that the traditional destroyer-building yards were completely filled with current orders for *Wickes* class destroyers. The only way to initiate the standardized destroyer program was for the yards to "remodel and enlarge their plants, ...change their methods, double their working forces, and train new personnel." Not only would these steps take time but their implementation would probably delay the completion of the *Wickes* class. As an alternative, the bureaus urged that the best results could be achieved by "duplicating the vessels now under construction. (*emphasis added*)" These measures, they concluded would result in the completion of approximately 40 or 50 destroyers by January 1919.*,[10]

In the meantime, private shipyards were also proposing methods to produce large numbers of destroyers. In July 1917 Bethlehem Steel Corporation submitted a proposal to accelerate production by building 150 small, 28-knot destroyers. This proposal received serious consideration because the proposed 28-knot design would

---

* Their estimate proved accurate. Fifty-one destroyers were completed by January 1919.

require only two boilers instead of the four in the *Wickes* class. However, after investigation it was determined that the construction of boilers was not the time-controlling factor in destroyer production and Bethlehem Steel's proposal was rejected. In addition, BuC&R realized that it would be easier and more efficient to simply continue production of *Wickes* hulls but with half power. As a result, in August 1917 the design of the 150 destroyers was approved as a full-length *Wickes* hulls with half power. Shortly after, however, the shipyards involved in the *Wickes* program noted that any major changes to the current *Wickes* design would require preparation of new detailed drawings and cause lengthy production delays. As a result, in September 1917 the SECNAV approved the *Clemson* class design to be essentially a repeat of the *Wickes* design, but strengthened to take a 5-inch gun and with 35% more fuel capacity to increase cruising radius (see Figure 2 and Table 3). The increase in fuel oil capacity was achieved by the addition of bunkerage abeam the boilers and gave the *Clemson* a radius of 4,900 nautical miles at 15 knots - 1,300 nm more that the *Wickes.*

Figure 2: USS *Broome* (DD-210), *Clemson* Class Destroyer[11]

Table 3: Design Characteristics, *Clemson* Class Destroyers[12]

Design Displacement	1,215 tons
Length on Waterline	310' 0"
Beam	30' 11½ "
Draft (mean)	9' 10"
Speed	36 knots
Crew	101
Armament	4 x 4" 3 x 3" 12 x 21" tt

2.2 Pre-Construction Preparations Phase

2.2.1 Selection of Shipbuilders

Even before the Navy approved the 150 *Clemson* class destroyers, it searched for shipyards to build the 111 *Wickes* destroyers. At the outbreak of World War One, destroyers were still a relatively new ship type, the first U.S. Navy destroyer, *Bainbridge* having been laid down in August 1899. Sixteen years later when the USS *Caldwell* and here five sisters were authorized, only 68 destroyers had been built by eleven commercial yards and one government yard (see Appendix A for a key to shipyard abbreviations used in this report). While the United States' destroyer-building history was embryonic in 1915, five shipyards had already emerged as the "traditional" yards, having built over three-quarters (53 of 68) of all U.S. Navy destroyers:

- William Cramp and Sons (Cramp) - 16
- Bath Iron Works (Bath) – 13
- Bethlehem Steel, Quincy yard (BethQ) – 11
- New York Shipbuilding (NYSB) -- 9
- Newport News Shipbuilding (NN) -- 4

A sixth yard, Bethlehem Steel, San Francisco (BethSF), also had experience, having built three of the early destroyers in 1899-1903. The sole destroyer built at a government yard, Mare Island Navy Yard (MINY), was also the most recently commissioned, USS *Shaw* (DD-68). When in March 1917 the SECNAV opened bids for seventy-four of the *Wickes* class destroyers, bids were received for only twenty-four and all were from the six yards that had destroyer-building experience. In April the

SECNAV explored the possibility that shipyards inexperienced in combatant construction could be induced to build destroyers. No offers were received because these shipyards were filled to capacity with merchant ship orders. In any case, most shipyards preferred merchant ship contracts because they commanded a higher profit margin than combatants and were viewed as easier to build.[13] As a result, all but one of the *Wickes* class were built by the six private yards and MINY. The other was built at Charleston Navy Yard (CharNY).

2.2.2 Competing Building Priorities

After settling on continuing to use the existing destroyer shipbuilders the Navy had to free up occupied building ways. This took some time because the Navy leadership was divided in their assessment of construction priorities in the first months of the war. Many, including the Chief of Naval Operations (CNO), desired that capital-ship construction continue because these ship types would remain strategically important after the war ended. Their views were strong enough that the SECNAV let contracts for six *Omaha* class scout cruisers and five *Lexington* class battle cruisers in March 1917. Along with existing battleship orders, these contracts were given to the same shipyards that were to build destroyers. NYSB had contracts for three battleships and one battle cruiser, NN had three battleships and two battle cruisers, BethQ had one battle cruiser and one scout cruiser, and Cramp had five scout cruisers. With the American entry into the war, the Royal Navy revealed the extent of losses to U-boats and by June the CNO changed his stance and agreed that destroyer construction should be the first priority. In the meantime, shipyards discovered that the large number of skilled workers needed to build and launch battleships could not be spared if work on destroyers was to be accelerated. As a result, in June the SECNAV ordered that construction of battleships and cruisers should be delayed and destroyer production accelerated. By the end of July 1917, work on battleships and cruisers had largely halted, thus freeing up shipyard personnel and building ways for destroyer work.[14] This policy of delaying capital ship construction lasted for the duration of the war. As a result, only two of the nine battleships under construction at the outbreak of the war were delivered during the war. These two ships, USS *Mississippi* and *New Mexico*, were only finished because they were nearly complete, having been laid down in 1914. No cruisers were built during the war.*

2.2.3 Expansion and Creation of Shipyards

With the additional requirement of building 150 *Clemsons* (156 were eventually built) the only option available to the Navy was to pay for the traditional yards to expand capacity at their existing yards and build additional facilities. Bethlehem Shipbuilding Corporation was able to contribute the most to this expansion. It upgraded its BethQ and BethSF yards. Capacity at the BethSF yard was increased by the acquisition and reactivation of the adjoining Risdon Iron Works. The company also constructed an assembly yard at Squantum (BethSQ), near its Quincy yard, where thirty-five *Clemson* class destroyers were built. The funding mechanism for both the *Clemson* destroyers and the expansion of shipyard facilities came on October 6, 1917 when President Wilson signed the Urgent Deficiencies Act. The urgent need for destroyers was evidenced by the fact that Bethlehem broke ground on the new assembly yard at Squantum the following day. NYSB, Cramp, and NN all expanded their yards to be able to handle a few more destroyers. Bath, limited by space, could only offer to speed up construction on its ways as a means to increase production. But, in fact, Bath was only able to build three *Clemsons*. All but four of the 267 *Wickes* and *Clemson* class ships were built by eight yards -- the six traditional civilian yards, MINY and the newly built BethSQ yard (see Figures 3 and 4).

---

* In fact, all non-destroyer combatant construction during the war was of small ship types: 60 *Eagles*, 405 110-ft. wooden sub chasers, 17 minesweepers, and 8 submarines.

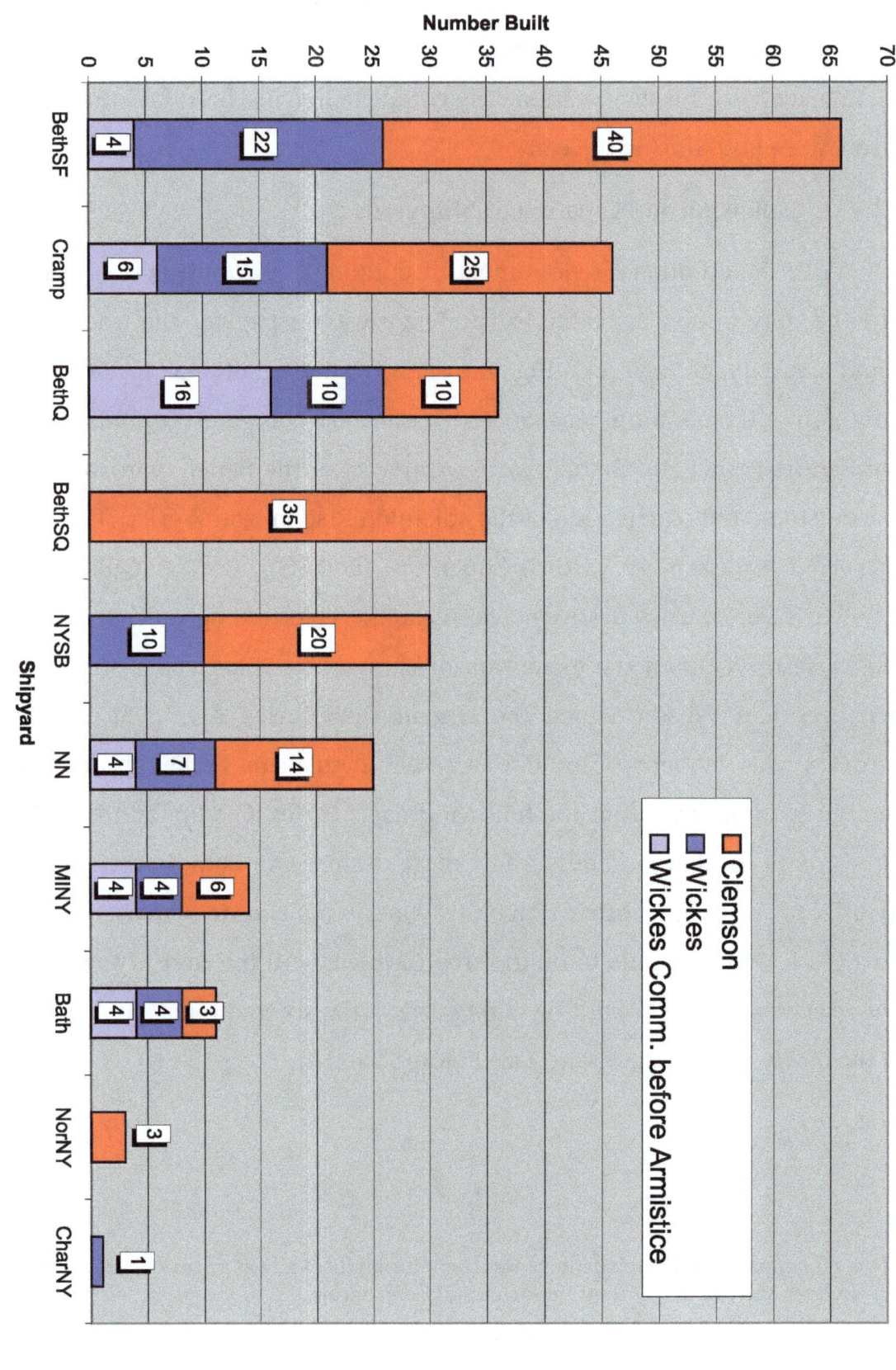

Note: No *Clemson* class commissioned before the Armistice. Five *Caldwell* class DD, contracted before the war crisis, also under construction during and after the war at Bath (1), Cramp (2), MINY (1), and NorNY (1).

Figure 3: WW I Destroyer Shipbuilders, By Class/Number Built

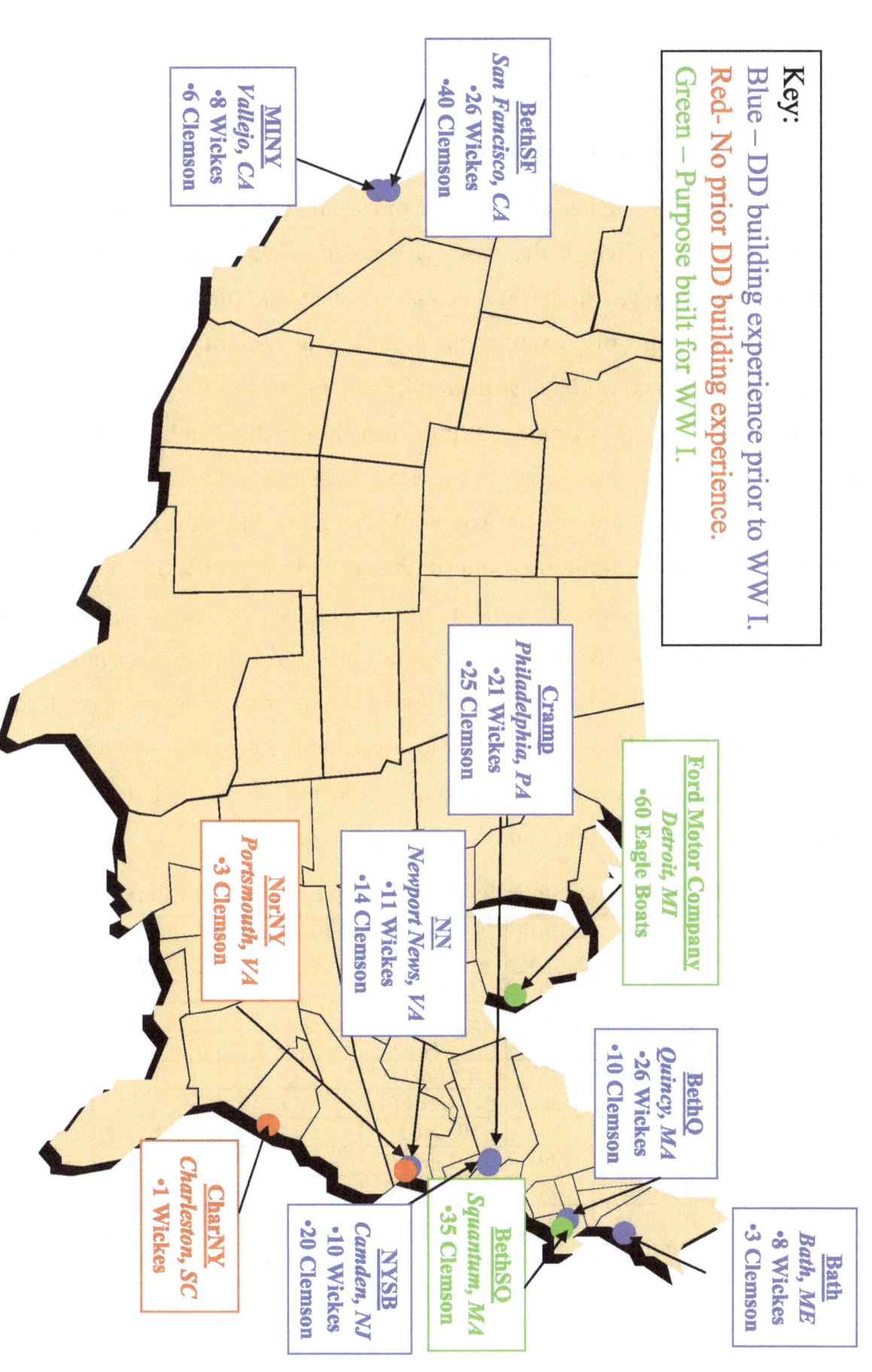

Also shown: Ford Motor Company's *Eagle* Boat plant.
Figure 4: World War I Destroyer Shipbuilders, Geographic View

2.3 Construction Phase

2.3.1 Number of Building Ways

With a finite number of shipyards to execute the emergency destroyer building program, the rate at which the destroyers could be constructed was limited by the number of building ways that could be made available at the shipyards. (This is true of all building programs discussed in this report). The sum of the maximum number of building ways at each of the destroyer shipbuilders was 85 ways. However, this level was never achieved concurrently because each shipyard began laying down destroyers and achieved peak usage of ways at different times (see Table 4). As a result, the most ways in use at one time was 77 in August 1918. With building priorities settled by June 1917, the destroyer building program commenced. Bath and BethQ began to lay down the first of the *Wickes* class the same month (see Figure 5). Cramp and MINY followed suit in July. However, BethSF, and NN did not begin laying keels until October 1917 and NYSB in December. BethSQ only began laying down *Clemson* class destroyers in April 1918 because of the time needed to construct the purpose-built facility. CharNY and NorNY began construction of its four destroyers late in the latter half of 1918 and never significantly contributed to the destroyer program.

Table 4: Building Way Statistics, WW I Destroyer Shipbuilders, by Start Date

Yard	# Built	1st Keel Laid	Most Ways in Use	Avg. Ways in Use
BethQ	36	18-Jun-17	10	7
Bath	11	26-Jun-17	4	3
MINY	14	10-Jul-17	3	2
Cramp	46	12-Jul-17	11	7
NN	25	1-Oct-17	11	6
BethSF	66	20-Oct-17	14	8
NYSB	30	1-Dec-17	18	10
BethSQ	35	20-Apr-18	10	9
CharNY	1	29-Jul-18	1	1
NorNY	3	18-Nov-18	3	3

Figure 5: USS *Colhoun* and *Stevens* on the building ways, BethQ, October 1917[15]

The peak of 77 building ways and construction productivity was achieved shortly before the Armistice in November 1918. At the time of the Armistice the building program had been underway for 17 months. During that period an average of 45 ways were in use and for over 50% of the time more than 51 were in use. After the war ended working hours were reduced and a concerted effort was made to return to peacetime conditions. As a result, the number of building ways in use quickly declined (see Figure 6) even though 97 of the *Wickes/Clemson* destroyers had yet to be laid down.

For the entire period of the building program when ways were in use (53 months) the average usage was 34 ways.

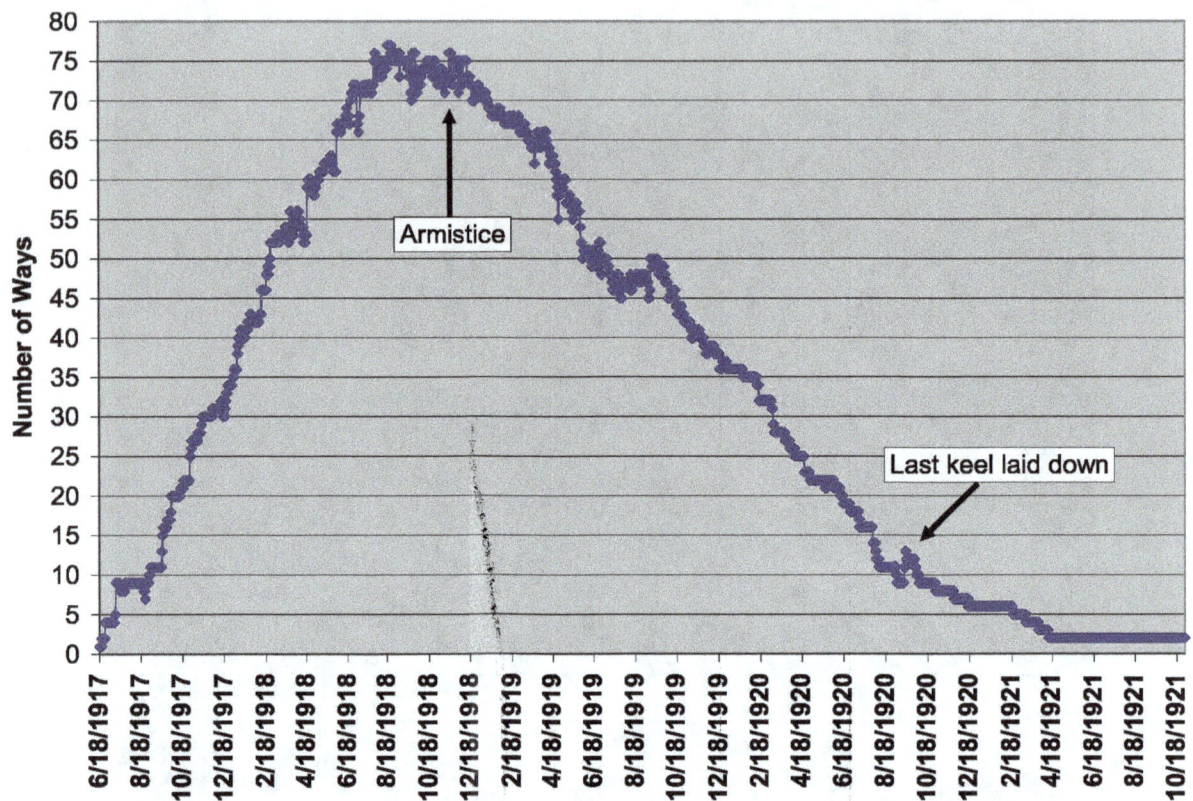

Figure 6: Number of Ways in Use, JUN 1917 – OCT 1921, All Destroyer Shipbuilders

2.3.2 Shortages and Industrial Expansion

The rate at which shipyards were able to lay down ships and make more building ways available was an important factor to get large numbers of ships built. An equally significant factor was the ability of the shipyards to get destroyers launched as soon as possible after laying them down, because all of the shipyards except CharNY and NorNY had many more destroyer orders than building ways. To speed up construction it was essential that the Navy coordinate standardization of design throughout the various shipyards to the greatest extent possible. To maximize production, three principles were followed:

- "The adoption of standard design covering general features of construction.

- The adoption of the smallest practicable number of detail designs of propelling machinery and auxiliaries, taking into consideration expansion of existing facilities.
- Study of materials of construction to determine where substitution of material could be made with the least possible sacrifice of efficiency.

"Standardization, where possible, was insisted upon and successfully accomplished with propellers, propeller shafts, turbine units, pumps, blowers, safety valves, evaporators and distillers, ice machines, electric generators, and searchlights."[16] Of primary importance when designing machinery was reliability and speed of construction. Simplification of design and use was also important because the unprecedented number of destroyers entering the fleet meant that most of destroyer crews were new to the Navy. Two basic plans evolved. All of the Bethlehem Steel yards built to one design, while all of the other shipbuilders used a design developed by Bath Iron Works. However, each yard made minor design changes to accord with its own construction methods.[17]

Shortages of major ship components, especially machinery and other auxiliaries that had to be installed while ships were on the building ways, posed the greatest threat to delaying hull construction. As a result, the Navy went to great effort to expand the industrial base that supplied the destroyers. Before the war, shipyards generally built the machinery and auxiliaries for the ships they were constructing (see Figure 7). Many continued this practice when building the *Wickes* and *Clemson* class destroyers. However, with so many destroyers on order it was inevitable that shortages would occur. And, many of the shipyards did not have the facilities to produce the outfit for all of the destroyers under construction. As a result, many shipyards used other industrial resources to help, in part or fully, to manufacture these components, sometimes under license. This had the benefit of freeing up the shipyard workforce to concentrate on hull construction and fitting out.

Figure 7: Boilers under construction at Norfolk Navy Yard, May 1917[18]

The most significant shortage encountered in the destroyer building program during World War One was that of reduction gears. The Bureau of Engineering's history of its war efforts states that "probably no other part of the machinery equipment of the entire DD program gave cause for more concern." The situation was serious enough that the American naval attaché in London was directed to ask the British for gears. However, an unsatisfactory response from British gear makers prompted BuEng to consider buying the plans for the Parsons gear hobbing machine and build the machines in the United States. Before such plans were carried out the British made existing machines available. But delays in the delivery of the promised machines led the Navy to expand facilities in Milwaukee, where gears were cut for all BethQ destroyers. While some of the engines for BethQ and BethSQ-built ships were built at BethQ, the majority was constructed by a newly built shop in Buffalo, New York. (The castings for the turbine casings were made at other points and shipped to Buffalo.) However, the building of the Buffalo shop was delayed because of severe cold and snow conditions during the winter of 1917-1918. Cramp built its own turbines for its destroyers. This was possible because the Navy purchased the entire stock of the De La Vergne Machinery Co. of New York City and transferred the operation of the works to Cramp in Philadelphia. Cramp-built destroyers had gears cut at De Laval Steam Turbine Co. of Trenton, NJ. Because of these shortages, Newport News opted to use paired Curtis direct-drive (nongeared) turbines for the *Wickes* destroyers it built, even though this configuration decreased these ships' maximum speed. Newport News was dissatisfied with their performance in the *Wickes* ships, so for the following *Clemson* class ships both they and New York Shipbuilding contracted with Westinghouse for geared turbines. General Electric and Westinghouse cut gears for the turbines which they manufactured, as did MINY for the turbines built at that yard. BethSF built a shop at Alameda, CA to facilitate construction of its original *Wickes* class contracts. When BethSF took on contracts for an additional 40 *Clemsons* it planned for the Alameda shop to build the machinery for these ships. However, it quickly became obvious that it could not. As a result, the Navy paid for a General Electric facility in Erie, PA that had just completed construction to be equipped to build turbines. It built the turbines for all 40 *Clemsons* built at BethSF.

A second source of concern for BuEng was the availability of boiler tubes, which for more than a year before the war were in scarce supply. The shortage was severe enough that the BuEng considered requesting that the President place an embargo on the exportation of tubes. After war was declared, many firms took up production and solved the supply problem. For example, about two-thirds of the boilers for the BethQ and BethSQ were built at a new shop at Providence, RI, which was specially equipped for manufacture of Yarrow boilers. The remainder was constructed at BethQ. For the construction of boilers for its ships, BethSF rented and equipped the adjoining Risdon Iron Works, which had been inactive before the war. All boilers were built to the Yarrow design.* Boilers for Cramp, NN, and NYSB were White-Forster type and built

---

* The Yarrow boilers installed on the BethSF destroyers were especially a problem. They had deteriorated in service to such an extent by 1929 that the Navy scraped all sixty of the destroyers with Yarrow boilers.

by Babcock & Wilcox at Bayonne NJ, whose works had to be greatly enlarged to meet a schedule of twenty a month. A delivery rate of one boiler a day was eventually achieved much later with the help of other Babcock & Wilcox-owned facilities.[19]

Because of these measures and the use of alternate machinery, the logistical shortages were kept to a minimum. As a result, in general, the destroyers' time on the building ways was not delayed because of a shortage of machinery and other major components that were installed before launching.

With the number of ways dedicated to the destroyer program increasing each month the number of ships laid down rose and had a cascading effect on the number of ships launched starting in November 1917. By July 1918 the shipyards involved in the destroyer building program reached both their peak number of keel layings and number of launchings (see Figure 8). By war's end, 170 of the 267 ships in the emergency building program had been laid down and 99 launched. For those 99 ships, the shipyards were able to launch them approximately five months on average after they had been laid down. This average grew to almost 7 months after the Armistice because of the work slowdown.

The decline of activity at the war's end, when so few of the destroyers had been commissioned, affected the average productivity of all shipyards. As can be seen in Table 5 the building times varied greatly for each shipbuilder. Contributing to the total construction time was that the winter of 1917-1918 in the northeastern United States was unprecedented in its severity. Temperatures were so cold that outdoor activity essentially ceased at East Coast shipyards during much of the winter months. This was reflected by the increased building times for ships that were laid down during the winter months of 1917-1918.

Figure 8: USS *Zane* (DD-337) launching at MINY, AUG 1919[20]

Table 5: Construction Times for WW I Destroyer Builders, By Number Built

Shipyard	# Built	Months from Keel Laying to Commissioning		
		Shortest	*Average*	*Longest*
BethSF	66	7.5	17.5	25.0
Cramp	46	8.0	12.1	16.1
BethQ	36	5.8	8.3	17.1
BethSQ	35	2.8	9.4	13.6
NYSB	30	15.5	20.8	28.4
NN	25	9.9	18.0	28.1
MINY	14	2.3	17.0	36.2
Bath	11	6.8	10.7	14.5
NorNY	3	21.5	24.1	27.3
CharNY	1	33.5	33.5	33.5

2.4 Delivery Phase

The war ended just as destroyer shipyards were beginning to reach a high level of productivity. At the time of the Armistice in November 1918, only 38 *Wickes* (and one *Caldwell*) class destroyers had been placed in commission (BethQ,16; BethSF, 4; Cramp, 6; BIW, 4; NN, 4; MINY, 4). Because of its late start the other "traditional" destroyer builder, NYSB, did not complete a single ship before the Armistice. The average building time for these *Wickes* was just under 10 months. This was better than the average time it took the same shipyards to build smaller prewar destroyer classes. The six-ship *Tucker* class (FY13 program) took an average of 20 months to build, while the six-ship *Sampson* (FY14 program) required on average 17 months to build. Because of the decrease in activity after the Armistice, most yards witnessed increases in the construction time of successive hulls (see Figures 9 and 10). The building time for the rest of the program after the Armistice was slightly more than 15 months.

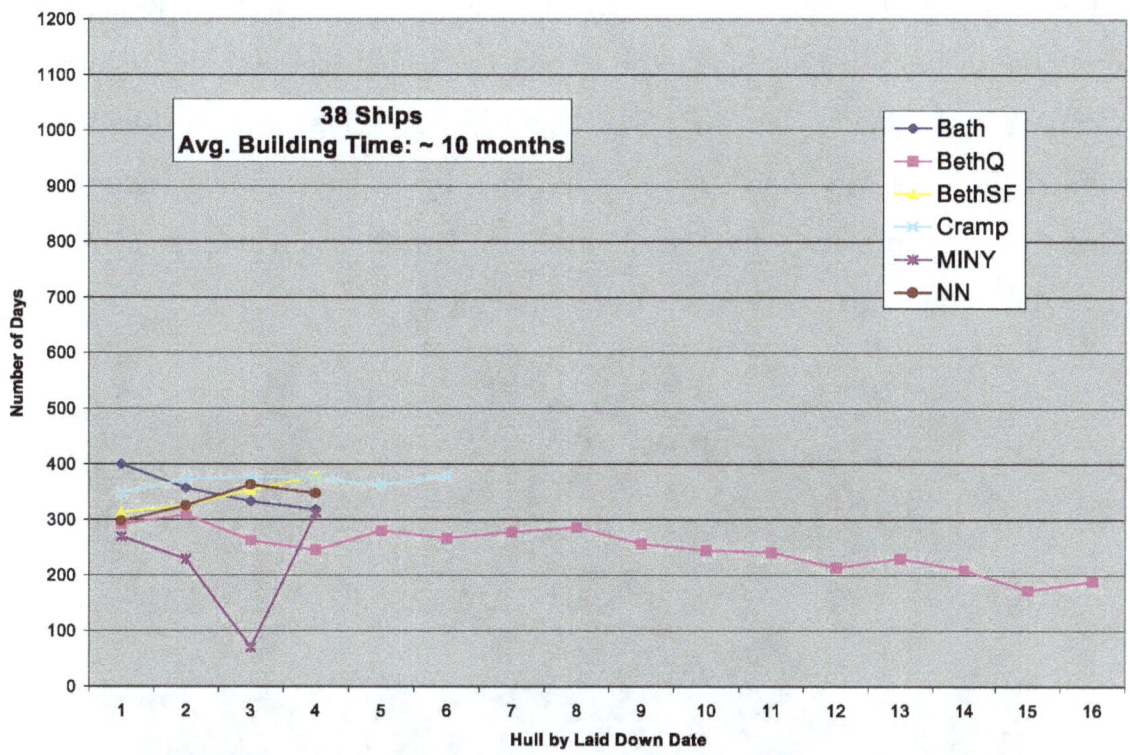

Figure 9: Building Times for Ships Laid Down Before Armistice

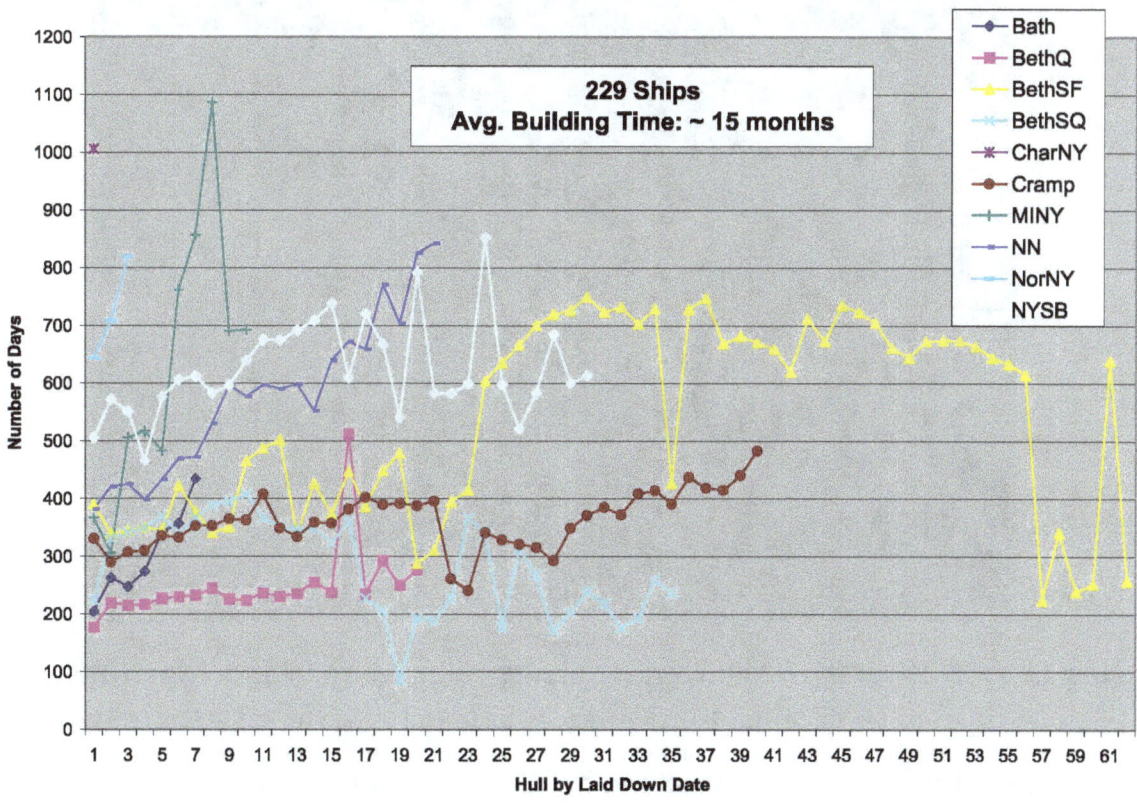

Figure 10: Building Times for Destroyers Laid Down After Armistice

Certain yards were able to build individual ships in very short periods through careful preparation, but were not able to do so on a consistent basis for all its ships. For instance, MINY was able to launch USS *Ward* only 17 days after keel-laying and commissioned the ship less than two months later by pre-assembling material and maximizing the use of prefabrication (see Figure 11). However, on average MINY took 17 months to build the fourteen *Wickes/Clemson* assigned to it.

Note: Many hull plates still held in place with bolts.

Figure 11: USS *Ward* (DD-139) Under Construction, Mare Island, May 1918[21]

Likewise, Bethlehem's Squantum yard was able to build the USS *Reid* in less than three months, but the average construction for its 35 *Clemson* class destroyers was over nine months (see Table 5).[22] However, its average was still below the total average of all shipyards. Still, BethSQ was able to build its ships quicker than the norm because it was essentially an assembly yard. As mentioned previously, the BethSQ plant was purposed built for the emergency destroyer building program (see Figure 12) and staffed by experienced shipbuilders from Bethlehem's Quincy yard. The main assembly building had ten building ways for initial construction and wet slips for fitting out (see Figure 13 and 14). All material for building the destroyers was shipped from other facilities owned or operated by Bethlehem Shipbuilding. This allowed material to be carefully prepositioned (see Figure 15) and left the work force to concentrate on construction.

Note: Left half of building contained dry building ways and right half had wet slips for fitting out. To the far right is an open dock, also for fitting out.

Figure 12: Bethlehem Shipbuilding's Victory Destroyer Plant, Squantum, MA[23]

Figure 13: Unidentified destroyer launching at BethSQ [24]

Figure 14: Interior View of (Dry) Building Ways, BethSQ[25]

Note: barrels, mountings, shields and base rings for 4"/50 guns.
Figure 15: Interior View of Wet Slips, BethSQ[26]

Emergency Production Historical Study

The ability of the Navy and the shipyards to achieve an average destroyer construction time of 10 months by November 1918 was a significant achievement. Had the war lasted until into 1919, as was generally assumed, more than 10 destroyers a month could have been commissioned (see Figure 16). The complexity of the ship fleet destroyer design was not conducive, on average, to construction breakthroughs that would result in increasingly shorter construction times. Such limitations were anticipated by the Navy's shipbuilding specialists, BuC&R and BuEng, who predicted to a remarkably accurate degree the rate at which destroyers could be delivered (see Figure 17).

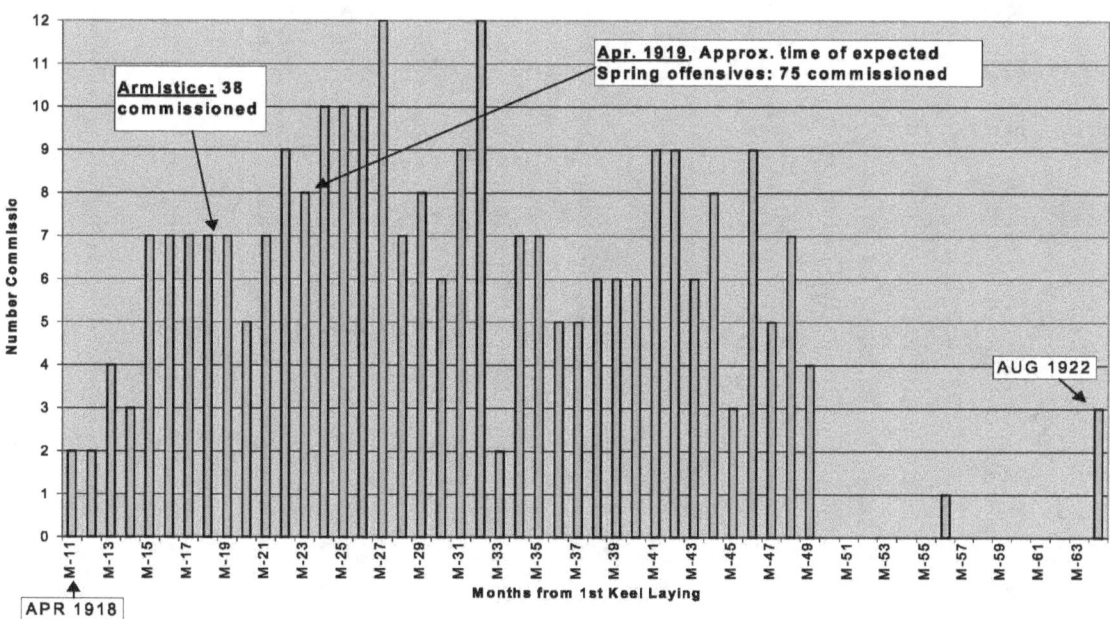

Figure 16: Monthly Commissionings of Wickes/Clemson Destroyers, 1918-1922

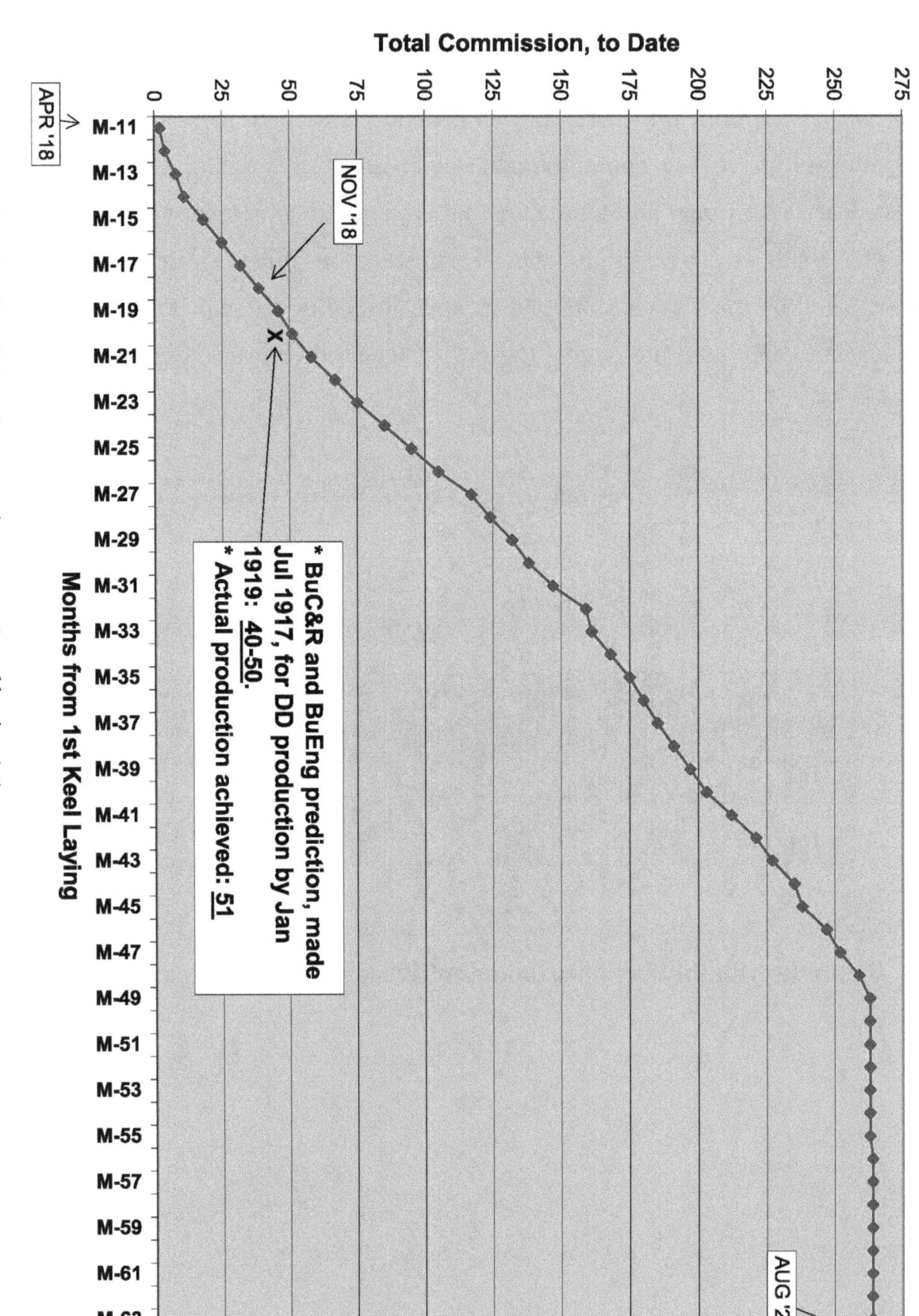

Note: 1 Caldwell class destroyer also commissioned by Armistice.
Figure 17: **Cumulative number of Wickes/Clemson Destroyers in Commission, 1918-1922**

Because of the urgency of the building program most of the *Wickes* and *Clemson* class were quickly built and, as a result, many did not meet peacetime standards of workmanship. One source cites the commissioning officer for the USS *Little* (DD-79) recording that "'leaky seams and loose rivets were the rule; boiler tubes had to be re-rolled wholesale; and a bushel basket-ful of nuts and bolts was collected from inside steam and water lines during shakedown.'"[27] This situation resulted when workers were not assigned to the same area of construction that they had been the previous workday. However, the Navy anticipated such problems and because of the variety of propulsion packages and the differing experience levels of the shipbuilders initially the Navy's primary acceptance criteria were the speed and cruising radius of each ship. The General Board demanded 35 knots on trial at a displacement of about 1,150 tons, and a steaming endurance of 2,500 nm at 20 knots. (The contracts specifically stipulated 3,600 nm at 15 knots.) The *Wickes* class generally achieved the desired speed within displacement limits.[28] Their displacement varied from 1,020 to 1,190 tons. Their "normal" displacement, the designed figure for a completely outfitted with half the consumables on board, varied from 1,125 to 1,215 tons. Actual trial displacements ranged up to 1,370 tons.[29]

However, results did vary by shipyard. The USS *Wickes*, built by Bath Iron Works, exceeded these requirements. On trial this ship achieved the equivalent of 5,000 nm at 15 knots or 3,400 nm at 20 knots. She was commissioned with a displacement of 1,300 tons. Ships built by Cramp, which followed the Bath design, also did well in their trials. However, ships built at New York Shipbuilding, also using the Bath design, were not able to achieve the same success as Cramp. Bethlehem, Quincy and Mare Island-built destroyers had disappointing trial results.

The shipyards generally did not lay down *Clemson* class ships until they had completed the *Wickes* class. Sixty-three Clemson were laid down between February 1918 and the Armistice. As a result, the *Clemson* class felt more keenly the wartime shortages of power plants and skilled workmen. As a result, the "only performance guaranteed was the delivery of the specified shaft horsepower". They "produced a range of shaft horsepower between 19,700 and 27,000 for rated speeds of 32 to 35 knots." [30] And due to the shortages in skilled workmen and hurried conditions, the *Clemsons* averaged 5 to 6% overweight.[31]

Because of the sharp reduction in budgets, workforce, and less rigorous schedules, many of the destroyers were not completed and commissioned until the early 1920s – long after they had been launched (see Figure 18). The last was commissioned in August 1922. Many ships were commissioned with a 50% complement and put in reserve status. Twenty-four of the destroyers saw almost no service. They had been laid up in 1922 and remained in this status until they were scrapped in the 1930s.[32] While the *Wickes* and *Clemson* destroyers did not see much service in World War I, they formed the backbone of the Navy's destroyer force for much of the interwar period. Forty-four were transferred to Great Britain and six to Canada in 1940 and many more were modified by the U.S. Navy for a variety of roles in World War II.

Figure 18: Destroyers fitting out at BethSF in 1920[33]

3. EAGLE BOATS

In contrast to the decision to continue the current design of fleet destroyers the Navy opted to design a radically simplified, less capable, small combatant and selected an inexperienced builder to execute the program.

3.1 Design Decision Phase

3.1.1 Strategic Background

As mentioned in the previous section, upon entry into the war the Navy decided that the three highest priorities for emergency construction should be: (1) Destroyers, (2) Submarine chasers, and (3) Small destroyers (the *Eagle* Boat).[34] To meet the first priority, the Navy embarked upon a destroyer building program, which is discussed in the previous section. Next, the Navy, working with yacht builders, designed a 110-foot, 75-ton submarine chaser. To reduce the competition for scarce materials the Navy opted for a wooden boat with gasoline engines. Because major shipbuilders were fully engaged with merchant and combatant construction the Navy selected a large number of boat builders located on both coasts, the Gulf of Mexico and the Great Lakes. A total of 440 wooden submarine chasers were built quickly. While these vessels were effective, patrol tactics alone did not reduce the losses to U-boats in the summer and fall of 1917. A convoy strategy was then emphasized, but the submarine chasers did not have the range to make transatlantic voyages, and destroyers were in short supply and had other missions.* In the meantime, the SECNAV ordered in March 1917 design work to commence on a large steel patrol boat for mass production. At first a 156-foot design was explored but this was rejected by the General Board in May 1917 because intelligence indicated that new 2,400 ton U-boats armed with three 5.9-inch guns had entered service. To meet this threat a design approaching the size, speed, and

---

* Large numbers of destroyers were held in readiness as a "fleet in being" on the east coast of England and Scotland in case German surface combatants attempted to sortie in force from the Baltic.

armament of a destroyer was necessary. And by the fall it was clear that only a larger steel design could provide the range and durability necessary for transatlantic patrols. In addition, new submarine detection devices had become available and platforms designed for their use were preferred. As such, the Navy desired that a ship between the size of a destroyer and submarine chaser be designed and built as quickly as possible. By November 1917 design work began on the *Eagle* Boats, although ship characteristics had not been formally approved.[35]

3.1.2 Simple Design for Rapid Construction

While a notional ASW ship was desired quickly, by late 1917 the nation's shipyards were filled to capacity with combatant and merchant ship construction. As such, developing a complex design that would require experienced builders and significant construction time was not a viable option. Only small maritime firms and/or inexperience builders were available, necessitating a radically simplified design for the *Eagle* Boats. It was hoped that the simple design would expedite construction. However, when the SECNAV canvassed the nation's smaller ship and boat builders – expecting that the project could be accomplished in a similar manner to the submarine chaser program – he discovered that none were available. Faced with this dilemma the Navy chose the Ford Motor Company to execute the <u>entire</u> *Eagle* Boat program.

3.2 Pre-Construction Preparations Phase

3.2.1 Selection of Ford Motor Company

The selection of Ford, a firm with no maritime experience whatsoever, was certainly unconventional, and a brief examination of the selection process will give an appreciation of the critical urgency surrounding the nation's building programs by late 1917. In June 1917, Henry Ford was invited to join the U.S. Shipping Board, which had been organized to oversee the allocation of resources for the national shipbuilding effort. Experienced with the intricacies of mass production, Ford was a natural choice, and he accepted membership in November. In this capacity he became aware of the

Navy's plans for what would eventually become the *Eagle* Boats and the SECNAV's difficulty in finding a builder. At that time he recommended the use of flat hull plates to speed construction and convinced the Navy to settle for steam turbines instead of reciprocating steam engines.[36] Influenced by his high regard for the car maker, the SECNAV asked Ford "if he could build such a ship under contract at Ford River Rouge plant, using mass production techniques and factory workers, instead of the various shipbuilding skilled trades normally required."[37] The SECNAV was not alone in his almost reverential regard for Henry Ford's abilities. In 1917, Ford was one of the most famous and respected men in American and his company's capacity for mass production was a matter of national pride.[38] The previous year, Ford Motor Company produced almost 600,000 Model T automobiles by using the principals of mass production. In addition, Ford was already heavily engaged in war production having manufactured a wide variety of materiel, including tanks, twelve-cylinder aircraft engines, armor plate, gun caissons, and helmets.[39] Confident that his company could apply the principles of mass production, especially the assembly line, to the construction of a small combatant, Ford formally offered to build all of the *Eagle* Boats on December 24. Reflecting the urgency of the time, design work moved rapidly. On December 26, BuC&R began preliminary design work and over the next four days three design conferences were held. Before the new year, Ford was provided with preliminary design drawings and by January 8, 1918, the design was completed. With the design in hand, on January 14 Ford submitted a proposal to build 100 to 500 *Eagle* Boats, with the first to be delivered in five months or less. Three days later, the Navy issued a contract with Ford for 100 *Eagle* Boats. After contract award, "work on the general and detail plans was prosecuted vigorously, often until late hours of the night, and as soon as they were ready were placed in the hands of the builder."

Both BuC&R and the General Board were extremely skeptical of Ford's ability to meet the promised production schedule. They noted that the supply of experienced shipyard workers was meager because most were engaged in destroyer, submarine and merchant ship construction. New workers would require training and guidance by a nucleus of experienced shipbuilders, which would take time and was no guarantee of success. BuC&R noted, for example, that the new American Shipbuilding Corporation, on the Great Lakes, was taking two years to complete tugs of an established design that previously required only a year. Nevertheless, the *Eagle* Boat program went forward with Ford Motor Company as the sole builder, largely because of the SECNAV's personal enthusiasm for Ford. Resigned to the decision, all that the General Board could do in December 1917 was "place on record its view that both the subchaser and the new patrol boat were emergency designs, neither of which would have been acceptable in a less urgent situation."[40]

3.2.2 *Eagle* Boat Design

Because Ford Co. was wholly inexperienced as a shipbuilder and to enable rapid production the design of the *Eagle* class was radically simplified. Detailed design was accomplished at the Highland Park plant of the Ford Motor Company under the direction of naval officers. To oversee construction of the hull, the Navy hired an experienced marine engineer as the Supervising Constructor. The Navy developed the hull with the goal of reducing curved sections as much as possible. Straight lines characterize the design throughout to a great degree:

> "The form was devised so that the waterlines were absolutely straight for a considerable length in the forward and after bodies [see Figure 19], thus maintaining a constant bevel for the frame angles; the sides were straight [see Figure 20], the rise of floor in the forebody and both the frame lines were also straight. Only one strake of plating, that at the turn of the bilge, required bending, and the straight frames at the side and bottom were bracketed together to avoid anglesmith's work [see Figures 21 and 22]. The deck beams had no round up and the sheer was provided by two straight lines so that the deck erections could be built as square houses, brought to the ship complete, and fastened down immediately. The number of different sections and plate thicknesses were kept to a minimum."[41]

Because Ford's engineers were inexperienced shipbuilders, "scantlings were fixed with a view to allowing a margin of strength to cover possible bad workmanship rather than to reducing the hull weight to a minimum. On account of the scarcity of special ship steel shapes and the unavoidable delay in getting them, flanged plates and structural angles were used instead. The flanged plates could be rapidly fabricated from plate stock and while the distribution of metal and consequent physical properties are inferior to those of regular rolled shapes the difference is not of serious importance. Flanged plates have the advantage over rolled shapes that they can be made to any dimension required and choice is not limited to the regular mill patterns. The strakes, angles, frames and gussets were drawn up and the positions of all rivet holes were laid out. No detail was omitted that would hamper manufacturing if left to be laid out in the shop."[42]

Figure 19: *Eagle* **Boat Under Construction, View 1**[43]

Figure 20: *Eagle* Boat Under Construction, View 2[44]

Figure 21 *Eagle* Boat Under Construction, View 3[45]

Figure 22: *Eagle* Boat Under Construction, View 4[46]

The resulting ship was 200 feet long and displaced over 600 tons (see Figure 23 and Table 6). While in March 1917 the Navy had intended to build a small patrol boat*, its design now approached that of a destroyer. In fact, the *Eagle* Boats were larger than any USN destroyer built before 1903.[47] It should be emphasized that the Navy used a manufacturer that was completely inexperienced in shipbuilding to execute this program.

---

* Even after the design grew to that of a small ship the designation "Boat" was retained.

Figure 23: *Eagle* Boat No. 2 on Trials[48]

Table 6: *Eagle* Boat Characteristics[49]

Length (water line)	194 ft.
Length Overall	200 ft. 9 in.
Extreme beam	33 ft. 1 in.
Max draft	8 ft. 6 in.
Max speed	18.32 knots
Displacement	615 tons
Engines	2,500 shp Poole geared turbines
Boilers	(2) Bureau Express
Armament	Two 4-inch/50-caliber One 3-inch/50-caliber Two .50-caliber machine guns 2 x dct 1 x Y-type gun (*Eagle* 4- 7 only)
Complement	5 officers, 56 enlisted.

3.2.3   Development of the River Rouge Plant

Believing that his company could rapidly produce *Eagle* Boats using mass production methods and the assembly line, Ford set an ambitious building schedule. He promised to deliver the first *Eagle* Boat no later than mid-July 1918. The schedule called for ten the following month, 20 in September, and 25 each month thereafter. Thus, in January 1918 Ford promised that he could deliver at least 56 *Eagle* boats by mid-October 1918. This schedule became part of the formal contract between Ford and the Navy executed on March 1, 1918.[50] To realize this promise the Ford Motor Company immediately began to design and construct special facilities at its River Rouge site outside of Detroit. It also began to dredge the River Rouge and drain surrounding marshes to provide adequate area for fitting out the *Eagle* Boats. All of these upgrades were made at the government's expense.[51] Among the new facilities were a 150 x 600 ft. fabricating shop and tool room (A-Building) where steel sheets were formed and many other parts fabricated. The most impressive accomplishment was the construction of the 350 x 1,700 ft. main assembly building (B-Building). More than half a mile long "with steel-framed, hundred foot tall walls which were nothing but undisturbed expanses of glass"[52] the B-Building accommodated three parallel assembly lines, each with seven stations, and two large outfitting buildings (see Figure 24). At the end of the B-Building was a 202-foot long transfer table (essentially a flatcar) that was supported on eleven railroad rails. The transfer table, with an *Eagle* Boat loaded, was then drawn by a tractor out of the assembly building and then perpendicularly for 300 to 600 feet (depending on which assembly line the *Eagle* boat was built) and then placed on a 225 foot steel trestle at the water's edge (see Figure 25). They were then lowered by hydraulic jacks into the channel and moved to the fitting out basin (see Figures 26 and 27).[53,54] The design and construction of the River Rouge plant was completed in under five months and was a considerable engineering feat. The first keel was laid in May 7, 1918 – only 132 days after BuC&R was tasked with developing the preliminary design for the *Eagle* Boat.

Figure 24: Main *Eagle* Boat Assembly Building ("Bldg. B"), River Rouge Plant[55]

Figure 25: Transfer Table, River Rouge Plant[56]

Figure 26: *Eagle* Boat No. 60 Launching, View 1[57]

Figure 27: *Eagle* No. 60 Launching, View 2[58]

While the River Rouge plant was under construction, the Ford Motor Company built a full-scale model of the *Eagle* at its Highland Park factory. With guidance from

Navy supervisors a number of changes were made to improve the rough design developed only in January to fit production requirements. The model was then used to build "special jigs, fixtures, templates, and other patterns for parts" of the ship in order to speed production. The model also allowed the builders to determine the position of all rivet holes. Afterward, the pattern boat was completely disassembled and each part marked to signify its location and to correspond to the detailed drawings.[59] With all of this information in hand, Ford's production engineers wrote operations sheets for all of the steps in the construction process. Each operation sheet precisely detailed the sequence of steps that a worker had to take in a given manufacturing process. This method had been perfected with the Model T and its success made Ford believe that factory workers with no shipbuilding experience could quickly gain a high degree of productivity.

Contributing to the optimistic estimates was the use of other manufacturers to construct the machinery and other auxiliaries. This left the River Rouge plant to concentrate on hull construction and outfitting. For instance, the turbines and reduction gear were from the design of the Poole Engineering Co., Baltimore, Md. Some of the boilers were built in the works of the Ford Motor Co., but the majority was constructed by the Brennan Boiler Works in Detroit. Companies that specialized in destroyer work manufactured most of the other auxiliary machinery and equipment.[60]

3.3 Construction Phase

3.3.1 Production Problems

On May 7, 1918, the keel of the first *Eagle* boat was laid down. However, almost immediately Ford's engineers had to revise their envisioned method of production. Initially, they believed that each *Eagle* boat could be built on a moving assembly line like the Model T. However, the size of the ships and the sheer number of different construction steps made this impossible. Instead, a step-by-step approach was developed and each of the three parallel assembly lines was divided into seven stations (essentially 21 building ways). Ford eventually determined that seven stations were inadequate and the B-Building was extended 200 feet to accommodate an initial preassembly stage before the ships moved along the seven stations. Even so it took many months before the River Rouge plant reached full capacity because of longer-than-expected construction times at each station. It was not until mid-September 1918 that all twenty-one stations were in use (see Figure 28). As a result, the plant's ways were at full capacity for less than a third of the total building program (see Table 7).

Table 7: Percentage Days Ways in Use, *Eagle* Boats

Number of Ways	% in Use Up to Armistice (6.3 months)	Total Building Program (15.5 months)
1-10 Ways in Use	35.4	27.7
11-20 Ways in Use	44.4	41.2
21-22 Ways in Use	20.1	31.1
Most Ways in Use	*21*	*22*
AVG Ways in Use	*14*	*15*

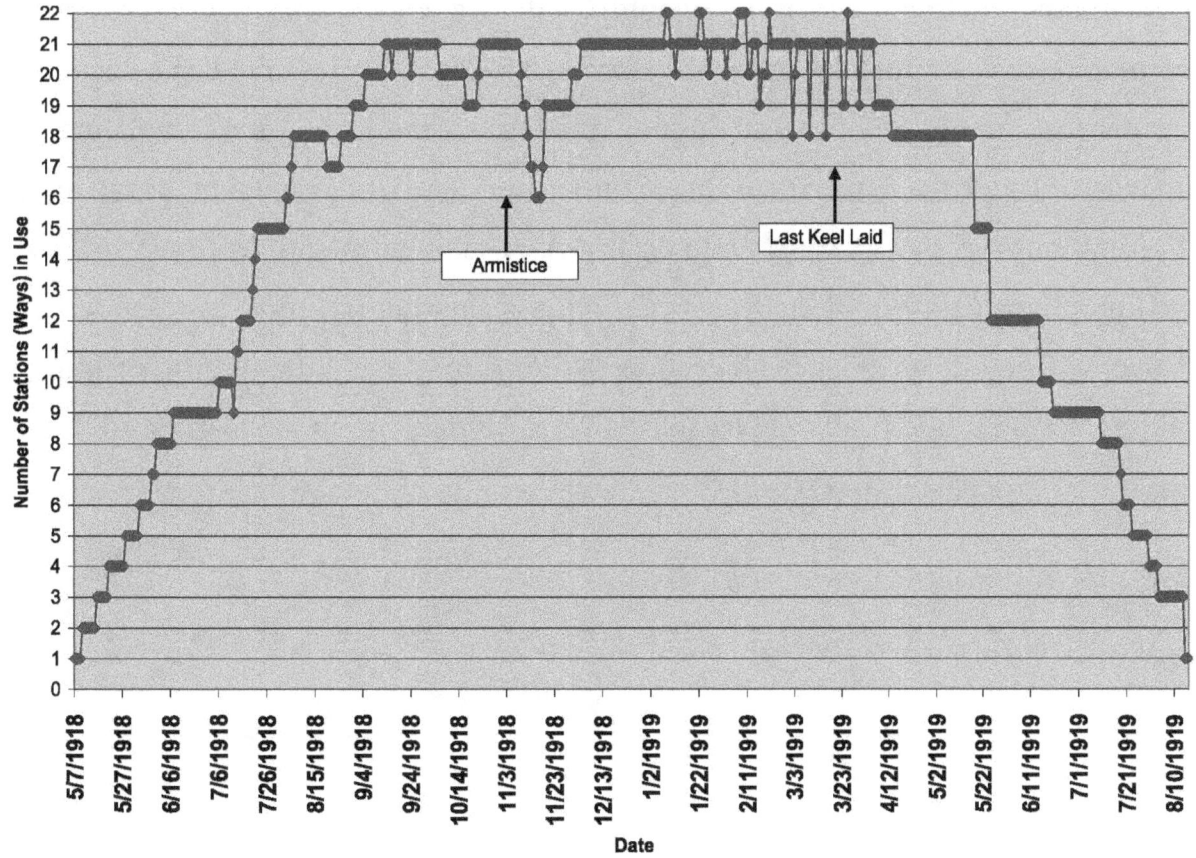

Figure 28: Number of Stations in Use, Ford River Rouge Plant, MAY 1918 – AUG 1919

Because of the construction delays Ford managers realized that they could not built 100 *Eagle* Boats in the time promised. As a result, they requested the Navy pay $2.5 million for a second plant to be built near Newark, NJ. Reflecting the Navy's desire to get large numbers of small ASW combatants into service, they agreed to this request sometime before July 1918. However, the plant was never built because of continual delays and the Armistice in November 1918.

The longer-than-expected building times at each station were the result of problems with construction techniques that arose from the start. The first seven *Eagle* Boats had inferior riveting because Ford's workforce found the task more difficult than anticipated because of their pre-riveting preparations. Workers would stand on ladders and try to bolt steel plates together using short-handled wrenches. However, their technique did not bring the plates together in a sufficiently tight manner. As a result, metal shavings worked in between the plates and prevented the rivets from pulling the plates together to form a strong enough seal (see Figure 29). As a result, the Superintending Constructor's team of inspectors found that the first *Eagle* Boats were not water-tight or oil-tight because of poor riveting techniques.* After complaints from both workers and the Superintending Constructor, Ford management began to use scaffolding but the use of ladders still occurred. The Superintending Constructor also noted the poor quality of electric arc welding, a technique not used in previous Ford endeavors. The officer "specifically requested Ford to 'do as little electric welding on oil and water tight bulkheads as possible as your welders are so inexperienced that the welds are both defective and porous' "[61]

---

* The *Eagle* Boat was designed with ten separate fuel oil compartments.

Note use of ladders.

Figure 29: Hull Construction on *Eagle* Boats[62]

Because of the initial construction problems only five keels were laid down by the end of May 1918 and only eleven more over the next two months – well behind Ford's initial schedule. Such delays meant that *Eagle* Boat launchings for final fitting out were also slow in coming. By August only two were launched (see Figure 30) and none had been completely fitted out. Because of these delays the Navy requested Ford to provide a realistic schedule for the completion of the *Eagle* Boat program. Ford replied that it could complete only twenty-six *Eagle* Boats by the end of 1918 and the rest, which included twelve more ordered by the Italian government, by April 1919.[63] This revised schedule was also not realized.

Emergency Production Historical Study

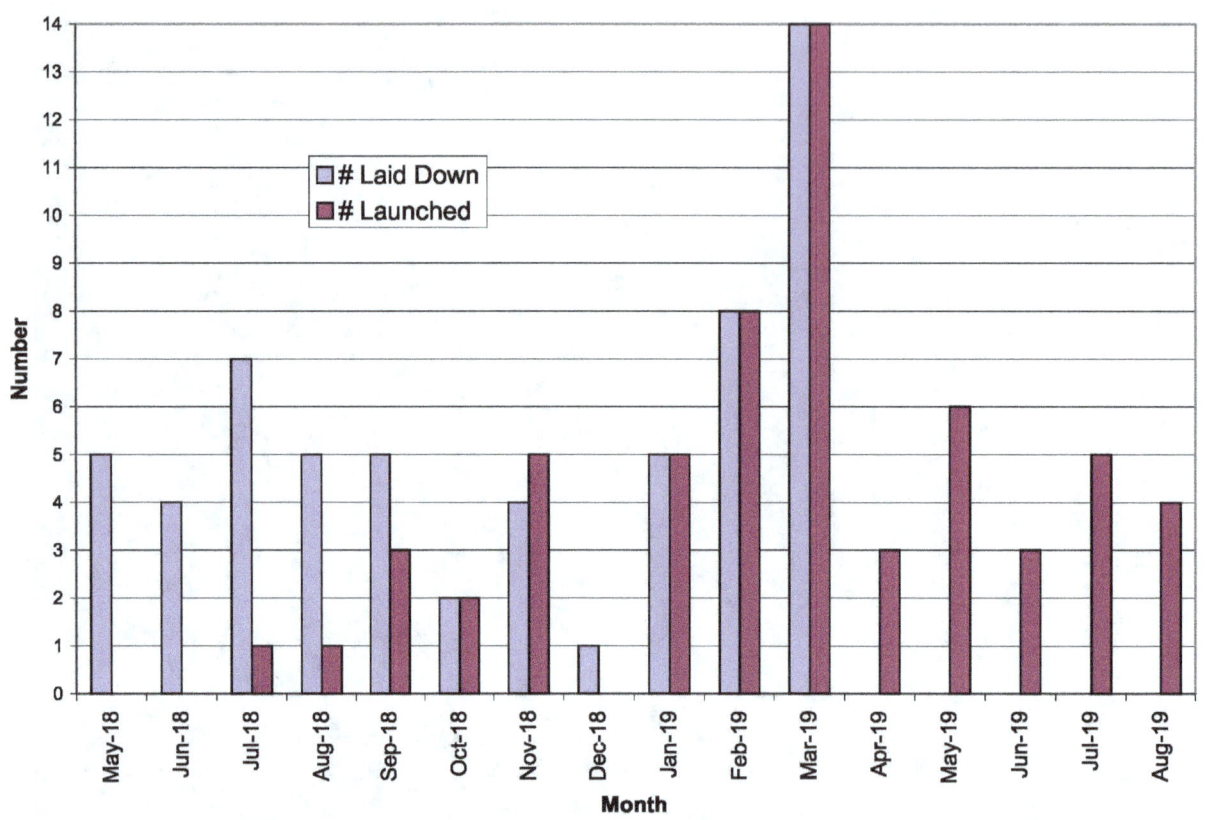

Figure 30: Monthly *Eagle* Boat Keel Layings and Launchings, MAY 1918-AUG 1919

Adding to the construction problems was the fact that working relations between Ford management and the Navy-hired Superintending Constructor were not always harmonious. The Superintending Constructor and his team of experienced shipbuilders attempted to provide advice to Ford's *Eagle* Boat program managers but were often met with resistance, especially at the outset of the program. As a Navy-appointee he was able to force Ford to hire more marine engineers, however, he wrote in September 1918 that "these men were being ignored."[64] The root of the problems arose from the Ford engineers' confidence that mass production methods could be applied to shipbuilding.

While the quality of riveting and welding improved with time and more building stations were used as more workers were hired[*], Ford's promise to rapidly built 100 *Eagle* Boats was defeated by the time required to complete outfitting of the ships. Ford engineers had initially assumed that each *Eagle* could be entirely

---

[*] By July 1918, Ford had 4,380 workers on the *Eagle* program. It later peaked at 8,000.

constructed at the assembly stations and ready for operational service upon launching. This assumption was based upon their experiences with automobiles, which came off the assembly line ready for sale. However, the *Eagle* Boats were a vastly more complex system. Ford was eventually able to standardize the construction of the *Eagle* hulls and devote large number of workers to the task. But the final outfitting tasks, such as installing turbines, boilers, piping, wiring, armament, and other equipment required more time on average than the construction of the hulls. The cramped interior spaces where the final outfitting work was accomplished did not permit large number of workers to be employed (see Figure 31). As a result, Ford was not able to achieve

Figure 31: *Eagle* Boat fitting out[65]

increasing efficiency – a hallmark of successful mass production – in the time needed from launching to commissioning during the course of the *Eagle* Boat program.[66] Therefore, by the Armistice, only three *Eagle* Boats were commissioned and only four more were finished by the end of November 1918. As shown in Table 8, the time from launching to commissioning of the first seven *Eagle* Boats was approximately three months shorter than the following 53 ships. This was the result of Ford's hurried and faulty construction techniques that resulted in leaky ships. Once proper techniques were incorporated after the first seven ships had been delivered, the total construction time, and especially the fitting out process, was considerably extended (see Figure 32).

Table 8: Construction Statistics, *Eagle* Boats

	First 7 *Eagle* Boats	Next 53 *Eagle* Boats	Total Program
Avg. time Laid Down to Launch (months)	3.7	4.0	4.0
Avg. time from Launch to Commissioning (months)	2.2	5.1	4.7
Total Construction Time (months)	5.9	9.1	8.7

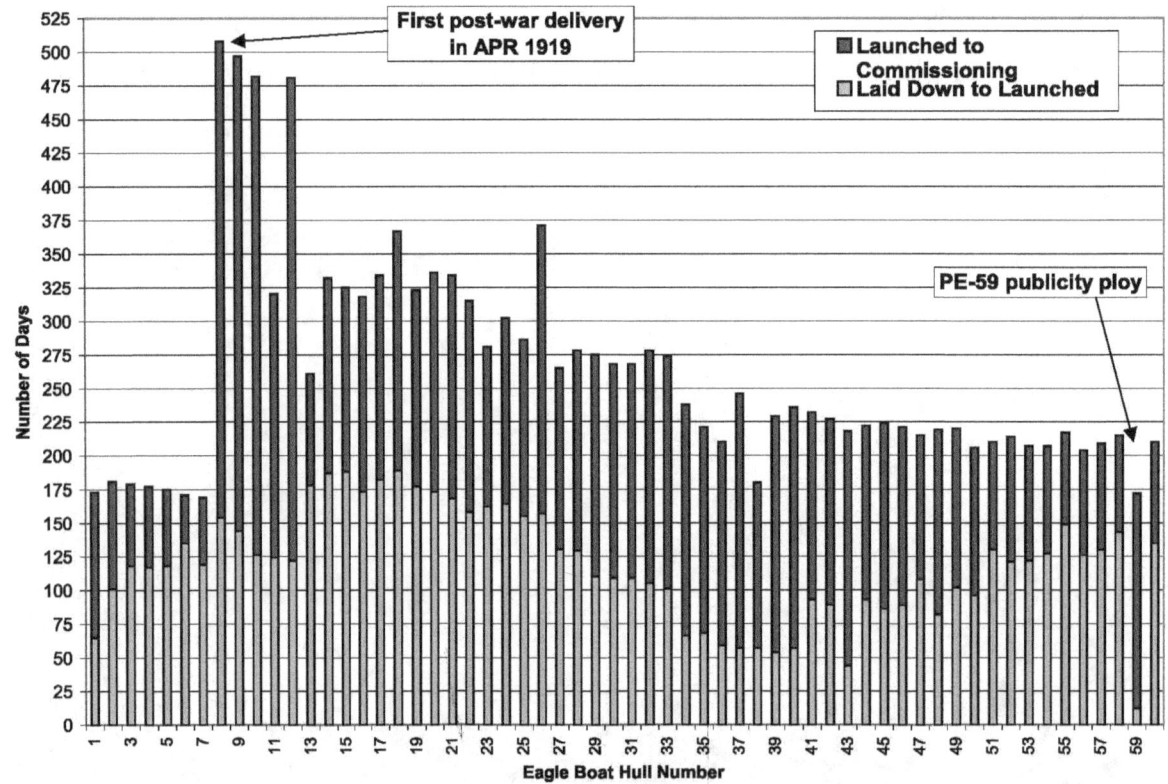

Figure 32: Length of Construct Milestones, *Eagle* Boats

3.4 Delivery Phase

All of these factors delayed the rest of the *Eagle* Boat program. After the initial deliveries in November 1918 the next *Eagle* Boat was not commissioned until April 1919. After the Armistice the Navy's need for *Eagle* Boats ceased and a reappraisal of the program led to the cancellation of fifty-two ships.[67] At the same time Ford sought to generate positive publicity after enduring severe congressional criticism of the program. Henry Ford assigned almost the entire workforce to work exclusively on the last keel laid (*Eagle* 59). The ship was launched, with much publicity, only twelve days later and Ford declared that the achievement was the norm. However, after the launching the workforce was redistributed to all of the other ships building and the *Eagle* No. 59 took until the end of August to finish (see Figure 32)[68] In general, the program moved slowly during most of 1919 and the rate of entry into the fleet was slow. Only three more *Eagle*s Boats were commissioned by mid-June. The last *Eagle* Boat was commissioned in November almost a year behind schedule (see Figure 33).[69]

Arriving too late for World War I, the majority of *Eagle* Boats saw little real service in the interwar period. *Eagle* number 25 capsized in a squall on the Delaware River in June 1920. A second *Eagle* was wrecked in 1922. By 1924, half of the ships were decommissioned, twenty-two were used to train naval reservists, and five were transferred to the Coast Guard. Probably because of the capsizing, the *Eagle*s in operation after 1924 were ballasted with many tons of concrete.[70] Eight *Eagle*s were still in service when World War II broke out. Because of their age, limited capability, and design shortcomings they were used only in the coastal United States during the war. One was lost during the war and the other seven were decommissioned after it ended.[71]

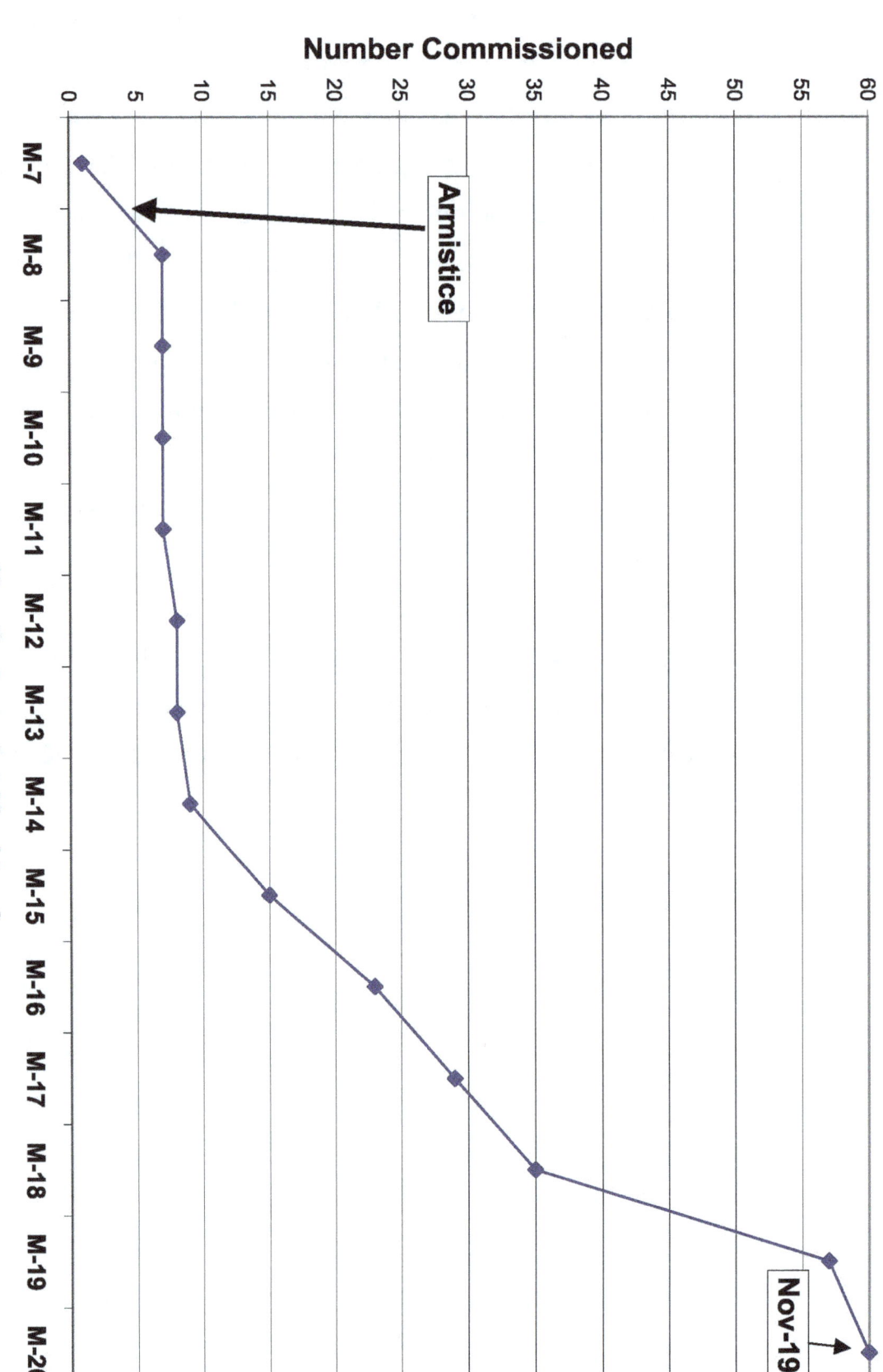

Figure 33: Cumulative Commissionings of *Eagles* Boats, 1918-1919

PART II: WORLD WAR TWO

"When the characteristics of the DD 445 class were established in January 1940, the importance of air attack was recognized and some features were incorporated in the design to provide both active and passive defense against this form of attack. Since that date, however, the seriousness of air attacks has been emphasized increasingly by experiences of ships in the present war... Active defense with heavy machine guns against dive bombing attack to the maximum degree practical is a necessity... It is now generally accepted that some sacrifices in other characteristics are warranted, even in destroyers, to attain these features, whereas this was not the case in January 1940."
~BuShips comment on design sketches for Allen M. Sumner Class, Oct, 1941~

"For American planners, the chief obstacle to embarking on an austere escort vessel program had been the difficulty of justifying the manufacture of ships that were similar in size and cost to the 1,630-ton (Benson-class) fleet destroyers already on the ways, but that were designed purposely to be less capable (e.g., slower, with fewer guns) in order to facilitate multiple production."
    *~Bruce Franklin – **The Buckley- Class Destroyer Escorts**~*

4. WORLD WAR II DESTROYERS

As they had in the First World War, the United States Navy used a dual approach to obtain large numbers of fleet destroyers and smaller ASW/convoy combatants during World War Two. For smaller combatants the Navy created simplified ships, whose designs lent themselves to quick production at inexperienced or purpose-built shipyards. (Sections 6 and 7 examine the simplified designs, the destroyer escort (DE) and patrol frigate (PF)). For fleet destroyers, the Navy opted to continue building complex designs and get more ships by increasing the number on order and the number of building yards.

4.1 Design Decision Phase

4.1.1   *Bristol* Class: Continuation of Existing Production Line

As in the first world conflict, the United States maintained official neutrality for more than two years after the outbreak of World War Two. In contrast to World War One, the United States reacted to world events and embarked upon a war emergency destroyer program before officially entering World War Two. When the European war began with the German invasion of Poland on September 1, 1939 the U.S. Navy was engaged in building the 24-ship *Benson* class (DD 421-444), sixteen of which had already been laid down. In the meantime, the Navy was preparing to develop a new destroyer design – what would become the *Fletcher* class. These ships promised to be larger and more capable than the *Bensons* because in late 1939 the U.S. Navy determined that the British renunciation of the Washington and London Navy Treaties meant that it was no longer obligated to limit the displacement of its ships.[72] (The Japanese renounced their treaty obligations in March 1937). In July 1940, with the fall of France and the threat from Japan intensifying, the Navy determined that it needed more fleet destroyers. The need was considered so acute that the Navy could not afford to wait for the *Fletcher* design to be completed before initiating more destroyer construction. As a result, in the summer of 1940 the Navy ordered twelve destroyers (DD 453-464) that were a slightly improved version of then-building *Benson* class, but with one 5-inch mount deleted to provide topside space and weight for more AA weaponry. While the resulting *Bristol* class proved to be less capable than the *Fletcher* class, they ensured that the existing production line would continue without pause (see Figure 34). To this end, ten of the twelve *Bristol* class contracts were awarded to shipyards (Fed, Bath, BosNY and CharNY) that were engaged in building *Bensons* (see Appendix A for a key to shipyard abbreviations used in this report). As the war crisis worsened the Navy periodically determined that even more destroyers were needed. Fifteen more *Bristol* class (DD 483-497) were ordered in September 1940, followed by forty-one more (DD 598-628, 632-641) in December 1940, and the final four of the class (DD 645-648) in February 1941. The *Bristol* class began to be laid down in September 1940. Seventy-two were eventually built.*

Figure 34: USS *Laffey* (DD-459), *Bristol* Class Destroyer[73]

---

* The *Bristol* class were later known as the *Benson-Gleaves* or *Benson-Livermore* class because war modifications erased design distinctions among the ships that existed when the *Bristol* class was first built. This report uses the "*Bristol*" designation because it examines only the 72 ships that were part of the war emergency building program.

4.1.2 *Fletcher* Class: Backbone of the War Emergency Program

With the release from the limitations imposed by the Washington Limitation of Armament Treaty of 1922 and succeeding treaties the U.S. Navy set out to design a more capable destroyer. At the beginning of 1940 the General Board selected a design and it was approved by the SECNAV on January 27, 1940.[74] The *Fletcher* class was approximately 30 feet longer and 500 tons greater displacement than the *Bensons* (see Figure 35). It was this design – which had been under development when the war crisis arrived – that formed the bulk of the Navy's destroyers during the war. Like the *Bristol* class the *Fletchers* were ordered piecemeal as the international situation got progressively worse.* By mid-1940 at least twenty-four *Fletcher* class destroyers were ordered. The number increased to a total of 100 by the end of the year. By the time the United States entered the war in December 1941 an additional seventy-five *Fletchers* had been ordered, bringing the total number eventually built to 175.[75] The *Fletcher* class began to be laid down in March 1941. Thus, the U.S. embarked upon a war emergency building program of 247 destroyers even before it entered the war. By December 7, 1941, eighty-nine *Bristol* and *Fletcher* class destroyers had been laid down at fourteen shipyards.

Figure 35: USS *Fletcher* (DD-445)[76]

---

* This is why the *Bristol, Fletcher, Allen M. Sumner*, and *Gearing* classes are not numbered sequentially.

4.1.3   *Allen M. Sumner*: Design Modification Due to War Experience

Once the initial war emergency building program had been put in place the Navy faced many of the same types of decisions regarding the design of succeeding fleet destroyers that had occurred in World War One. As discussed in Section 2, in mid-1917 the Navy debated the design type of the *Clemson*. A modified repeat option of the *Wickes* class was eventually chosen because the war crisis was at hand and there was no time to develop a new design, be it complex or simplified. Because the Navy had begun its war emergency building program more than a year before America's entry into World War Two, the General Board was able to begin deliberations on its next destroyer design in October 1941. Two years of conflict had shown the seriousness of air attacks. As a result, the Navy's primary design goal was an improvement to the anti-aircraft battery and a reduction of the silhouette (see Figure 36). Two basic options were explored. The first was a reversion to the medium-sized destroyer, the 1,630-ton *Gleaves* class. The second was an improved 2,100-ton *Fletcher*. The former was rejected because improvements to the AA battery increased the size of the ship to 1,800 tons with only a small increase in firepower. In addition, it was argued that a reversion to the smaller destroyer type would be "unacceptable from both the material and production standpoints."[77] (Although, it should be repeated that as late as February 1941 the smaller *Bristol* class destroyer were still being ordered because of the urgent need for more destroyers.) Instead the improved *Fletcher* design was chosen because it was "ideally suited to the current production program in that their hulls and machinery were essentially the same as the *Fletchers*. The hull and machinery could not be altered without changing the shipyards' facilities and the engine builders' tooling, changes that would in turn disrupt the wartime shipbuilding program and cause an intolerable increase in production time."[78] The ultimate design was a close derivative of the *Fletcher* hull but of higher displacement (2,200 tons) (see Table 9) and was a compromise between more offensive firepower at the sacrifice of speed and steaming radius. In April 1942, the General Board approved and forwarded the *Allen M. Sumner* class design to the SECNAV, who, in turn, approved the characteristics in May. The CNO also approved the design "recommending that the new ship and the DE be the only destroyer type ships laid down for the present (referring to proposals to build improved *Gleaves* type destroyers) since 'the current and prospective material and production situations will not allow any further diversification of destroyer types'" (emphasis added).[79] The first group of *Allen M. Sumner* class destroyers were ordered in August 1942 followed by a second block in June 1943. The ships began to be laid down in January 1943. Eventually seventy *Allen M. Sumner* class ships were built.

Note: Reduced silhouette of bridge structure compared to *Fletcher* class in Figure 35.

Figure 36: USS *Soley* (DD-707), *Allen M. Sumner* Class Destroyer[80]

4.1.4 *Gearing* Class

As the *Allen M. Sumner* class began to be constructed in 1943 the operational experiences of *Fletcher* class ships, especially in the vastness of the Pacific, showed that their cruising radius was much lower than officially stated. This was the result of the numerous additions of AA armament, which increased displacement, and the frequent high formation speeds necessary under combat conditions. As a result, the Navy explored ways to increase the fuel capacity of its destroyers. As early as 1942, a new destroyer design was under consideration. However, development was still ongoing when war ended. Any increase in fuel capacity would have to be achieved by modifying existing designs. An increase to the *Fletcher* class destroyers was dismissed because the majority had already been laid down and modifications to those yet to lay down would lead to unacceptable construction delays. The same conclusion was reached with regard to the first batch of *Allen M. Sumner* class destroyers. However, construction had yet to begin on the second group. As a result, BuShips* lengthened the *Allen M. Sumner* design by fourteen feet and added fuel tanks between the forward and after halves of the engineering plant. The resulting *Gearing* class destroyers had 168 tons more fuel and 30% longer cruising radius than the *Allen M. Sumner* class. These modifications divided the 2,200-ton destroyer design into the "short hulled" *Allen M. Sumner* class and the "long hulled" *Gearing* class (see Figure 37). The CNO approved this step but with the caveat that the construction of the improved ships not seriously interfere with the completion of the *Bristol, Fletcher* or *Allen M. Sumner* class destroyers under construction. Thus the Navy chose to modify an existing design versus creating a new design because they were in the midst of a war emergency. The Gearing class began to be laid down in March 1944. Forty-five were commissioned by August 1945, but not many saw actual service in the war. Over fifty were canceled in 1945. Ninety-eight were eventually built.

Figure 37: USS *Benner* (DD-807), *Gearing* Class Destroyer[81]

---

* "C&R and BuEng merged in 1940 and became BuShips.

Table 9: World War II Destroyer Class Characteristics

	Bristol	*Fletcher*	*Allen M. Sumner*	*Gearing*
Length on Waterline	341' 0"	369' 0"	369' 0"	383' 0"
Displacement	1,630 tons	2,100 tons	2,200 tons	2,425 tons
Beam	36 ft. 1 in.	39 ft. 8 in	39 ft. 10 in.	40 ft. 10 in.
Draft	17 ft. 6 in.	13 ft.	15 ft. 8 in.	18 ft. 6 in.
Speed	35 knots	36 knots	34.2 knots	34.6 knots
Armament (typical)	5 x 5 inch 10 x 50 cal. AA 1 depth charge projector (dcp) 2 dct 5 x 21 inch tt	5 x 5 inch 2 x 40mm 6 x 20mm 10 x 21 inch tt. 6 x (dcp) 2 x dct	6 x 5 inch 12 x 40mm 11 x 20mm 10 x 21 inch tt. 6 x dcp 2 x dct	6 x 5 inch 12 x 40mm 2 x 21 inch tt. 6 x dcp 2 x dct
Complement	276	273	345	345

4.2 Pre-Construction Preparations Phase

4.2.1 Selection of Shipbuilders

As in World War I, the Navy needed to find additional shipyards because its strategy to obtain large numbers of fleet destroyers was to increase both the number on order and the number of builders. However, the Great Depression and the interwar treaties limiting gross tonnage seriously affected the shipbuilding industry. By 1933, only six private shipbuilding companies remained in existence; Bethlehem Shipbuilding, New York Shipbuilding, and Newport News were large shipyards, while Bath Iron Works, Federal Shipbuilding and Electric Boat were smaller. Government owned Navy Yards were also still in operation but they too had been affected by the decrease in shipbuilding during the 1920s and 1930s. While six navy yards, at Portsmouth, Boston, Philadelphia, New York, Norfolk, and Puget Sound, were able to regularly build ships during the lean years, Mare Island had become mostly a repair yard and Charleston had essentially closed down in the early 1930s. In the late 1930s the industry began to rebound as orders increased. Against this backdrop the U.S Navy searched for shipyards to build the seventy-two *Bristol* and almost 100 *Fletcher* class destroyers that had been ordered in 1940. Within two years it would need builders for a total of 415 destroyers of the *Bristol, Fletcher, Allen M. Sumner*, and *Gearing* classes.

When the war emergency destroyer building program began in 1940 three private shipyards and three Navy Yards were engaged in building the twenty-four *Benson* class destroyers. These were Bath (6), Federal, Kearny (Fed) (4), BethQ (2), BosNY (6), CharNY (4) and PSNY (2). All of these yards were awarded contracts to build *Bristol* and/or *Fletcher* class ships. Federal Shipbuilding in Kearny was assisted by Gibbs and Cox, who did all of its plan work, etc. Bethlehem Shipbuilding Corporation's San Francisco and Staten Island yards, which had each built a few destroyers in the mid-1930s, were also given contracts. And the Navy Yards at Philadelphia and Norfolk each built two *Bristols*. However, even more yards were needed so the Navy awarded contracts to shipyards with little or no experience in destroyer building and paid for the reactivation or upgrading of other yards. Gulf Shipbuilding of Chickasaw, Alabama, with no prior experience, was awarded contracts for seven *Fletchers*. Bethlehem Shipbuilding's San Pedro yard was reactivated and eventually built twenty-six destroyers of all classes. Many yards received upgrades, including Bethlehem, Staten Island, which in 1942 had a 700 foot pier built in a record 43 days. As in the First World War, the Navy also paid for the construction of shipyards from the ground up to participate in the program. These were Consolidated Steel of Orange, TX (which also built destroyer escorts, see next section) and Todd-Pacific Shipyards of Seattle, Washington – both of which built over 30 destroyers.[82] Fourteen shipyards in total participated in the building program. As in World War I, a core group of experienced shipyards executed the Navy's destroyer building program. Eighty-five percent of all 415 destroyers were built by just seven private yards (see Figures 38 and 39).

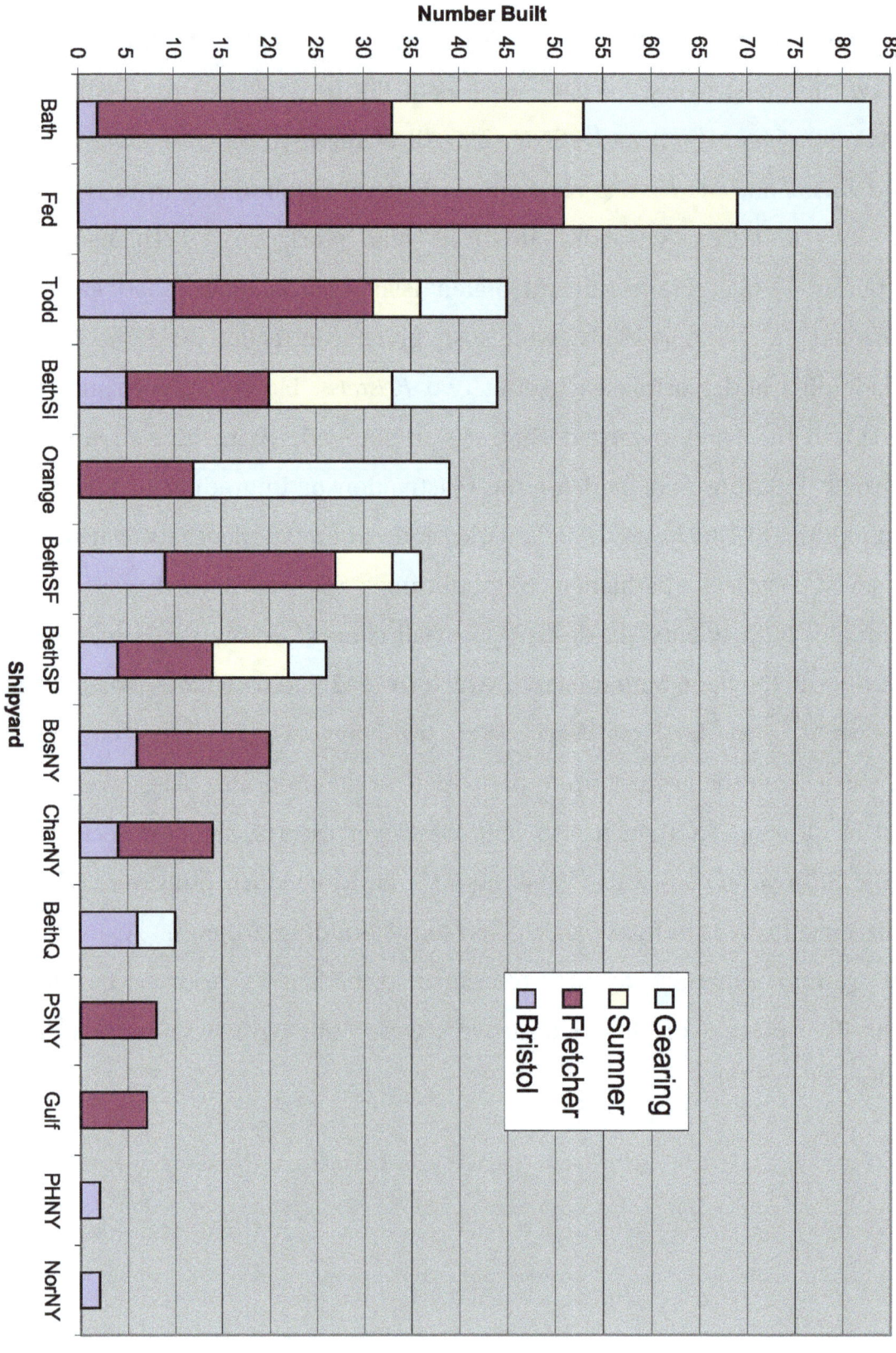

Figure 38: WW II Destroyer Shipbuilders, By Class / Number Built

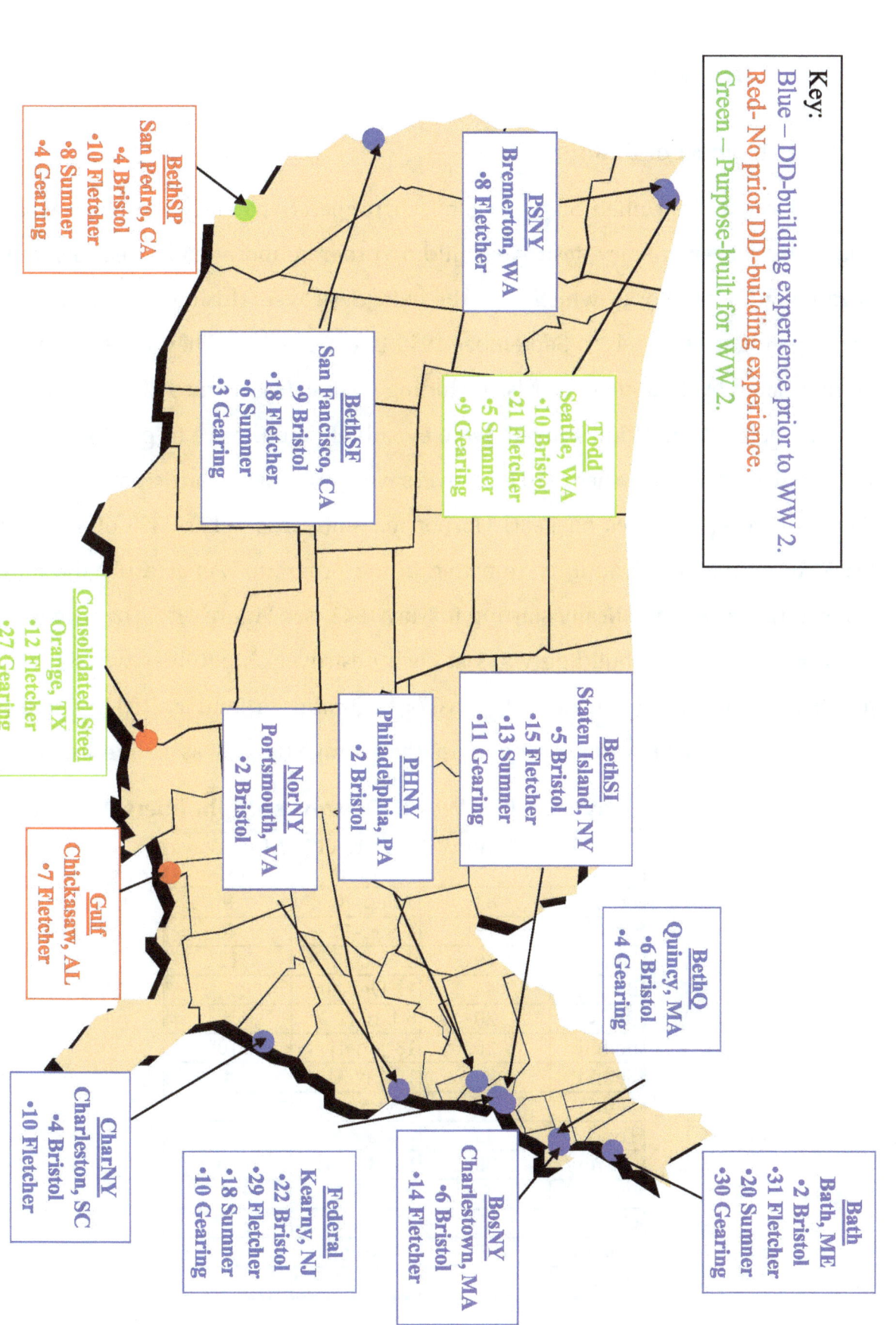

Figure 39: WW II Destroyer Shipbuilders, Geographical View

4.3 Construction Phase

4.3.1 Number of Building Ways

Because the United States began war preparations early the Navy was able to initiate its war emergency destroyer building program more than a year before the war began. Bath Iron Works, which built the most destroyers during the war, and CharNY began laying down keels in September 1940 (see Table 10). They were followed a few months later by four more yards, including BethSI (see Figure 40). By January, six yards, where 276 of 415 destroyers were eventually built, were in production. By May 1941, four more yards, where 120 destroyers were built, were participating. Thus, seven months before the attack on Pearl Harbor ten shipyards, where 396 of 415 destroyers (95%) were eventually built, were active in the program. As a result, the number of ways in use rose dramatically starting in May 1941 (see Figure 41). The sum total of the maximum number of building ways at each destroyer shipbuilder was 83. The peak number of ways used concurrently was 74 beginning in January 1942. For the entire building program when ways were in use the average usage was 41 building ways.

Table 10: Building Way Statistics, WW II Destroyer Shipbuilders, By Start Date

Yard	# Built	1st Keel Laid	Most Ways in Use
Bath	83	3-Sep-40	9
CharNY	14	4-Sep-40	5
Fed	79	2-Dec-40	12
BethSI	44	11-Dec-40	5
BosNY	20	6-Jan-41	4
BethSF	36	13-Jan-41	10
BethSP	26	1-May-41	4
BethQ	10	1-May-41	2
Todd	45	1-May-41	11
Orange	39	14-May-41	10
PSNY	8	3-Jun-41	4
Gulf	7	12-Jun-41	4
NorNY	2	26-Aug-41	1
PHNY	2	16-Sep-41	2

Emergency Production Historical Study

Note: View looks aft along ship's keel, with some bottom plating in place and a bulkhead erected amidships.

Figure 40: Construction of USS *Meade* (DD-602), *Bristol* Class, BethSI, JUN 1941[83]

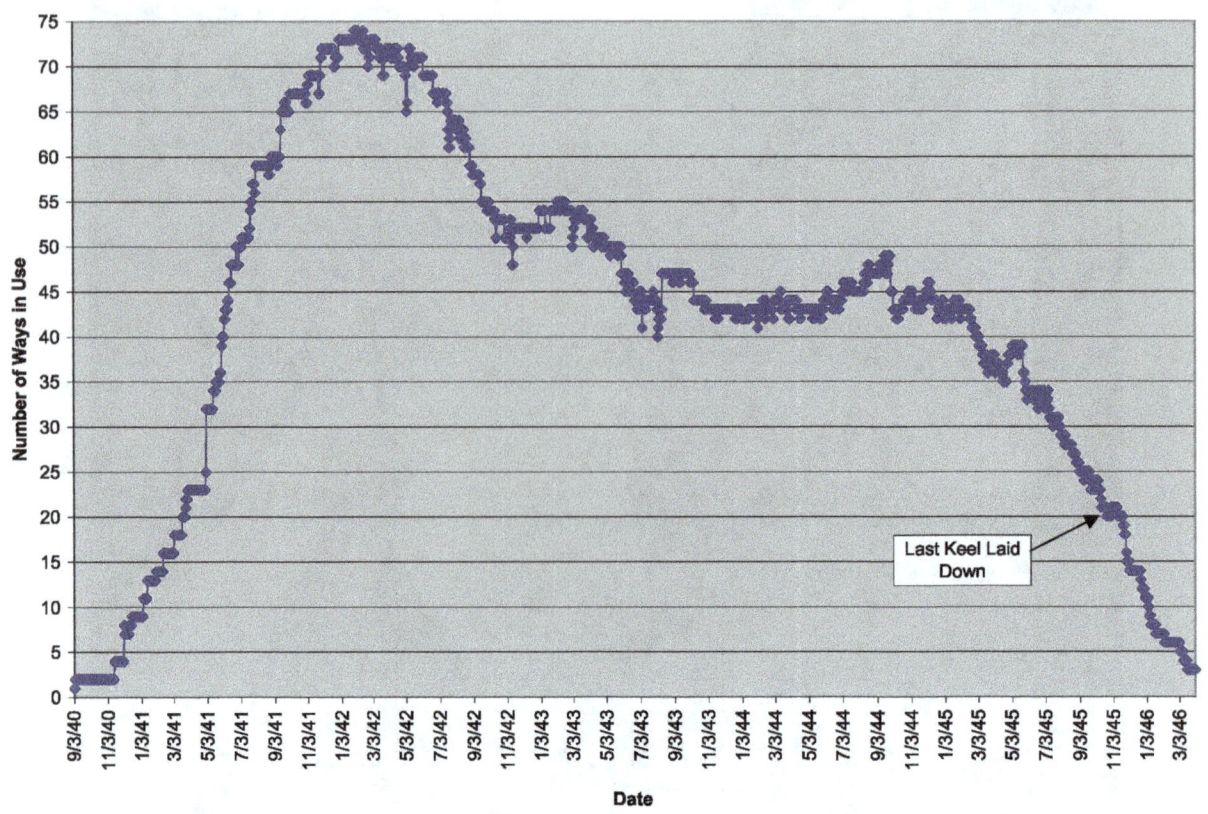

Figure 41: Number of Ways in Use for DD Construction, All Shipyards

4.3.2 National Shipbuilding Effort in World War II

Unlike World War One, when destroyers were the largest combatants built, the destroyer building program in World War Two had to share priority with many other combatant types and merchant ships. Reflecting the variety of programs the number of shipbuilders participating in building and repair programs was enormous. By December 1941, 156 shipyards were engaged in new construction and 76 in conversion and repair work. A year later the number of yards involved in new construction reached a wartime peak of 322. A wartime peak 248 yards engaged in conversion and repair was achieved in September 1944. These yards were dispersed throughout the United States. For instance, during World War I fourteen shipyards on the Great Lakes area participated in the war effort. By comparison, there were fifty shipyards active in the same area by July 1943. By the same month there were eighteen shipyards active along the length of the Mississippi and twenty-one others on the Gulf Coast. All told

BuShips helped develop yards in 34 out of 48 states. While there was an enormous number of yards, a core of twenty-eight private shipyards and eight Navy Yards performed the bulk of construction during the war. As the BuShips history of World War II states, "in these plants alone could the necessary management and facilities be combined to do the tremendously complex work required for the construction of major combatant types."[84] The majority of these large yards were well established before the war, but ten were built from the ground up in response to the war crisis. As mentioned above, two of these purpose-built yards built destroyers, but the majority was dedicated to merchant and auxiliary work.* By February 1943, almost seven million tons of vessels were under construction. A year later the over 8,600,000 tons of vessels of all types were building or being converted in American yards. The number of workers engaged at the shipyards building and repairing U.S. Navy vessels rose from 443,500 in January 1942 to 1,049,981 in July 1943. By mid-1943 the supply of labor had become so scarce in most industrial areas that the War Production Board and War Manpower Commission established Area Production Urgency and Manpower Priority Committees to assign manpower based on need.

All of these statistics emphasize the point that the war emergency destroyer building program (and the destroyer escort and patrol frigate program discussed later) was subject to competition for material to a degree not seen in World War I. As the BuShips history states, ""In peacetime, when materials, facilities and labor were abundant, the Navy and the Bureau could decentralized detailed shipbuilding and component scheduling to contractors and manufacturers. Under war conditions neither contractors nor the Navy had full control of the planning and scheduling of ship programs. There programs competed with Army, aircraft, Maritime, Lend Lease, civilian, and other needs for materials, machines and men, there not being enough to go around. The problem faced by the Bureau therefore was new, both in magnitude and in complexity."[85]

---

* Two others, Federal, Newark and Bethlehem, Hingham built destroyer escorts (see next section.)

4.3.3 Shortages and Industrial Expansion

As in World War I, the requirement to build large numbers of ships meant that the Navy's efforts to expand and construct shipyards had to be coupled with the development of an industrial base to supply the shipyards with the vast quantities of material to build the ships. BuShips assessed that "its greatest headache centered on the problem of upland facilities capable of manufacturing the components and materials necessary to keep the shipyards supplied. It is not unreasonable to state that the Bureau devoted as much effort to the increase of production capacity in supporting industries as to the increase of the shipbuilding facilities." The instances of material shortages and the efforts taken to resolve them in World War II were numerous. For instance, early in the national shipbuilding effort an acute shortage of turbo-electric propulsion machinery led to the construction, beginning in May 1942, of an enormous plant in a 50 acre cornfield. As in World War I, the war emergency led to large building projects being completed in astoundingly short times. Because of the urgent need for the turbo-electric machinery the plant began delivering machinery by the end of the year. Shortages were also experienced with the supply of steel. By 1942 the shortage was so severe that there was not enough steel to build all of the ships in the national building effort. After a review of the programs in April 1942 forty-eight minesweepers and fifty-eight subchasers were canceled and several other programs switched from steel to wooden construction.

Unlike World War I, these shortages led to delays in construction early in the destroyer program. A September 4, 1942 memorandum from VADM Robinson, Chief of the Office of Procurement and Material to Chief of Operations, on "Delays in Shipbuilding Program" states "Expansion of facilities to produce ships' components had proved to be much more onerous than that of providing the ship ways themselves. It has also been a much heavier contributor to shipbuilding delays up to date. This is due to two reasons: it is normally much simpler to build a shipbuilding way than it is to build a factory for the manufacture of a machine; and the need for expanded facilities for many components was not apparent in time to prevent a shortage of that component form causing a delay in ships' construction. Among the delays from this cause which can be cited are delays in some destroyers because of lack of facilities for the production of turbines and gear, and for forced draft blowers."[86] To rectify these and other shortages, between June 1940 and November 1945 the U.S. Navy spent $1,500,000,000 on shipyard and other navy establishments and $400,000,000 on the industrial base, such as manufacturers of motors, turbines and gears.

4.3.4 Mid-War Design Changes

The effort to get large numbers of destroyers into commission as rapidly as possible was complicated by the numerous mid-war alterations to the destroyer's design. America's involvement in World War II was over twice as long as that of the First World War (46 versus 20 months). With almost four years of direct wartime experience, plus two more observing as a neutral, many shortcomings in the designs of the destroyers were discovered and improvements were implemented. As discussed earlier, these shortcomings spurred the evolution in the Navy's destroyer design from the *Fletcher* to the *Allen M. Sumner* and finally the *Gearing* class. Because of the size of each destroyer class, their building spans were concurrent for at least part of their duration (see Figure 42). As such, when design alterations were approved they were incorporated into ships then under construction and during availabilities for ships already in commission. However, the need for rapid construction meant that partial solutions sometimes had to be accepted. For instance, early war experience showed that the original closed-in rounded bridge with platform wings restricted the field of view of the ship's commander. When air battles were taking place on both sides of the ship, the commander could not view it in its entirety. The ideal solution was an open bridge. However, this required a complete redesign of the bridge and would have entailed a delay in the construction schedule. As a stopgap the platform wings were extended around the entire bridge.[87]

Emergency Production Historical Study

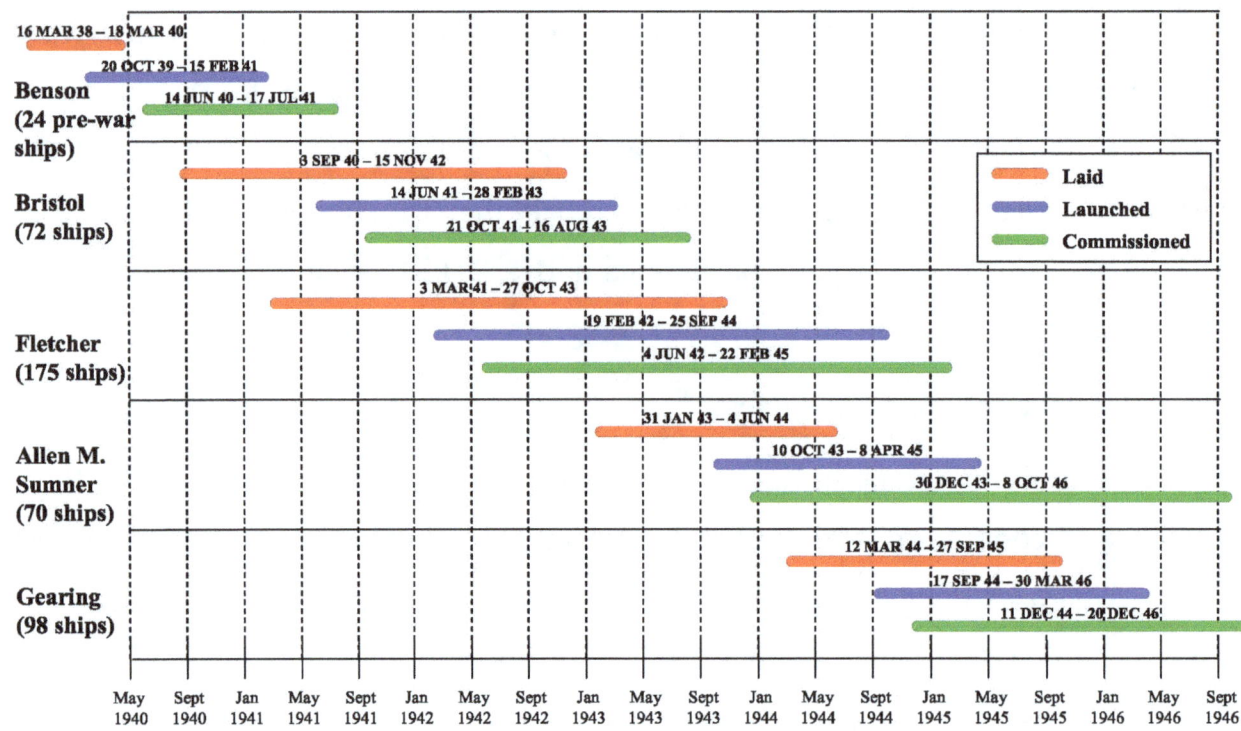

Figure 42: Construction Spans of Destroyer Classes during World War II

Regardless of when alterations were made in the construction process, they could only be implemented if there were no shortages of the desired component. For instance, by the end of 1941 the AA armament of the *Fletcher* class was modified because of Britain's wartime experience. The quadruple 1.1-inch cannon initially intended for the *Fletcher* class was replaced by one twin 40-mm Bofors gun and the original four single 0.5 inch machine guns were replaced by single 20-mm mountings.[88] The 1.1-inch gun was a mechanically unreliable mount. Frequent jams prevented its consistent use. However, because of the scarcity of Bofors guns the first three *Fletchers* completed had 1.1 inch cannon installed. These ships received their Bofors replacement guns after trials and working up. In other instances the Bofors guns were unaccompanied by the associated MK 51 director because they were not available. These ships then had to return to government owned Navy Yards when the equipment became available to be fully fitted out. As a result, even though they began commissioning in June 1942, it was not until the fall of 1942 that the first *Fletchers* reached the Pacific where they were desperately needed off Guadalcanal.[89] Operational experience gained in 1942 revealed that an even greater increase in AA firepower was

71

desirable. By January 1943, the *Fletcher* class's AA armament was increased to eight single 20mm and two twin Bofors (see Figure 43). The first ships to receive these modifications were those completing construction at the time and those receiving repairs from battle damage.[90]

Circles mark recent alterations, including addition of 40mm twin mounts on each side of the forward and midships superstructure

Figure 43: USS *Fletcher* (DD-445) at MINY, AUG 1943 showing recent alterations[91]

All of these weight additions, coupled with the hurried construction of the war emergency building program, negatively affected the performance of the *Fletcher* class. For instance, the first *Fletcher* class destroyer to commission, USS *Nicholas* (DD-449), displaced 2,589 tons and could make only 37 knots versus a desired 38 knots. Furthermore, trials revealed that the ships could reach a maximum continuous sea speed of about 32-33 knots, which only equaled the *Benson* class destroyers.[92] Because of the *Fletcher* class was redesigned in 1942 to reduce topside weight, included lowering the director, decreasing STS protection, and reducing the height of the aft superstructure. However, topside weight growth was exacerbated by periodic shortages of aluminum. Shipyards had to use mild steel for the superstructure when aluminum was unavailable, which made those *Fletcher* class ships about 50 tons heavier that those with aluminum superstructures.[93]

The *Allen M. Sumner* class was also subject to revisions in design because of operational experience. This was especially true with regard to AA weaponry. For instance, in March 1943, only two months after the first of the class were laid down, their AA armament was increased to four 40mm twins and eleven 20mm guns. And, in June 1943, two of the 40mm twin mounts on the after superstructure were replaced by two 40mm quad mounts. However, of more importance with regard to construction time was the relocation of the Combat Information Center (CIC) on the *Allen M. Sumner* class in September 1943. Wartime experience had showed the great need for this relocation and it was approved even though it delayed the construction program by five months.

4.3.5 Total Construction Time

As discussed earlier, shortages of material did lead to delays in construction in the early part of the war. However, once these initial delays were overcome, the construction time of destroyers was steady. Because modifications to designs were implemented first to destroyers under construction and then later backfitted when possible to those already built, the building ways were continuously turned over and the shipyards were able, on average, to steadily produce destroyers. As in World War I, the complex design of the fleet destroyer precluded large numbers of ships being constructed in a short amount of time. The average construction time for all 415 destroyers was slightly under one year.

Nevertheless, there was a significant difference in productivity attained at each shipyard based upon shipyard experience and the number built. These factors are interrelated, in many instances, because experienced shipyards were generally awarded more contracts than inexperienced yards. For instance, four private shipyards with pre-war destroyer-building experience, Bath, Fed, BethQ, and BethSI, were able to build destroyers quicker than the entire program average of eleven and a half months (see Table 11). These four yards built over half of all 415 destroyers. However, not all shipyards that built large numbers of destroyers were able to match this performance. For instance, the two purpose-built yards, Orange and Todd, which built eighty-one destroyers, averaged had much longer average building times. This was partly the result of the time needed to gain experience. The destroyers built early in the program at these and other yards took longer than later ships (see Figures 44 and 45).

Table 11: Construction Times for WW II Destroyers, By Average Per Yard

Shipyard	# built	# of Months from Keel Laying to Commissioning		
		Shortest	*Average*	*Longest*
Fed	79	4.6	7.7	14.8
Bath	83	4.1	8.2	19.0
BethQ	10	6.8	9.4	12.1
BethSI	44	8.6	10.4	15.9
PHNY	2	11.1	11.6	12.1
BethSP	26	9.3	11.9	19.0
CharNY	14	9.3	12.5	15.7
BosNY	20	6.9	12.6	15.4
Orange	39	9.0	12.7	18.8
Todd	45	8.9	15.5	22.9
BethSF	36	10.5	16.6	33.7
PSNY	8	15.1	22.7	33.5
Gulf	7	12.5	23.7	30.9
NorNY	2	11.8	13.9	16.0
Avg. for all DD builders			11.5	
Avg. for builders of 30 or more			10.8	
Avg. for builders of less than 30			13.8	

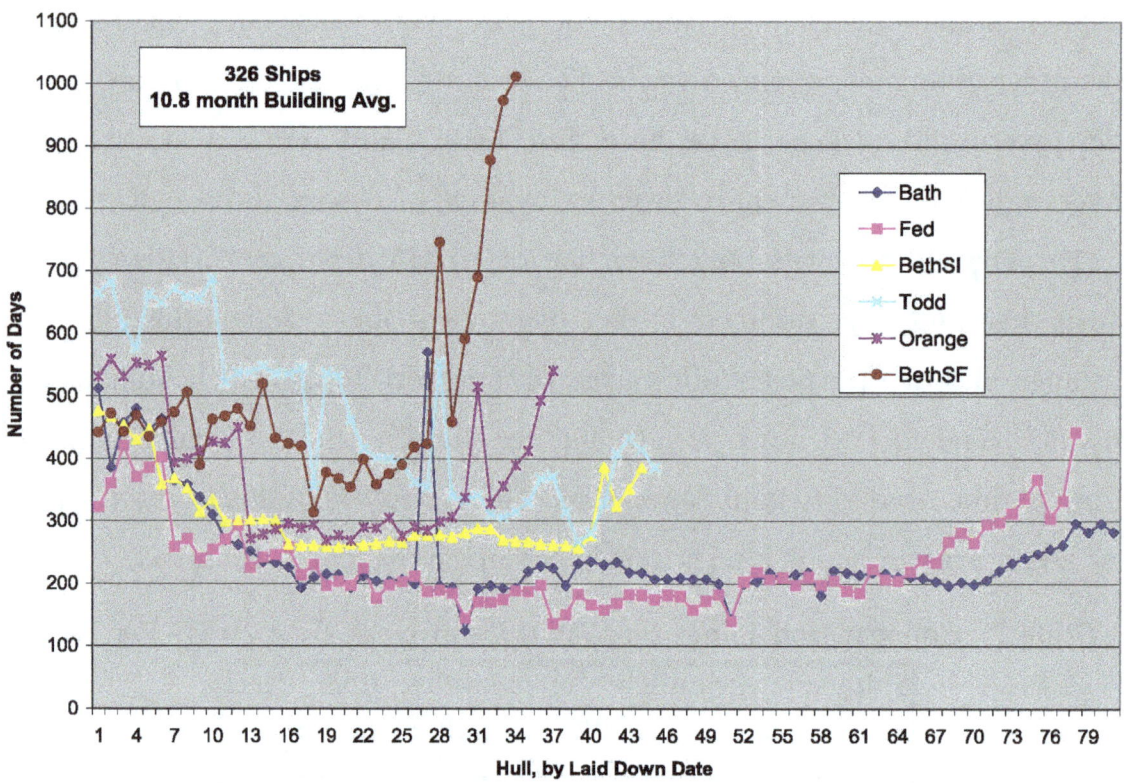

Figure 44: Construction Time, Builders of 30 or more Destroyers

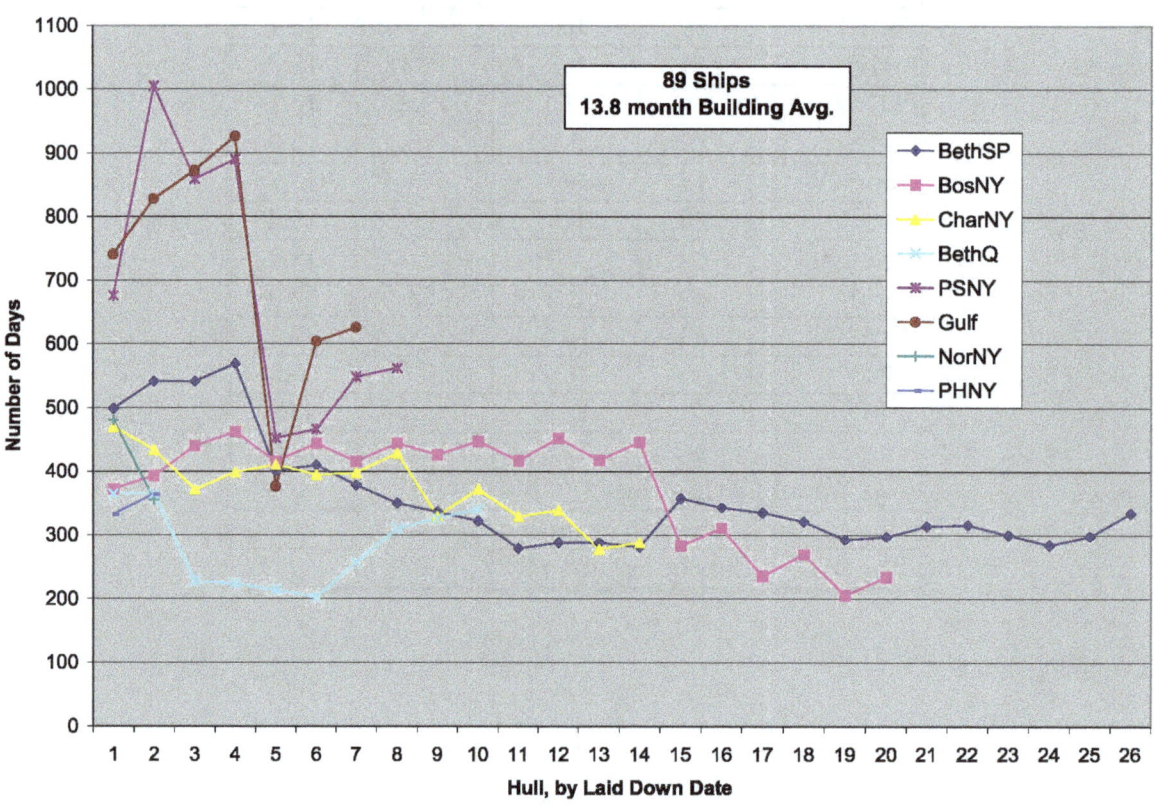

Figure 45: Construction Time, Builders of Less than 30 Destroyers

The Navy's goal was to get <u>large numbers</u> of destroyers into service as rapidly as possible. As such, while the faster construction times at certain yards was encouraging, their finite number of building ways meant that they could only build so many destroyers in a given period. And, because the complex design of the fleet destroyers was not conducive to rapid production, of more import to the Navy was the proper management of resources to enable experienced, inexperienced and purpose-built shipyards to construct as many destroyers as possible at a steady rate. In this they were successful. Once initial construction delays were overcome, throughout the course of the war the shipyards were able to maintain consistent average building times (see Figure 46). This consistency translated into a steady rate of commissionings over the course of the war (see Figure 47).

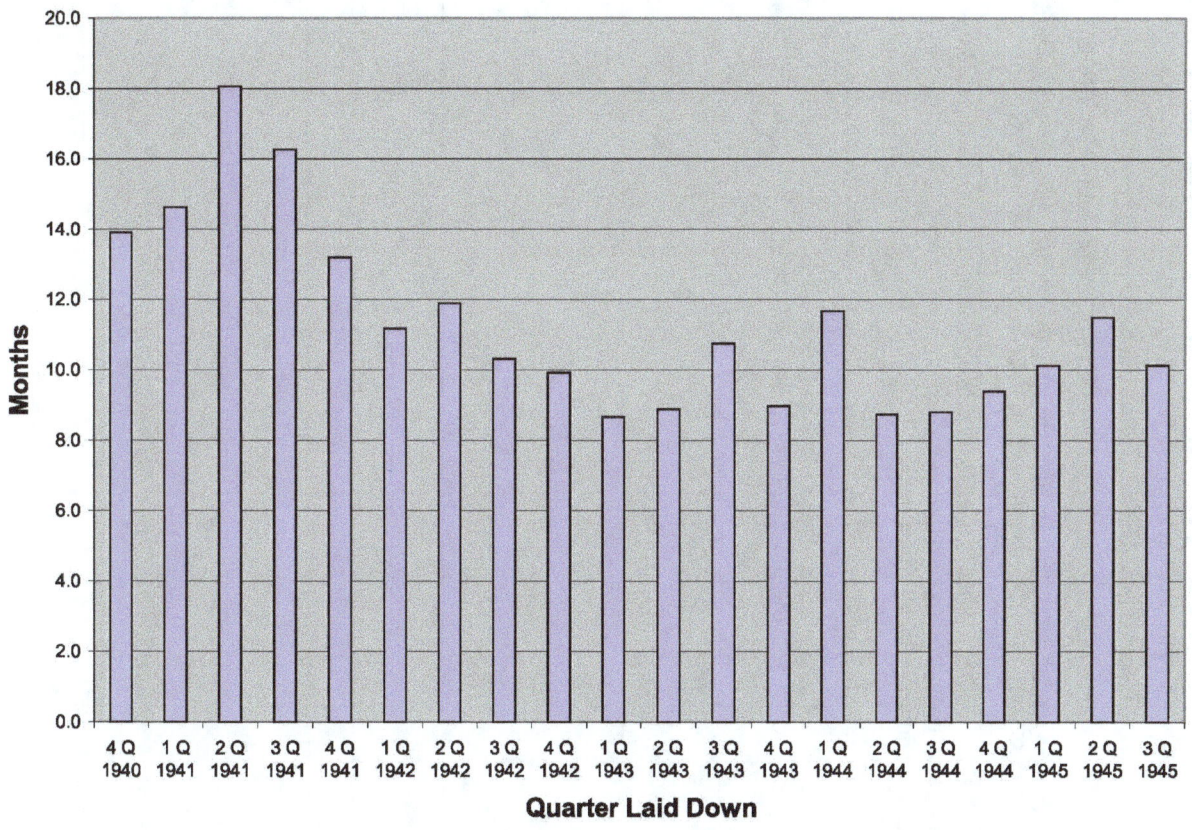

Figure 46: Construction Time for World War II Destroyers, By Quarter

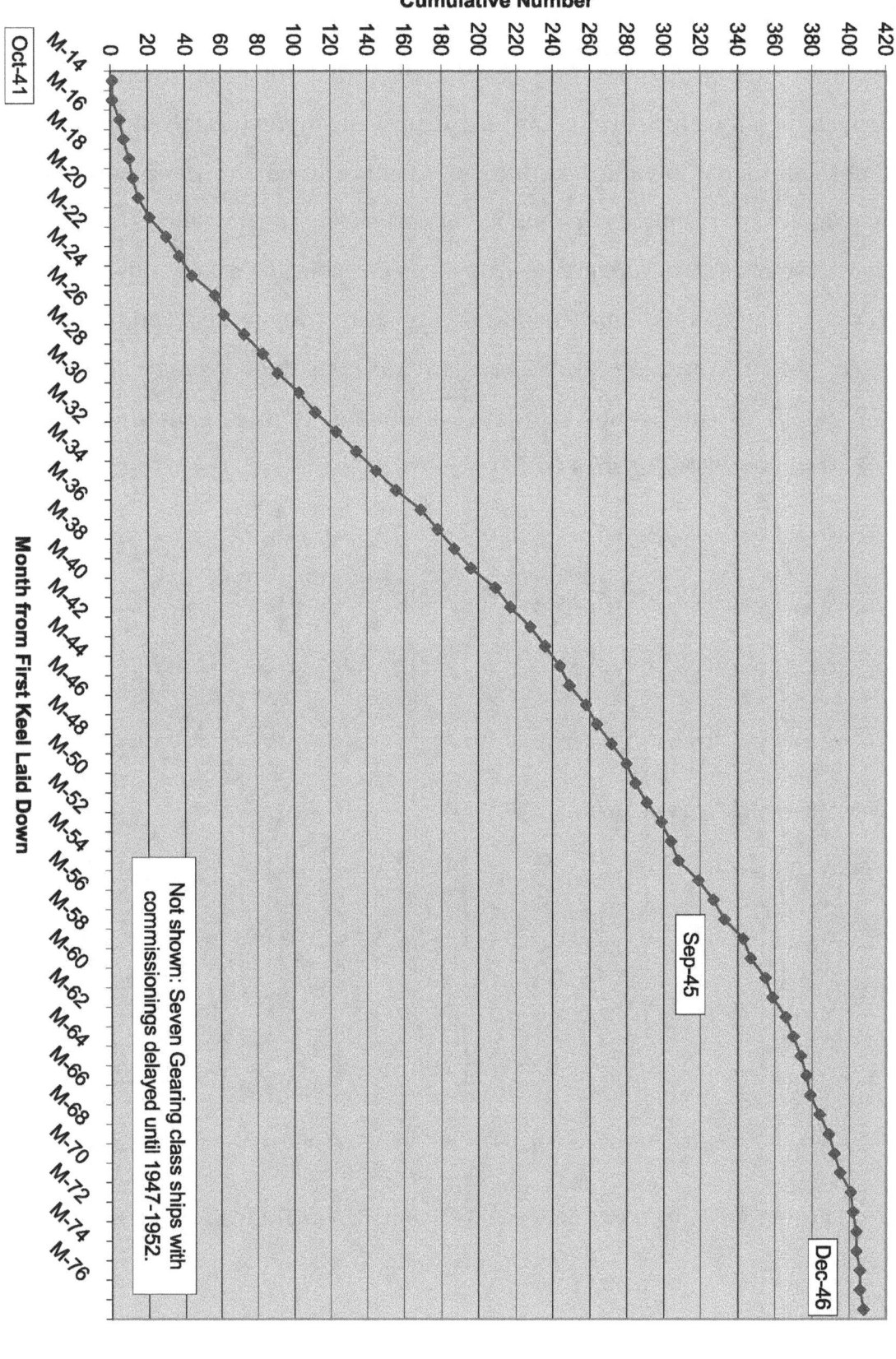

Figure 47: Cumulative Commissionings of World War II Destroyers

5. Destroyer Escorts

In contrast to the decision to base the war emergency destroyer program on complex designs, the Navy chose simplified designs for its smaller combatant programs, the destroyer escort and patrol frigate. And it chose mostly second-tier shipyards to build the ships. This section discusses the destroyer escort, while Section 7 discusses the patrol frigate.

5.1 Design Decision Phase

5.1.1 Strategic Background

As tensions increased in Europe, in the spring of 1939 the U.S. Navy considered constructing destroyer escorts. The Navy reasoned that a European war would produced a submarine threat similar to that of World War I and would necessitate large number of convoy escorts. A number of design concepts were developed but were not pursued further because no imminent threat existed. Likewise, the Royal Navy did not deem destroyer escort construction a priority before mid-1940 because they assumed that a war with Germany would be fought in France. The British assumed that coastal patrol boats could largely contain the U-boat threat in home waters and indirectly protect trans-Atlantic convoys. For the nine months before France's defeat the average monthly loss of shipping to U-boats was 62 ships (194,500 tons). However, when Germany gained Atlantic ports with the fall of France in mid-1940, the naval strategy of the United States and Great Britain was considerably altered. In the nine months after the fall of France, U-boats sank a monthly average of 100 ships (413,351 tons). For the British, the protection of convoys, and thus the construction of destroyer escorts, became of the highest national priority. However, Britain's shipyards did not have the capacity to build the required number of convoy escorts. Only the United States had the industrial base to build a large number of destroyer escorts, but American neutrality prevented the initiation of the program in 1940. Instead the U.S. eased toward an open alliance with Great Britain, one of the first steps being the agreement to give the British and Canadians fifty *Wickes/Clemson* destroyers in return for leases on British bases. An outright alliance became more open with the passage of the Lend-Lease Act on March 11, 1941. By June, the Royal Navy urged the U.S. to begin construction of destroyer escorts using Lend-Lease funding. In August, President Roosevelt authorized construction of destroyer escorts and in November orders for 50 destroyer escorts were placed. The attack on Pearl Harbor the following month quickly altered the United States' strategic outlook. The U.S. Navy itself now required a large number of destroyer escorts. Within the next year 1,005 destroyer escorts were ordered. Such was the urgent need of ASW ships that Great Britain only received six of the original 50 destroyer escorts ordered under Lend-Lease. The U.S. Navy retained the remaining ships. Eventually, 98 destroyer escorts were loaned or given to other countries. The Royal Navy received 78 ships (32 *Evarts* and 46 *Buckley* class), and France and Brazil received eight and twelve *Cannon* class destroyer escorts, respectively. In February 1942, the first destroyer escorts were laid down – six months after presidential authorization. By war's end 504 destroyer escorts, comprising six subclasses, were built. Fifty-six more ships were completed as APD's and three destroyer escorts were completed after the war. All told, 563 ships were built – the largest Allied combatant ship building program during World War II.

5.1.2 Simple Design for Rapid Construction

When the British request for destroyer escorts came in June, the characteristics for the ship were already developed. In the spring of 1941, the General Board had approved the Navy's design for a destroyer escort. BuShips' design was influenced by a close study of both British ASW operations during America's two-year neutrality and the design of the Royal Navy's *Hunt* class DE and *Flower* class corvette. The Navy's goal, as in the case of the *Eagle* Boat in World War I, was to simplify the hull and superstructure for rapid and economical construction and to enable second-tier yards to do most of the construction. The initial design work was assigned to Gibbs & Cox, who had accomplished a similar goal on the Liberty ship design. The resulting design incorporated a number of features that enhanced producibility.* Prefabricated sections were utilized throughout and the ships were entirely welded. The design called for a flush-deck and the use of thin steel plate throughout the ship. The majority of hull and deck plating was ¼" steel plate, superstructure bulkheads were 3/16", while ½ inch plate was used around the outboard strake about the keel. Stronger plate up to 7/16" was used in areas of greater stress. The resulting *Evarts* class destroyer escorts were 290 feet long and displaced almost 1,200 tons -- only 60 feet shorter and about 400 tons lighter than the *Bristol* class fleet destroyers then being laid down (see Figure 48). However, they were 14 knots slower and had fewer guns than the *Bristol* class. This relatively slight difference in size but significant difference in offensive capabilities created some misgivings about embarking on the destroyer escort program for Great Britain. However, these concerns were offset by the need to get large numbers of ASW/convoy assets into Allied service as quickly as possible – which the simplified design promised to accomplish. In addition, while the *Evarts* class had fewer guns, it had a much more robust ASW battery than fleet destroyers, including sonar echo ranging gear, which was the most up-to-date ASW equipment available.

The Royal Navy initially requested that the destroyer escort design include a bank of torpedo tubes. They were deleted from the design before any *Evarts* class ships had been laid down in order to install additional AA guns. All other World War II destroyer escorts were designed with torpedoes. However, the *Evarts* never received the additional AA armament because there was a shortage of guns and mounts when the ships were fitting out in mid-1942. As mentioned in the previous section, this shortage also affected the *Fletcher* class program at this time. This was but the first of many shortages that would impact the destroyer escort program. These shortages resulted in six classes of destroyer escorts, and large number of variations in design and

---

* These methods were used later by Great Britain for the *Castle* class corvette and *Loch* class frigate.

armament within and among the classes. Perhaps no other ship type's design was affected more by shortages in World War II.

Figure 48: USS *Canfield* (DE 262), *Evarts* Class Destroyer[94]

5.1.3 Design Variations

Even before any of the *Evarts* class were laid down the DE program was affected by shortages. The most significant shortages occurred with power plants. As a result, diesel geared engines, diesel electric, steam turbo geared and steam turbo electric engines were all used for different destroyer escorts. The differences (along with variations in bridge structures and armament) were significant enough that they defined the different destroyer escorts classes. In fact, the classes were commonly known by abbreviations based on their propulsion systems rather than their proper class names (see Table 12).

Table 12: DE Class Hull and Propulsion Differences[*]

Hull Type	Class	Abbreviation	Propulsion System
"Short Hull"	Evarts	GMT	General Motors diesel-electric tandem drive
"Long Hull"	Buckley	TM	Turboelectric drive
	Cannon	DET	Diesel-electric tandem drive
	Edsall	FMR	Fairbanks-Morse diesel reduction gear drive
	Rudderow	TEV	Turboelectric drive with 5-inch guns
	John C. Butler	WGT	Westinghouse geared turbine drive

The first shortage appeared during the detailed design of the *Evarts* class in late 1941. Around that time the Navy selected General Motors V12 diesel engines in tandem with electric drive for the *Evarts* class (97 ships) in order to avoid the need for reduction gears, which were experiencing a bottleneck in production. However, diesel engines were also in short supply. As a result, while the original *Evarts* design called for eight diesel engines, they received only four. This reduced shp 12,000 to 6,000 and lower the design speed of the class from 24 to 19 knots. The Navy also halved the number of diesels in what would become the *Edsall* (85 ships) and *Cannon* (72 ships) class destroyer escorts. As a result, these classes also had top speeds well under the original design goal of 24 knots. [95]

Despite halving the number of diesels in 254 of the ships, it was apparent that there would not be enough diesel engines for the hundreds of other destroyer escorts on order. In response, in January 1942 the Navy contracted with General Electric to create a turboelectric plant. GE produced a plant that consisted of a high-pressure, superheated boiler in a fire room and a main GE 4,600-kW steam turbine-generator, synchronous propulsion motor, and motor-generator set in an adjacent engine room. Each ship was fitted with two plants and together they produced the equivalent shp of the originally envisioned eight linked diesels (12,000 shp). However, the GE machinery needed greater longitudinal space than the *Evarts* class could accommodate so a longer destroyer escort design was developed by Bethlehem Shipbuilding. The new design, what would become the *Buckley* class, was about 17 feet longer and 2 feet beamier than

---

[*] DEs with similar propulsion systems were generally kept in the same operational divisions during the war to simplify logistical support.

the *Evarts* class (see Figure 49 and Table 13). The longer hull and more powerful propulsion gave the *Buckley* class the desired 24 knot speed. All subsequent destroyer escort classes, *Cannon*, *Edsall*, *Rudderow*, and *John C. Butler*, were based on the 306 ft. *Buckley* hull design, although, as mentioned above, they had different propulsion plants. While the use of turboelectric plants alleviated the need for reduction gears and provided excellent acceleration and maneuvering characteristics, the turboelectric equipped ships had only about half the endurance of the "long hull" *Cannon* and *Edsall* with diesel plants. In addition, electric drive was more expensive to produce, operate, and maintain than the geared steam turbine power plant installed in *John C. Butler* class. However, the wartime emergency necessitated that these deficiencies be tolerated.

Like the *Evarts* class, the design of the *Buckley* and follow on classes incorporated techniques that enhanced producibility. The hull consisted of thirteen prefabricated sections and the basic deck layout and superstructure of the *Evarts* class were retained to avoid a lengthy redesign process. Although, the *Buckley* superstructures were extended from the bridge to the number three gun position on the quarterdeck and they received three torpedo tubes amidships.[96]

Figure 49: USS *Darby* (DE 218), *Buckley* Class Destroyer[97]

Table 13: *Evarts* Class Characteristics

	Evarts "Short Hull" Class	Five "Long Hull" Classes
Length Overall	289 ft. 5 in.	306 ft.
Displacement	1,140 tons	1,400 tons (standard) 1,740 tons (full load) 1,800 tons (wartime)
Beam	35 ft. 1 in.	36 ft. 10 in.
Draft	8 ft. 3 in.	13 ft. 6 in.
Max speed	19-21 knots	24 knots
Armament (typical)	3 x 3" 2 x dct 8 x dcp 1 x hedgehog	3 x 3" 3 x 21" tt 2 x dct 8 x dcp 1 x hedgehog
Complement	156	188 - 225

5.2 Pre-Construction Preparation Phase

5.2.1 Selection of Shipbuilders

With over 1,000 destroyer escorts ordered the United States needed a large number of shipbuilders to complete the program. As mentioned above, the contracts for the first 50 destroyer escorts were placed in November 1941. They went to four Naval shipyards, at Boston, Mare Island, Philadelphia and Puget Sound. However, other building projects contributed to a delay in the start to the program. Philadelphia and Mare Island did not lay down the first destroyer escorts until February – six months after the president had authorized their construction. Boston Navy Yard laid down its first DE in April and Puget Sound only in September 1942. In the meantime the Navy searched for other private shipyards. Seventeen shipyards eventually participated in the destroyer escort program (see Figures 50 and 51). Eight of these yards, Orange, BethSF, BosNY, CharNY, PHNY, PSNY, NorNY and BethQ, also built destroyers during World War II.

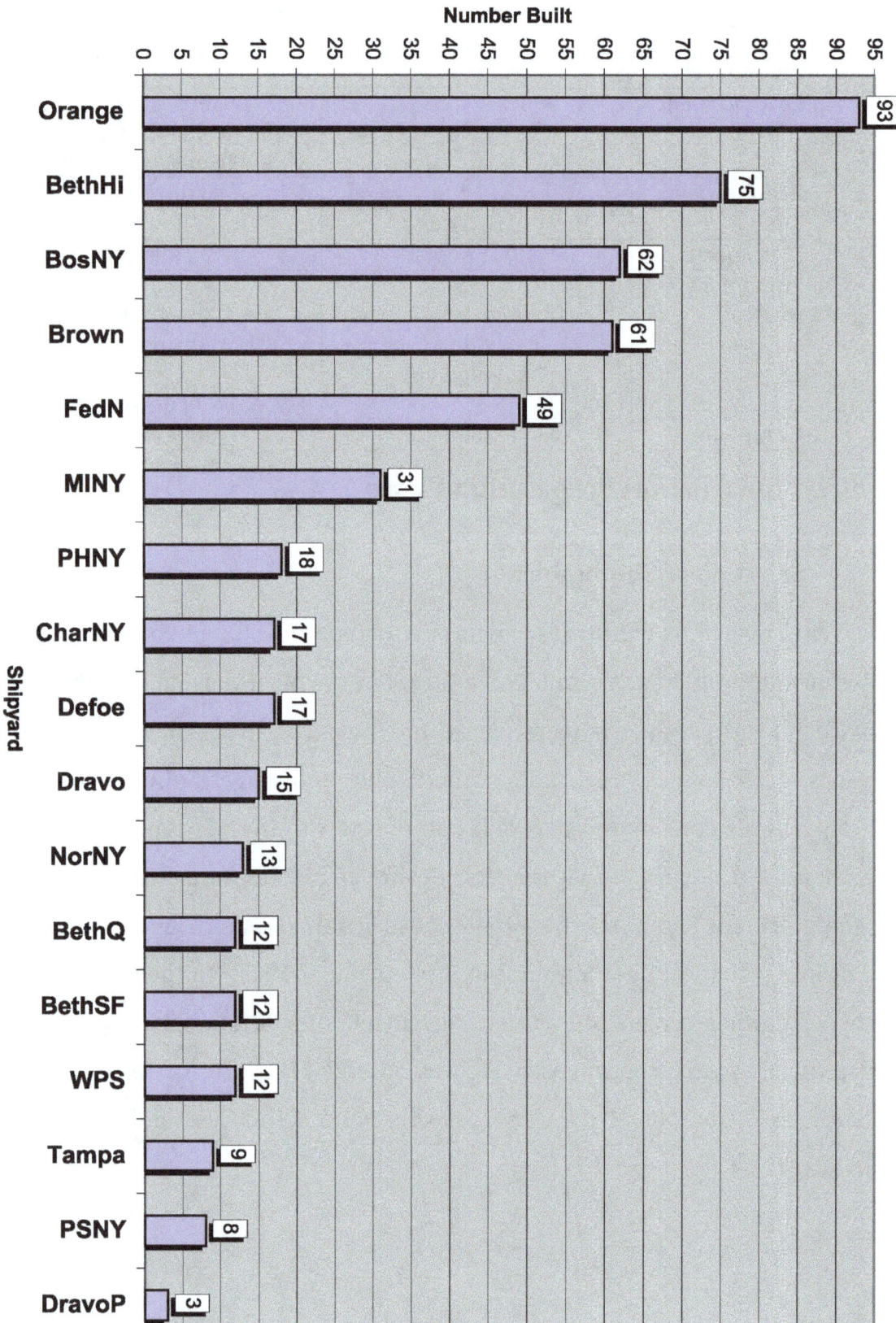

Figure 50: Destroyer Escort Builders, By Number Built

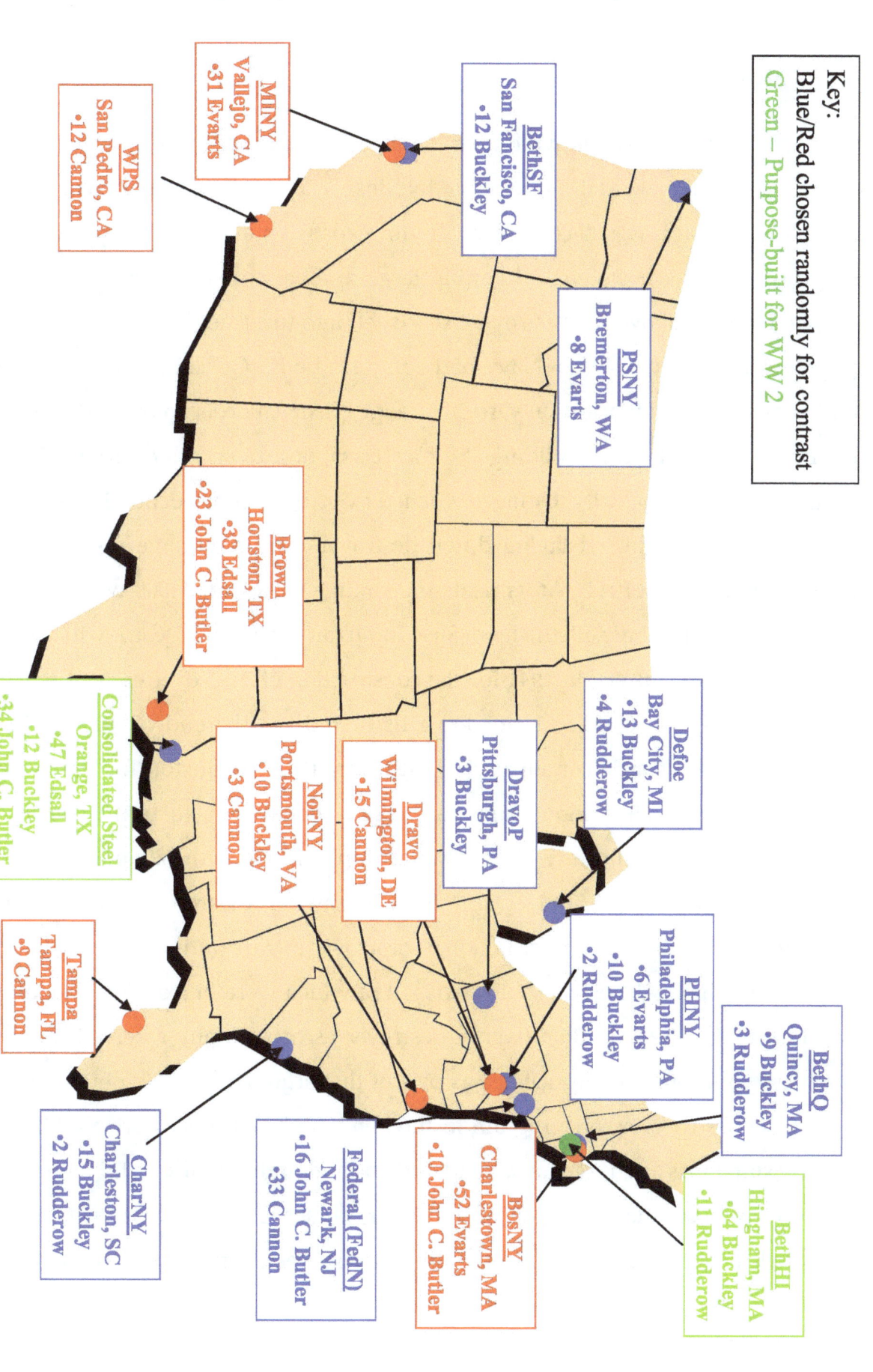

Figure 51: Destroyer Escort Shipbuilders, Geographical View

5.3 Construction Phase

While seventeen shipyards participated in the program, 73% were built by just six yards, Orange, BethHi, , Brown, FedN, BosNY and MINY. As in World War I, the Navy found that it was necessary to pay for expansion and/or construction of private shipyards to achieve its goal of getting large numbers of ships constructed. All four private builders of over 30 destroyer escorts fell into this category. As mentioned in the previous section, in 1940 the Navy had contracted with Consolidated Steel to upgrade and expand a small fabrication yard in Orange, Texas in order to build destroyers. The Orange yard had been building *Fletcher* class destroyers since May 1941. With destroyer escorts a priority, Orange switched over to DE construction beginning in June 1942. After it completed laying down destroyer escorts, Orange resumed destroyer construction in May 1944. At its peak, the Orange yard had 20,000 workers. With $35 million from the Navy, Bethlehem Steel built an emergency yard with 16 ways at Hingham, Massachusetts in 1941 for the construction of destroyer escorts. It achieved a peak workforce of 23,000. It laid down its first DE at the end of June 1942. Brown Shipbuilding built an emergency yard, also in 1941, in Houston for destroyer escort construction with $9 million from the Navy. It was able to begin construction of destroyer escorts by mid-July 1942. Federal Shipbuilding, with $20 million provided by the Navy, built a yard in Newark, New Jersey for destroyer escort construction. However, it did not begin construction of destroyer escorts until October 1942.

The other eight private shipyards, all of which were in existence before the war, would each build fewer than twenty destroyer escorts. Many received funding from the Navy to improve their facilities as part of the larger national shipbuilding effort, of which the destroyer escort program formed only a part of their work. While the eight private shipyards and three naval shipyards did not individually build large number of destroyer escorts the aggregate of 136 ships was a significant contribution. These shipyards began to participate in the program between September 1942 and May 1943 (see Table 14).

5.3.1 Number of Building Ways

Table 14: Building Way Statistics, DE Shipbuilders, By Start Date

Yard	# Built	1st Keel Laid	Most Ways in Use
PHNY	18	12-Feb-42	8
MINY	31	28-Feb-42	10
BosNY	60	5-Apr-42	8
Orange	93	26-Jun-42	13
BethHi	75	29-Jun-42	16
Brown	61	15-Jul-42	9
PSNY	8	7-Sep-42	8
NorNY	13	7-Sep-42	6
FedN	49	19-Oct-42	12
Dravo	15	14-Nov-42	9
Defoe	17	15-Dec-42	4
WPS	12	11-Feb-43	8
CharNY	17	15-Feb-43	8
BethQ	12	22-Feb-43	2
Tampa	9	1-Mar-43	9
BethSF	12	21-Mar-43	7
DravoP	3	12-May-43	3

This staggered entry of shipyards in the destroyer escort program was reflected in the number of building ways in use. By May 1943 all 17 yards had building ways in use for destroyer escorts and it was in this month that the peak of 122 building ways were in use simultaneously (see Figure 52). However, over the course of the 31 months that DE were on the building ways, only half that number were average ever in use because of the gradual entry of the different shipyards into the program and the tapering off of the program beginning in late 1943.

Emergency Production Historical Study

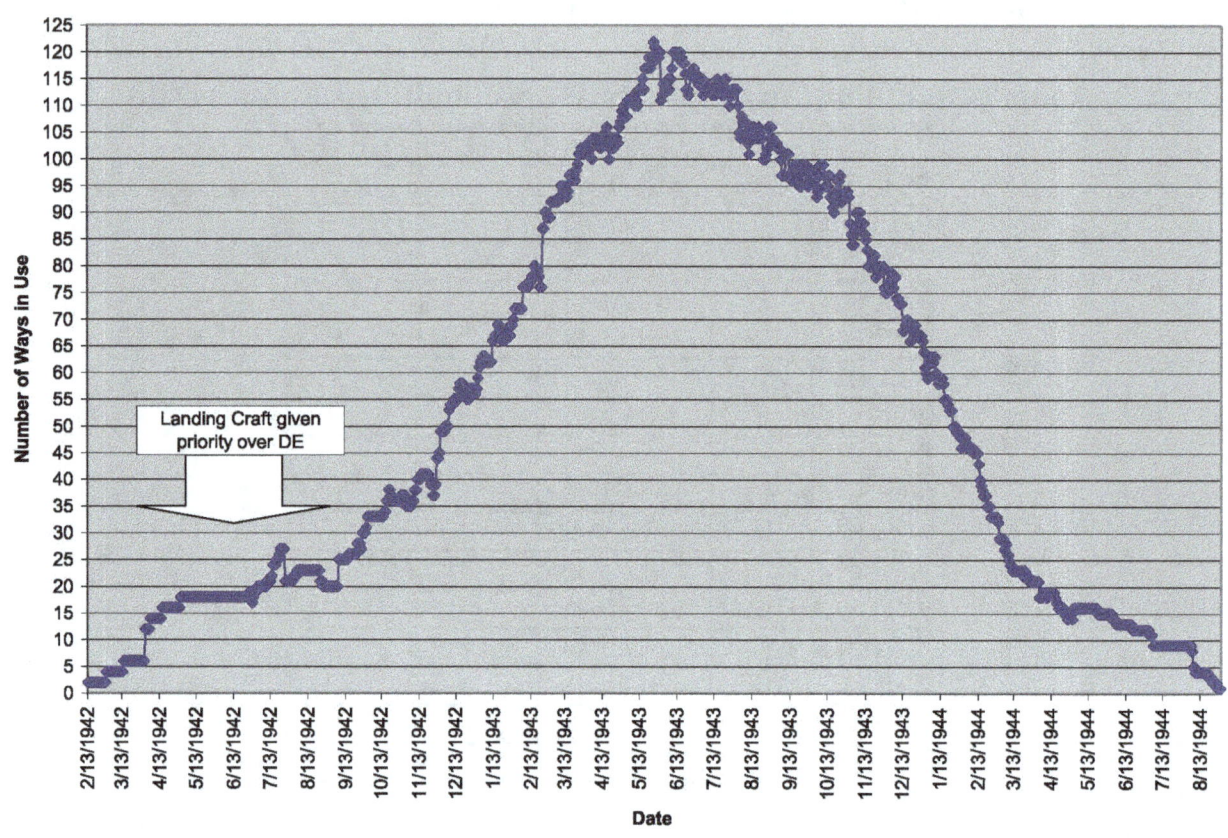

Figure 52: Number of Ways in Use for DE Construction, All Shipyards

5.3.2 Initial Construction Delays

The buildup in 1942 of the number of building ways dedicated to DE construction was also affected by landing craft construction. In 1942 President Roosevelt issued an executive order that assigned a higher priority to landing craft construction than destroyer escorts because it was hoped that an amphibious assault on Western Europe could be launched in September 1942. The building ways at Philadelphia and Boston Navy Yards were directly affected by this change in priority because both were assigned orders for LST construction. As a result, both ceased laying down destroyer escorts after April 1942 and switched over to LST production. DE keel layings did not resume until September 1942 at Boston and January 1943 at Philadelphia – a delay of six and nine months, respectively. The Navy Yards at Norfolk and Charleston were also assigned to build LSTs. In addition, Norfolk Navy yard prematurely launched a double-bottom section of the USS *Kentucky* (BB-66) to free up a building way for LST construction.

Landing craft, in particular LST and LCI(L), shared may vital mechanical components with destroyer escorts and a shortage of these components in 1942 meant that both programs could not be supported simultaneously. As a result, work on destroyer escorts effectively ceased at yards that had already begun construction and keel laying were slowed or delayed at shipyards that were just then entering the program. This delay lasted for almost the rest of 1942 until the Allies recognized that more preparations were needed for the invasion of France.* It was not until November 1942 that the DE program received the Navy's highest priority ranking and the Navy's logistics specialists were reassigned from landing craft programs to DE work. However, the shifting of these assets came too late and it was impossible to realize the original program goals. When the destroyer escort program was slowed in April 1942 only eighteen destroyer escorts had been laid down. No ships were laid down the following month and only 34 more were laid down and 15 launched between June and October (see Figure 53). As a result, the projected number of destroyer escorts for January 1943 was not reached until the end of 1943. In fact, only two were in commission by the end of January 1943 – almost twelve months after the first destroyer escorts were laid down. By mid-June less than forty ships were in commission. With so few operational ready, the destroyer escorts were not able to play a significant role in the convoy battles that occurred in the spring of 1943. By the time large numbers of destroyer escorts entered service the Allies were firmly in control of the Atlantic shipping lanes and the need for the 1,000 ships had passed. As a result, in late 1943 over 400 destroyer escorts were canceled and landing craft production for the planned invasion of France received priority again.

---

* The disastrous Dieppe raid in August 1942 showed that the Allies were not ready to assault mainland Europe.

Emergency Production Historical Study

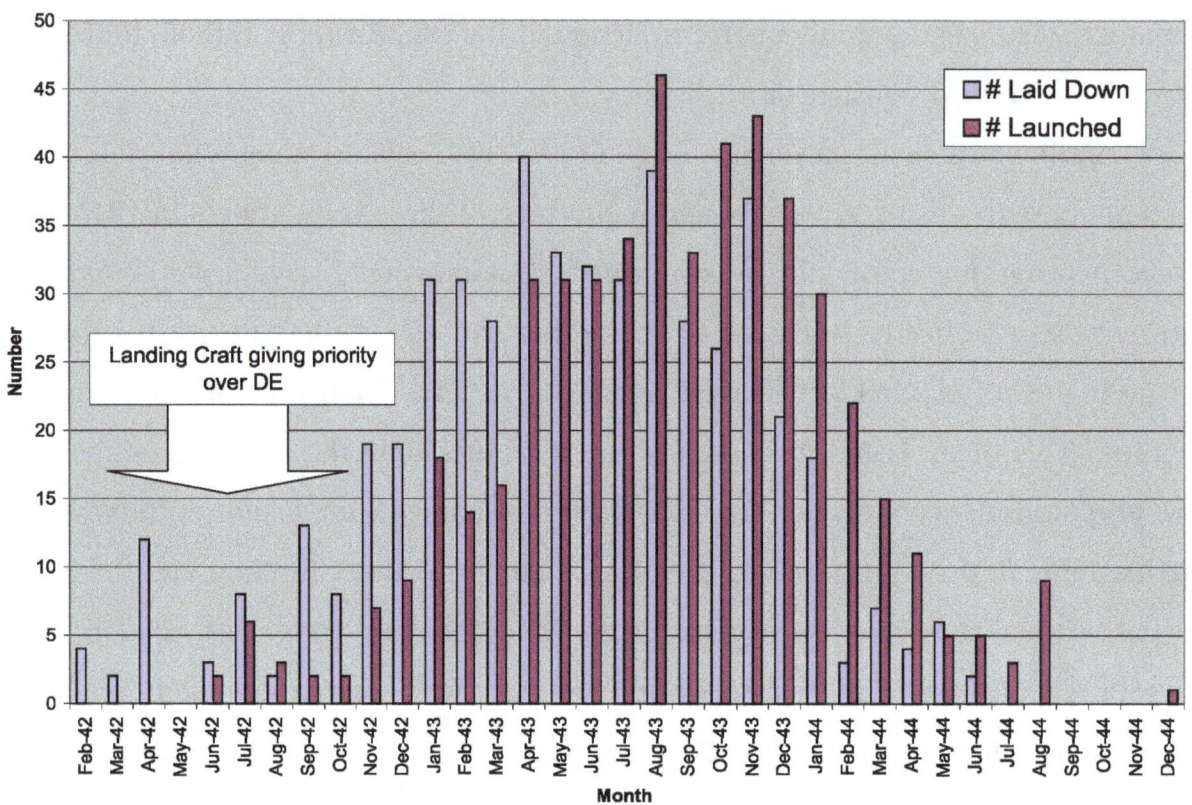

Figure 53: Monthly Keel Layings and Launchings of DE, FEB 1942-DEC 1944

The delayed entry of large numbers of destroyer escorts were the result of competing national priorities and were not a negative reflection of the producibility of the destroyer escort design. While the ships laid down before November 1942 took almost 11 months on average to build, once priority was given to the destroyer escort program in November 1942 and all shipyards began to reach full capacity, the ship were able to be produced rapidly because of their simple design. An average of 31 destroyer escorts were laid down and launched each month during 1943 (see Figures 54 and 55).

Ships laid down beginning in November 1942 took approximately 6.5 months on average to build. It should be noted that this includes all shipbuilders and covers the period after November 1943 when destroyer escorts were less of a priority and were beginning to be canceled by the hundreds. During the same period the builders of 30

Figure 54: USS *Swasey* (DE-248) launching at Brown Shipbuilding, MAR 1943

Figure 55: USS Leopold (DE-319) launching at Orange, TX, JUN 1943

or more destroyer escorts were able to achieve more rapid construction times on average (6 months) than those yards that built less than twenty (8 months) (see Table 15). Even with the delays of 1942 the average building time at all shipyards for the entire wartime program (505 ships) was only seven months because of the simplified design. Although, the builders of 30 or more destroyer escorts were able to achieve increased productivity compared to the other builders (see Figure 56 and Figure 57).

Table 15: Construction Times for DE, By Shipyard

Shipyard	# Built	# of Months from Keel Laying to Commissioning		
		Shortest	Average	Longest
Orange	93	3.8	6.6	11.5
BethHi	75	1.8	5.2	10.8
Brown	61	3.3	6.3	11.6
BosNY#	60	3.2	5.7	20.0
FedN	49	3.3	6.2	17.0
MINY	31	8.0	10.6	13.7
PHNY	18	6.7	11.5	22.0
Defoe	17	6.0	6.6	8.0
CharNY	17	5.7	7.2	8.7
Dravo	15	5.5	8.2	10.7
NorNY	13	3.3	5.9	8.9
WPS	12	8.7	11.8	14.2
BethSF	12	0.8	7.8	12.0
BethQ	12	2.0	2.9	5.1
Tampa	9	9.6	13.8	15.9
PSNY	8	9.3	11.1	13.0
DravoP	3	8.4	8.7	9.2

The rapid building time and the large number of shipyards and building ways dedicated to the program in 1943 produced a substantial number of ships in a relatively short time. While the first ships were not commissioned until the twelfth month after the first keel laying, only a year later in January 1944 more than 300 were commissioned (see Figure 58). Two hundred more were commissioned by the following January (the 36th month from the first keel laying).

Emergency Production Historical Study

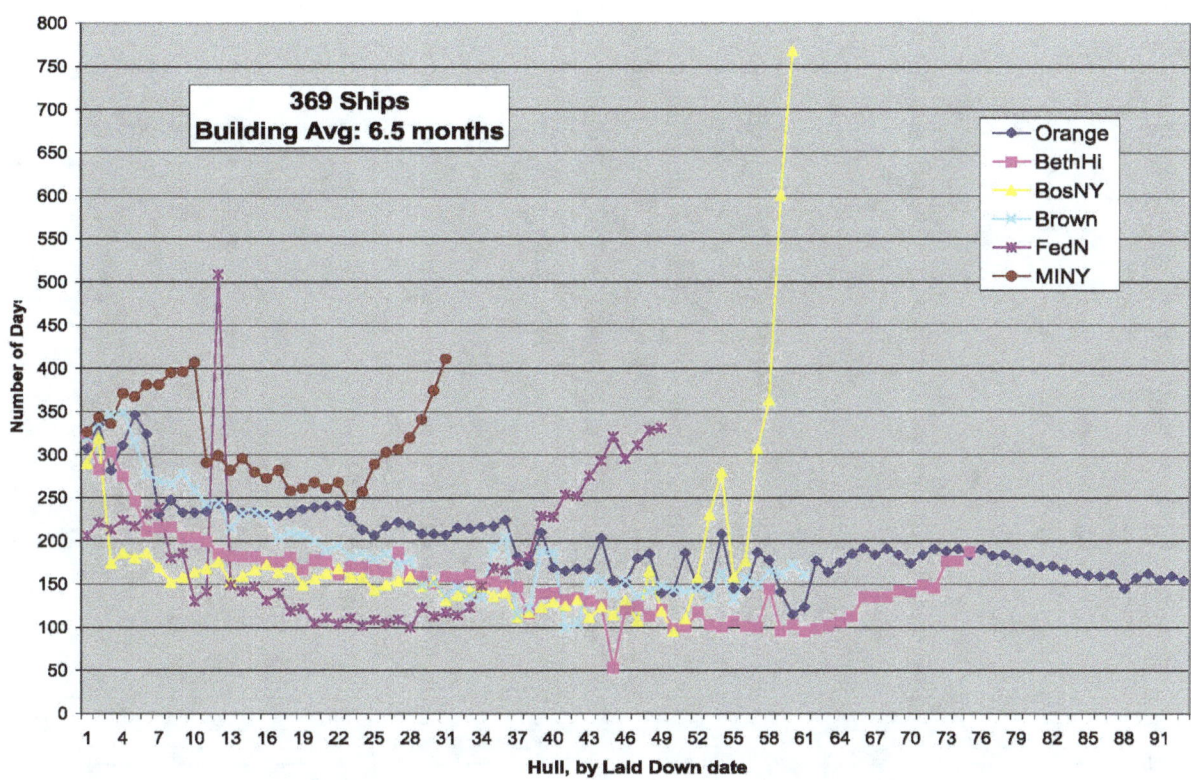

DE-540 & DE-539 not included because they were not commissioned until 1950 and 1955, respectively

Figure 56: Building Times for Shipyards that built more than 30 DE

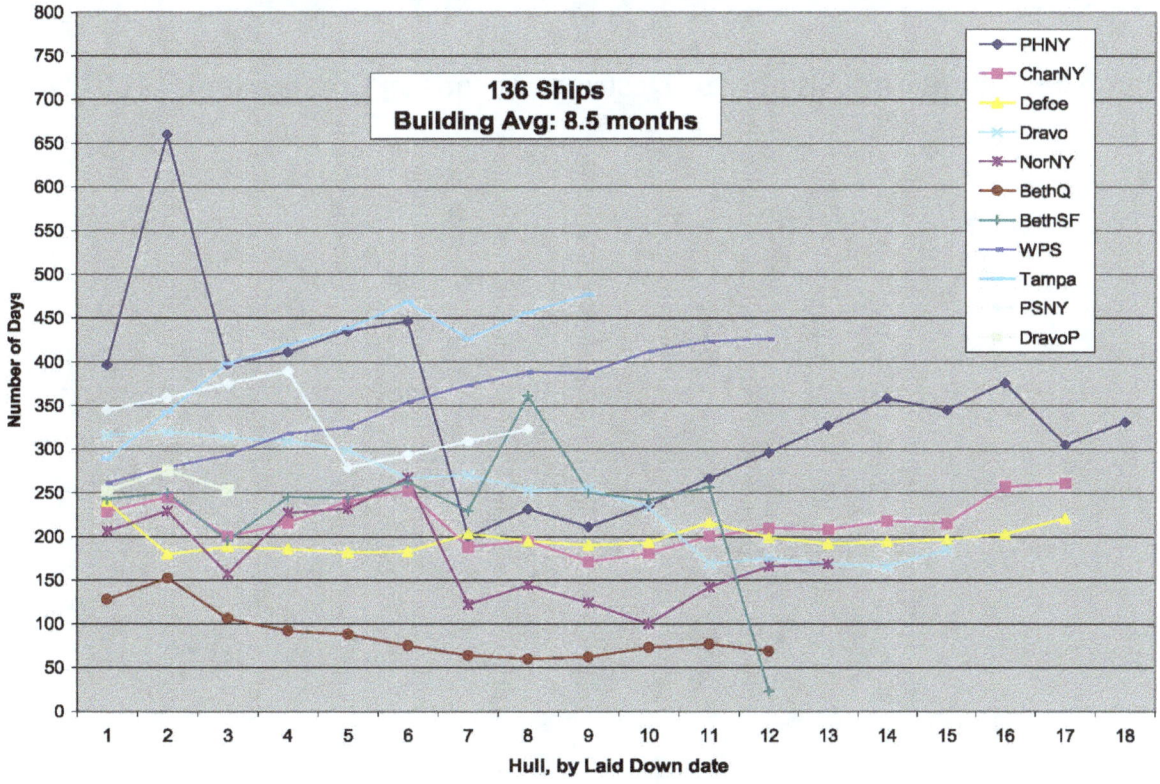

Figure 57: Building Times for Shipyards that built less than 30 DE

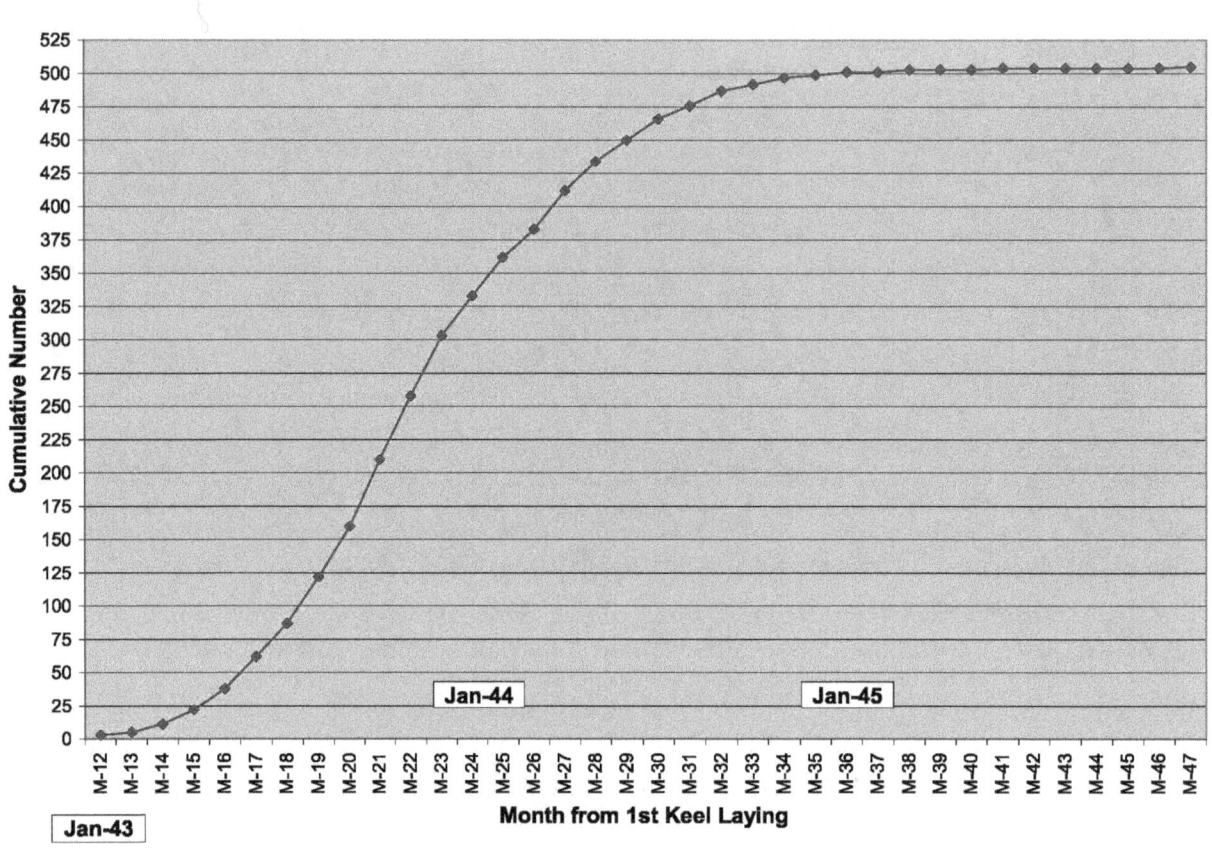

Figure 58: Cumulative Number of Destroyer Escorts in Commission, 1943-1945

6. Patrol Frigates

6.1 Design Decision Phase

As mentioned in the previous section, the destroyer escort program was initiated on behalf of the Royal Navy. Ironically, the United States' own urgent need for escort ships in early 1942 required the United States to seek help from the British. Starting in February 1942, the U.S. Navy accepted the transfer of twenty-two small ASW craft with British crews and the loan of ten *Flower* class corvettes (PG 62-71) under the Reverse Lend-Lease program.[98] In the same month the Hyde Park Agreement allotted to the United States forty-eight more escort ships built in Canada, including ten *River* class frigates (PG 101-110). Of the ten frigates only two were kept by the U.S. Navy. In the meantime, as mentioned in the previous section, in 1942 the United States assigned destroyer escort contracts to a large number of traditional combatant builders and purpose-built shipyards. Shipyards that traditionally built merchant ships were not considered for the destroyer escort program because they were full with orders for those types of ships. In June 1942, the Maritime Commission proposed that merchant shipyards could be put to better use if they built escort craft based upon a British corvette design. It was reasoned that more escort craft in service would lead to more U-boat sinkings, which would reduce merchant ship losses and, thus, the need for merchant shipbuilders.[99] Initially, this proposal was rejected because of the national shortage of steel and the lack of inactive shipyards. However, in December 1942, President Roosevelt verbally directed the Maritime Commission to initiate the program. By this time Maritime Commission yards on the Great Lakes had become available after completing their mass production of 5,000 Gross Ton coastal freighters (C1-M-AV1) contracts. Many of the Great Lakes yards had been purpose-built for the small freighter program and there was considerable political pressure to assign them new work.[100] The *River* class frigates in U.S. Navy service, PF-1 and PF-2, were selected as the design prototype for an American-built patrol frigate program (see Figure 59 and Table 16).

Initially, the Maritime Commission planned to build sixty-nine patrol frigates, with a goal of completing fifty in 1943. The total program size was later increased to one hundred and named the *Tacoma* class. The ships were initially classes as patrol gunboats (PG 111-120) but were redesignated patrol frigates (PF 3-102) on April 15, 1943.

Figure 59: USS *Tacoma* (PF-3)

Table 16: *Tacoma/Hallowell* Class Characteristics

Displacement	1,430 tons (lt)
	2,415 tons (fl)
Length Overall	303 ft. 11 in.
Beam	37 ft. 6 in.
Draft	13 ft. 8 in.
Max speed	20 knots
Armament	3 x Single 3"/50 gun mounts
	2 x twin 40mm gun mounts
	9 x 20mm gun mounts
	2 x dct
	8 x dcp (Y-gun)
	1 x dcp (Hedgehog)
Propulsion	2 x 5,500 HP turbines
	2 x shafts
	3 x boilers
Endurance	5,500 miles @ 18 knots
Complement	190

6.2 Pre-Construction Preparations

Unlike the Navy-led destroyer and destroyer escort efforts, the patrol frigate program was run by the Maritime Commission and followed its methods. As such, the

Maritime Commission employed Gibbs and Cox to adapt the *River* class design to merchant versus military standards. Kaiser Cargo was awarded the contract to develop the ship specification and working plans. A number of alterations to the design were necessary to accommodate American versus British standards, including incorporating bunks versus hammocks, and altering electrical circuits to work on alternative rather than direct current so American industrial equipment could be used. A foot of beam was also added to the design to improve stability and the ship was lengthened to make machinery spaces less cramped.

6.2.1   Selection of Shipbuilders

As mentioned above, political considerations necessitated the awarding of patrol frigate contracts to Great Lakes yards. Seven yards in Wisconsin, Minnesota, and Ohio were awarded contracts for a total of forty-five ships, while three yards on the East and West Coasts built fifty-one (see Figure 60 and 61).

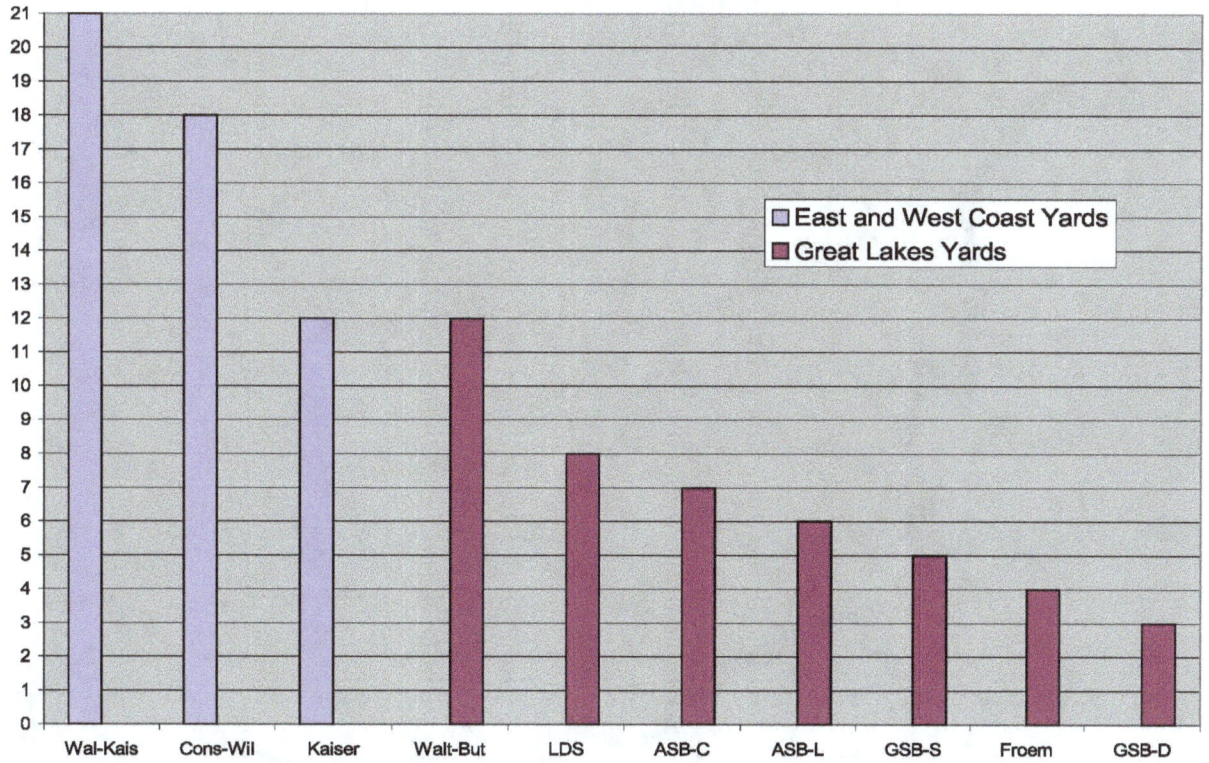

Figure 60: Number of Patrol Frigates Built, By Shipbuilder

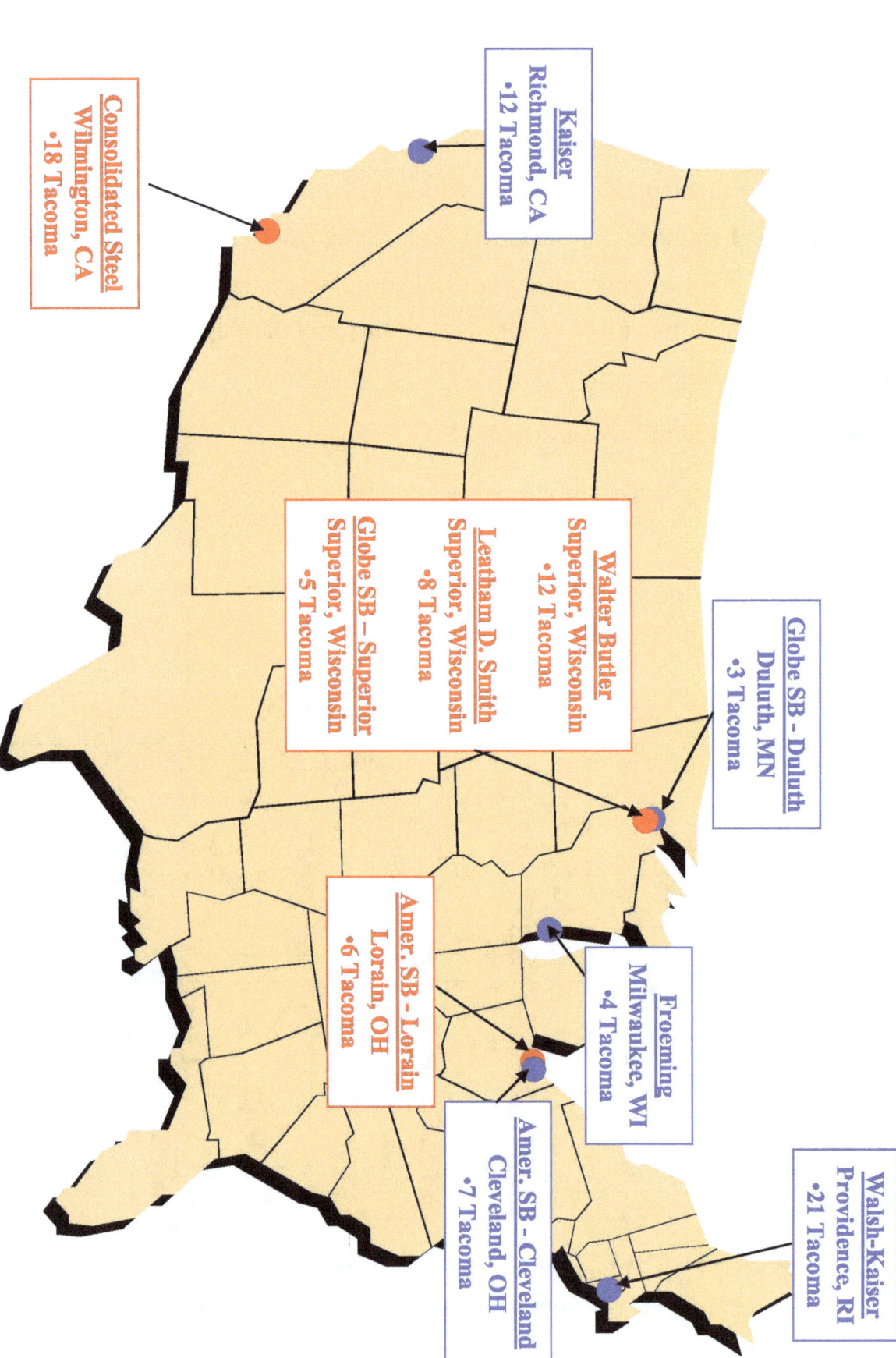

Figure 61: Patrol Frigate Shipbuilders, Geographical View

6.3 Construction Phase

The construction program began in March 1943 when six of the ten yards began laying down patrol frigates (see Table 17). Two more yards began building the following month, including Walsh-Kaiser which built the most ships. The last two yards were engaged by August 1943. The maximum number of ways at all shipyards devoted to patrol frigate construction was 38. Because most of the yards were engaged in construction from the outset of the program by June 1943 thirty-four building ways were in use (see Figure 62). As the program got under way, the Navy objected to the Maritime Commission's goal of 100 ships, arguing that building more than seventy patrol frigates would unbalance its national shipbuilding effort. In December 1943, four patrol frigates were canceled (PF 95-98) and twenty-one ships (PF 72-92) were transferred to Great Britain as the *Colony* class.

Table 17: Building Way Statistics, PF Shipbuilders, By Start Date

Yard	# Built	1st Keel Laid	Most Ways in Use	Months (Avg.) from Keel Laid to Launch	Months (Avg.) from Launch to Comm.
ASB-C	7	1-Mar-43	3	4.8	12.4
GSB-S	5	1-Mar-43	3	3.4	12.9
Walt-But	12	4-Mar-43	6	1.9	6.3
Kaiser	12	10-Mar-43	3	2.5	5.0
Cons-Wil	18	19-Mar-43	4	1.3	5.1
Froem	4	23-Mar-43	2	3.2	8.1
Wal-Kais	21	1-Apr-43	6	2.3	10.3
LDS	8	15-Apr-43	4	3.4	11.6
ASB-L	6	20-May-43	4	5.6	9.9
GSB-D	3	26-Aug-43	3	2.9	9.0

Note: Coastal shipyards are shaded.

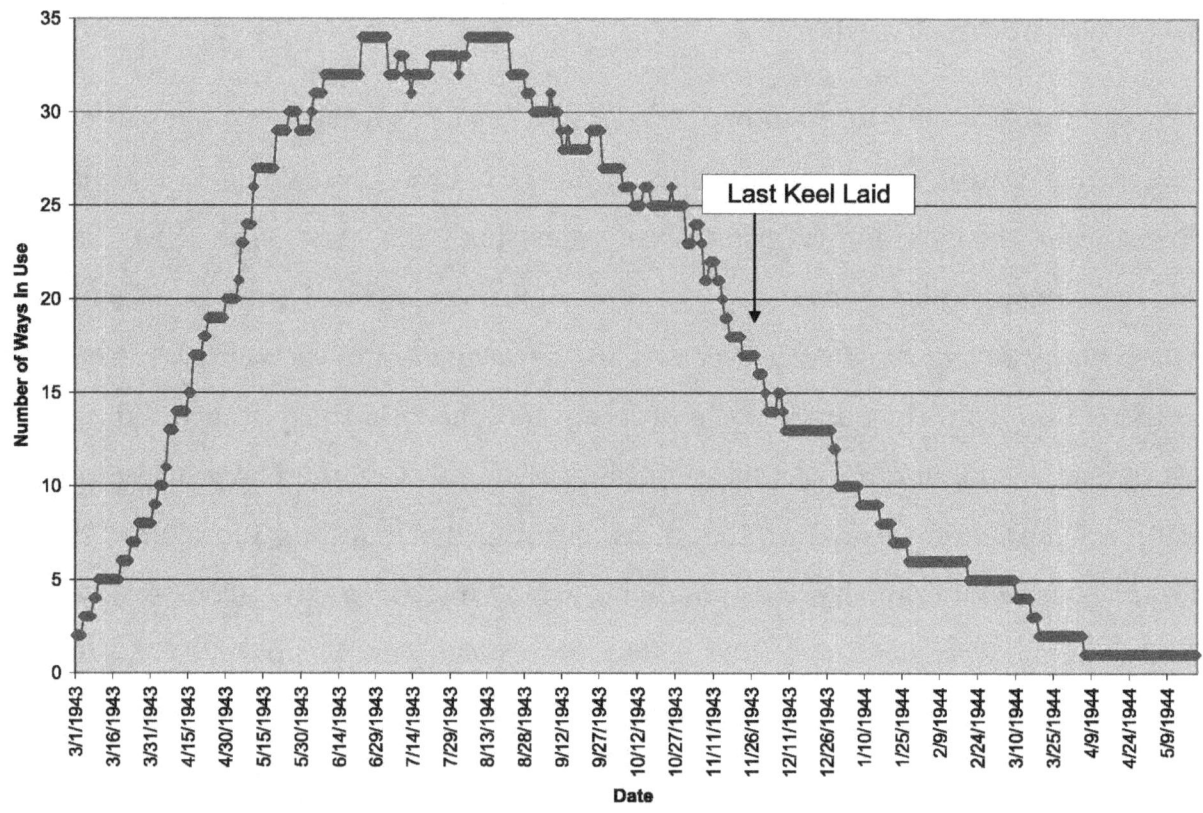

Figure 62: Number of Ways in Use, Patrol Frigate Shipbuilders

When Gibbs and Cox modified the *River* class to Maritime Commission standards it incorporated design alterations that enabled the use of mass production techniques. Because of these measures and the less stringent requirements for commercial versus military construction the time from keel laying to launching was very short. On average the ninety-six ships were launched only 2.6 months after they were laid down. The Great Lakes yards averages slightly more than this because of difficulties experienced when lining up the engines. They initially attempted to line up the engines while cold but this damaged the bearings. These problems were solved by the yards switching to lining up the engines while they were hot. Consolidated Shipbuilding's Wilmington, yard, which from the start had lined up its engines while hot, was able to achieve an average of only 38 days from keel laying to launching. The short time, coupled with the small ratio between the number of ways and the number of PF orders at most of the shipyards, allowed all ninety-six PF to be laid down by December 1943.

While the patrol frigates were quickly launched, final fitting out before commissioning took on average an additional eight months. The entire program averaged slightly less than eleven months total construction time. However, the average for each shipyard varied considerably (see Table 18). Kaiser and Consolidated Shipbuilding, both in California, and Walsh-Kaiser in Rhode Island were able to achieve total building times on average of six to eight months because there were able to quickly fit out and complete the ships after they were launched. These three shipyards built 51 of the 96 patrol frigates.

Table 18: Construction Times for PF, By Shipyard

Shipyard		# Built	# of Months from Keel Laying to Commissioning		
			Shortest	*Average*	*Longest*
East & West Coast Yards	Wal-Kais	21	5.0	8.2	12.3
	Cons-Wil	18	5.5	6.3	8.1
	Kaiser	12	5.1	7.5	13.1
Great Lakes Yards	Walt-But	12	7.3	12.6	15.6
	LDS	8	9.6	15.0	18.6
	ASB-C	7	14.4	17.1	21.7
	ASB-L	6	13.7	15.5	20.9
	GSB-S	5	13.5	16.3	18.2
	Froem	4	9.5	11.3	12.5
	GSB-D	3	10.0	12.0	15.6
Average Building Time at All yards				10.7	

The remaining shipyards, all located on the Great Lakes, had considerably longer average building times, which arose because of special requirements to enable the ships to reach the ocean. The four yards on Lake Superior could not deliver ships between November 15 and April 15 because of ice conditions in the locks at Sault Ste. Marie. All of the ships had to access the sea by being towed down the Mississippi because they were too long to use the locks of the Cardinal and LaChine ship canals, which accessed the St. Lawrence River. To get to the Mississippi the patrol frigates used the Chicago Drainage Canal ships to access the Illinois River. However, this created other requirements. To get under the bridges on the Chicago Canal the patrol frigates could not have their masts installed. Figure 63 and Figure 64 show two patrol frigates launching on the Great Lakes and California, respectively. Note that the Great Lakes ship does not have its pole mast erected. The passage down the Mississippi presented its own challenges. The Mississippi's shipping channel had a max depth of nine feet, but the patrol frigates had a draft of thirteen feet. Four pontoons were attached to each frigate to give them a draft of 8' 1.5".

Note: No pole mast at time of launching
Figure 63: USS *Lorain* (PF 93) Launching at ASB-L, March 18, 1944

Note: Pole mast installed. Kaiser's Richmond Yard in the background
Figure 64: USS *Grand Forks* (PF 11) Just Launched

All of these measures considerably increased the length of time before the Great Lakes ships were operationally ready (see Figure 65 and Figure 66). For instance, the USS *Hingham* (PF-30) was launched by Walter Butler Shipbuilders on August 27, 1943 but not commissioned until November 3, 1944 after outfitting at Plaquemine, La. Similarly, in October 1943 the USS *New Bedford* (PF-71) began construction at Leathem D. Smith Shipbuilding in Sturgeon Bay, Wisconsin. After launching in December 1943, the ship was towed to Houston to complete construction and did not commission until November 18, 1944.[101]

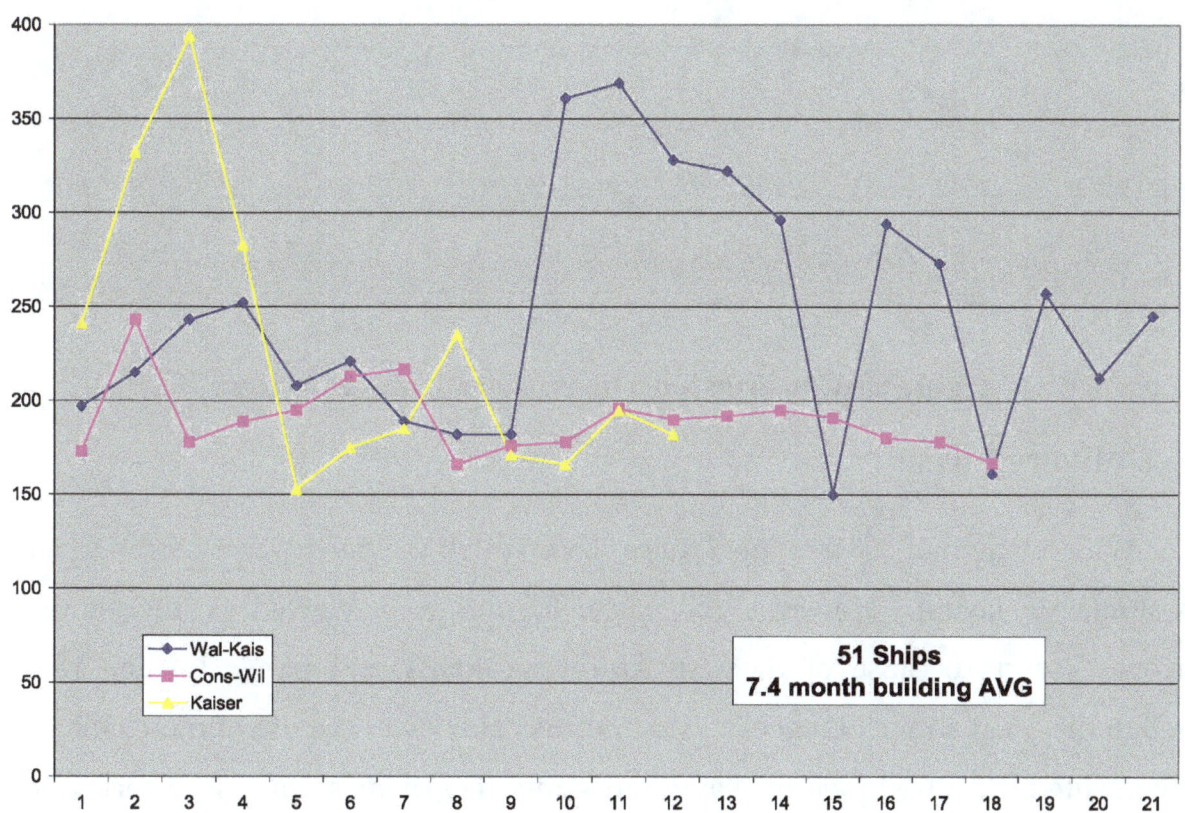

Figure 65: Construction Times, East and West Coast Builders

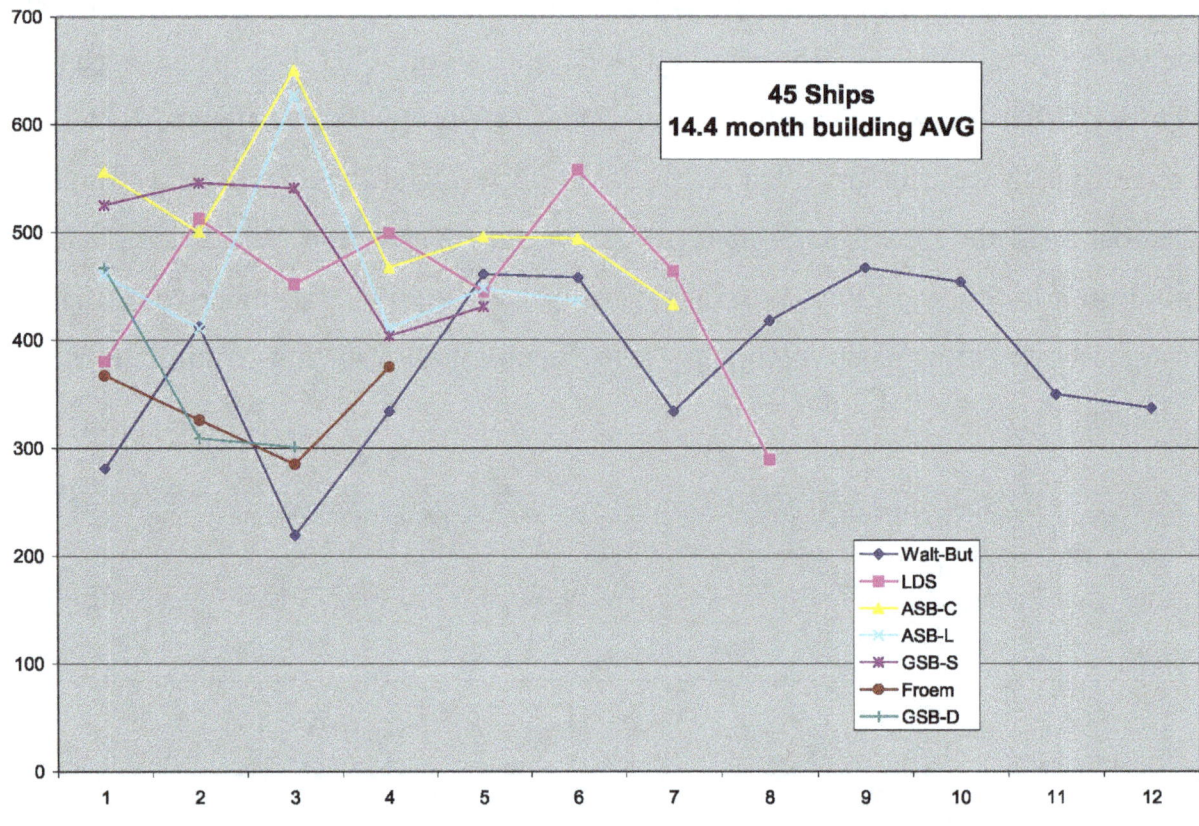

Figure 66: Construction Times, Great Lakes Builders

6.4 Delivery Phase

With a length of 303 feet the *Tacoma* class rivaled the destroyer escort in size and was similar in layout. However, the patrol frigates were viewed as inferior to the destroyer escorts because of their structural weakness and larger turning radius, although they had a much longer cruising radius. However, the use of merchant yards supplemented the capacity of the Navy Yards and the private shipyards experienced in combatant construction. Moreover, the mass production techniques, which were the source of PF design shortcomings, allowed the experienced shipyards on the East and West Coast to build the patrol frigates relatively quickly. The first PF from these yards were commissioned six months after the construction program began. However, the inexperience of many of the Great Lakes yards, which built 47% of the ships, coupled with the special needs of getting the ships to the sea, delayed delivery for a significant part of the program. The planned delivery of 69 patrol frigates by December 1943 was not attained until June 1944. The last of the patrol frigates were commissioned in October, two years after the program began (see Figure 67).

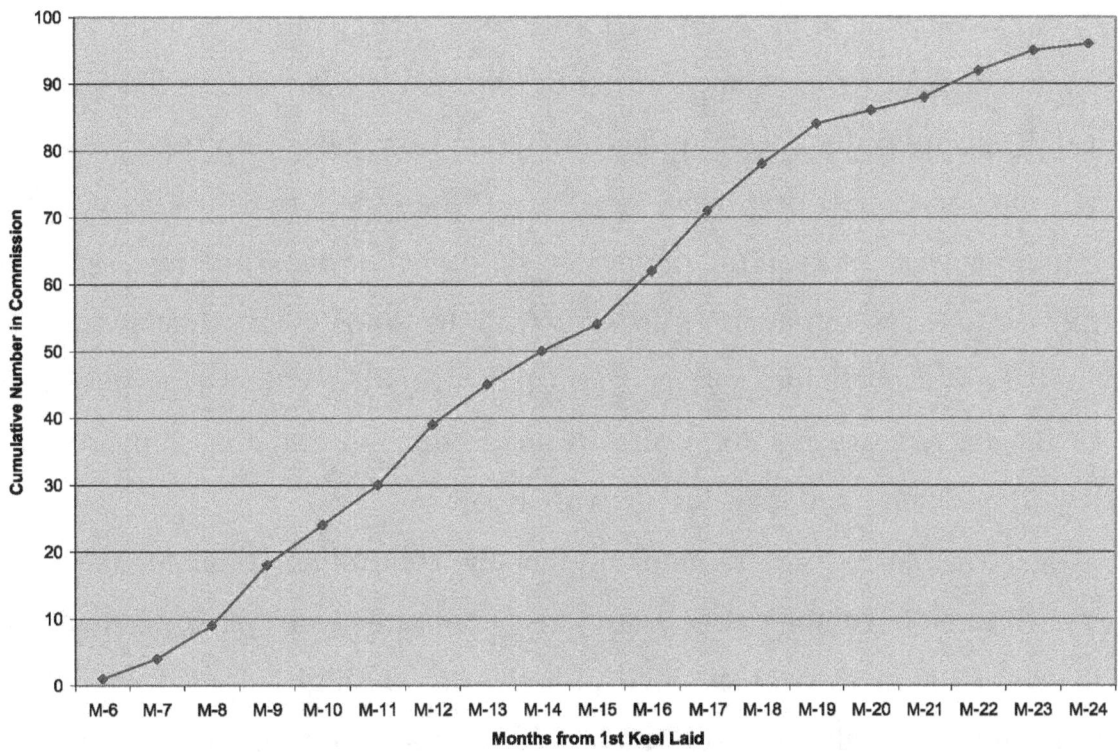

Figure 67: Cumulative Commissionings of Patrol Frigates

By the time the ships began to enter service in late 1943 the Battle of the Atlantic had shifted decisively in favor of the Allies and their usefulness had largely passed. Of the ninety-six ships built, twenty-one were transferred to the Royal Navy. The remaining seventy-five ships were manned by Coast Guard crews. Twenty-four of the patrol frigates were modified to operate as weather ships. The 3-inch/50 gun was replaced by a balloon hangar and five of the 20mm guns were removed. In the summer of 1945 twenty eight of the ships that had were not operating as weather ships were loaned to the Soviet Union for Operation Olympic, the planned invasion of Japan.[102]

7. CONCLUSION

The examination of the Navy's efforts to obtain large numbers of fleet destroyers and simplified smaller combatants during the two world wars shows that a simplified design did not markedly decrease the time needed for these ship types to first enter service compared to fleet destroyers (see Figure 68 and Figure 69). This was because significant time was first required to develop simplified designs, and then select, equip, and train second-tier shipbuilders to construct the ships. The time needed to get complex fleet destroyers into service compared favorably with the simplified design because the fleet destroyers were already in production and the shipyards had an experienced workforce and logistical network existing.

Logistical shortages were generally not the controlling factor for the length of time needed to build complex fleet destroyers or simplified smaller combatants. Long-term logistical shortages were avoided in both wars through an enormous industrial expansion that was only possible because of the magnitude of the war emergency. However, logistical shortages, especially of experienced, skilled laborers and available machinery, coupled with the urgencies of the building program, led to instances of workmanship that did not meet peacetime standards.

While the limited capability ship programs required more initial preparations, once in production their simplified design generally lent themselves to rapid production. As a result, a simplified design does allow larger number of ships to enter service at a faster rate once production experience is gained and the labor force becomes trained. However, to achieve this faster rate of production experienced second-tier shipyards must form the core of the building program, as was the case with the destroyer escort in World War Two. The simplified-design *Eagle* boat and patrol frigate did not achieve a rapid production rate because of the use on inexperienced builders to execute all of the *Eagle* boat program and half of the patrol frigate program.

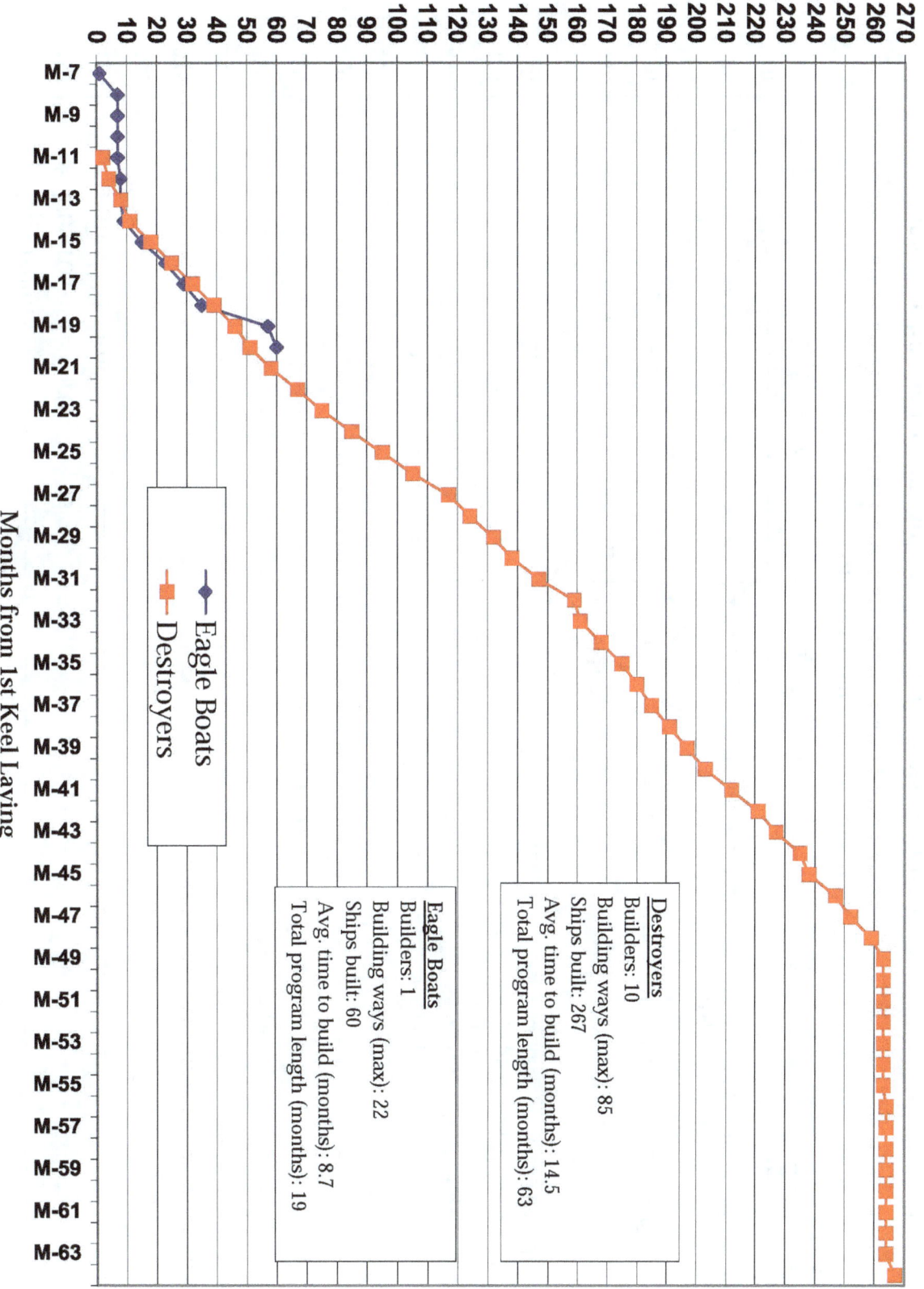

Figure 68: Rate of Commissioning of War Emergency Ships in World War I

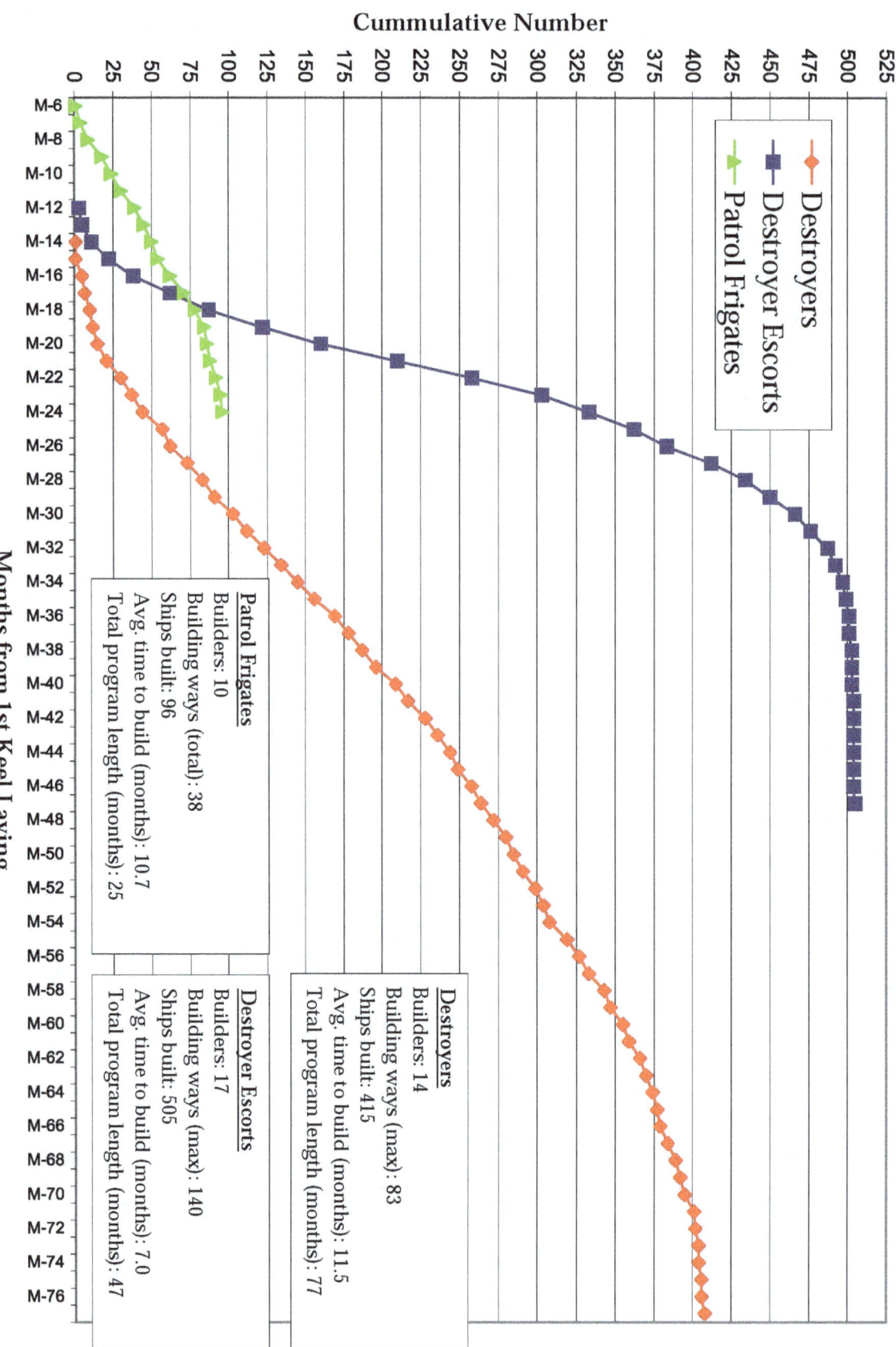

Figure 69: Rate of Commissioning of War Emergency Ships in World War II

APPENDIX A Key to Shipyard Abbreviations

Abbr.	Corporate Name/ Notes	Location	Ship Type(s) Built / (War)
Private Yards			
ASB-C	American Shipbuilding Co	Cleveland, OH	PF
ASB-L	American Shipbuilding Co.	Lorain, OH	PF
Bath	Bath Iron Works	Bath, ME	DD – (WW I & II)
BethHi	Bethlehem Steel Co.	Hingham MA	DE
BethQ	Bethlehem Steel Co. Known as Fore River Shipbuilding Co. at outbreak of World War I.	Quincy, MA	DD – (WW I & II) DE
BethSI	Bethlehem Steel Co.	Staten Island, NY	DD – (WW II)
BethSF	Bethlehem Steel Co. Known as Union Iron Works at outbreak of World War I.	San Francisco, CA	DD – (WW I & II) DE
BethSP	Bethlehem Steel Co.	San Pedro, CA	DD – (WW II)
BethSQ	Bethlehem Steel Co. Purpose-built in 1917 to meet emergency shipbuilding needs.	Squantum, MA	DD – (WW I)
Brown	Brown Shipbuilding Company	Houston, TX	DE
Con-Wil	Consolidated Steel Corporation	Wilmington, CA	PF
Cramp	William Cramp and Sons Ship & Engine Building Co.	Philadelphia, PA	DD – (WW I)
Defoe	Defoe Shipbuilding Company	Bay City MI	DE
Dravo	Dravo Corp.	Wilmington DE	DE
DravoP	Dravo Corp.	Pittsburgh PA	DE
Fed	Federal Shipbuilding & Dry Dock Co.	Kearny, NJ	DD – (WW II)
FedN	Federal Shipbuilding & Dry Dock Co.	Newark NJ	DE
Ford	Ford Motor Co.,	Detroit, MI	PE
Froem	Froeming	Milwaukee, WI	PF
GSB-D	Globe Shipbuilding	Duluth, MN	PF
GSB-S	Globe Shipbuilding	Superior, WI	PF
Gulf	Gulf Shipbuilding Corporation	Chickasaw, AL	DD – (WW II)
Kaiser	Kaiser Co.	Richmond, CA	PF
LDS	Leatham D. Smith	Superior, WI	PF
NN	Newport News Shipbuilding & Dry Dock Co.	Newport News, VA	DD – (WW I)
NYSB	New York Shipbuilding Co.	Camden, NJ	DD – (WW I)
Orange	Consolidated Steel Corporation	Orange TX	DD – (WW II) DE
Tampa	Tampa Shipbuilding Company, Inc.	Tampa, FL	DE
Todd	Todd Pacific Shipyards	Seattle, WA	DD – (WW II)
Wal-Kais	Walsh-Kaiser	Providence, RI	PF
Walt-But	Walter Butler	Superior, WI	PF
WPS	Western Pipe & Steel Co. of California	San Pedro, CA	DE
Government Yards			
BosNY	Boston Naval Shipyard	Charlestown, MA	DD – (WW II) DE
CharNY	Charleston Naval Shipyard	Charleston, SC	DD – (WW I & II) DE
MINY	Mare Island Naval Shipyard	Vallejo, CA	DD – (WW I) DE
NorNY	Norfolk Naval Shipyard	Portsmouth, VA	DD – (WW I & II) DE
PHNY	Philadelphia Naval Shipyard	Philadelphia, PA	DD – (WW II) DE
PSNY	Puget Sound Naval Shipyard	Bremerton WA	DD – (WW II) DE

APPENDIX B   SHIP DATA

World War I Destroyers

Class	Number	Name	Shipyard	Laid Down	Launched	Commissioned
Wickes	DD-75	Wickes	Bath	26-Jun-17	25-Jun-18	31-Jul-18
Wickes	DD-76	Philip	Bath	1-Sep-17	25-Jul-18	24-Aug-18
Wickes	DD-77	Woolsey	Bath	1-Nov-17	17-Sep-18	30-Sep-18
Wickes	DD-78	Evans	Bath	28-Dec-17	30-Oct-18	11-Nov-18
Wickes	DD-79	Little	BethQ	18-Jun-17	11-Nov-17	6-Apr-18
Wickes	DD-80	Kimberly	BethQ	21-Jun-17	14-Dec-17	26-Apr-18
Wickes	DD-81	Sigourney	BethQ	25-Aug-17	16-Dec-17	15-May-18
Wickes	DD-82	Gregory	BethQ	25-Aug-17	27-Jan-18	1-Jun-18
Wickes	DD-83	Stringham	BethQ	19-Sep-17	30-Mar-18	2-Jul-18
Wickes	DD-84	Dyer	BethQ	26-Sep-17	13-Apr-18	1-Jul-18
Wickes	DD-85	Colhoun	BethQ	19-Sep-17	21-Feb-18	13-Jun-18
Wickes	DD-86	Stevens	BethQ	20-Sep-17	13-Jan-18	24-May-18
Wickes	DD-87	McKee	BethSF	29-Oct-17	23-Mar-18	7-Sep-18
Wickes	DD-88	Robinson	BethSF	31-Oct-17	28-Mar-18	19-Oct-18
Wickes	DD-89	Ringgold	BethSF	20-Oct-17	14-Apr-18	14-Nov-18
Wickes	DD-90	McKean	BethSF	12-Feb-18	4-Jul-18	25-Feb-19
Wickes	DD-91	Harding	BethSF	12-Feb-18	4-Jul-18	24-Jan-19
Wickes	DD-92	Gridley	BethSF	1-Apr-18	4-Jul-18	18-Mar-19
Wickes	DD-93	Fairfax	MINY	10-Jul-17	15-Dec-17	6-Apr-18
Wickes	DD-94	Taylor	MINY	15-Oct-17	14-Feb-18	1-Jun-18
Wickes	DD-95	Bell	BethQ	16-Nov-17	20-Apr-18	31-Jul-18
Wickes	DD-96	Stribling	BethQ	14-Dec-17	29-May-18	16-Aug-18
Wickes	DD-97	Murray	BethQ	22-Dec-17	8-Jun-18	21-Aug-18
Wickes	DD-98	Israel	BethQ	26-Jan-18	22-Jun-18	13-Sep-18
Wickes	DD-99	Luce	BethQ	9-Feb-18	29-Jun-18	11-Sep-18
Wickes	DD-100	Maury	BethQ	25-Feb-18	4-Jul-18	23-Sep-18
Wickes	DD-101	Lansdale	BethQ	20-Apr-18	21-Jul-18	26-Oct-18
Wickes	DD-102	Mahan	BethQ	4-May-18	4-Aug-18	24-Oct-18
Wickes	DD-103	Schley	BethSF	29-Oct-17	28-Mar-18	20-Sep-18
Wickes	DD-104	Champlin	BethSF	29-Oct-17	7-Apr-18	11-Nov-18
Wickes	DD-105	Mugford	BethSF	20-Dec-17	14-Apr-18	25-Nov-18
Wickes	DD-106	Chew	BethSF	2-Jan-18	26-May-18	12-Dec-18
Wickes	DD-107	Hazelwood	BethSF	24-Dec-17	22-Jun-18	20-Feb-19
Wickes	DD-108	Williams	BethSF	25-Mar-18	4-Jul-18	1-Mar-19
Wickes	DD-109	Crane	BethSF	7-Jan-18	4-Jul-18	18-Apr-19
Wickes	DD-110	Hart	BethSF	8-Jan-18	4-Jul-18	26-May-19
Wickes	DD-111	Ingraham	BethSF	12-Jan-18	4-Jul-18	15-May-19
Wickes	DD-112	Ludlow	BethSF	7-Jan-18	9-Jun-18	23-Dec-18
Wickes	DD-113	Rathburne	Cramp	12-Jul-17	27-Dec-17	24-Jun-18
Wickes	DD-114	Talbot	Cramp	12-Jul-17	20-Feb-18	20-Jul-18
Wickes	DD-115	Waters	Cramp	26-Jul-17	9-Mar-18	6-Aug-18
Wickes	DD-116	Dent	Cramp	30-Aug-17	23-Mar-18	9-Sep-18
Wickes	DD-117	Dorsey	Cramp	18-Sep-17	9-Apr-18	16-Sep-18

Class	Number	Name	Shipyard	Laid Down	Launched	Commissioned
Wickes	DD-118	Lea	Cramp	18-Sep-17	29-Apr-18	2-Oct-18
Wickes	DD-119	Lamberton	NN	1-Oct-17	30-Mar-18	22-Aug-18
Wickes	DD-120	Radford	NN	2-Oct-17	5-Aug-18	30-Sep-18
Wickes	DD-121	Montgomery	NN	2-Oct-17	23-Mar-18	26-Jul-18
Wickes	DD-122	Breese	NN	10-Nov-17	11-May-18	23-Oct-18
Wickes	DD-123	Gamble	NN	12-Nov-17	11-May-18	29-Nov-18
Wickes	DD-124	Ramsay	NN	21-Dec-17	8-Jun-18	15-Feb-19
Wickes	DD-125	Tattnall	NYSB	1-Dec-17	5-Sep-18	26-Jun-19
Wickes	DD-126	Badger	NYSB	9-Jan-18	24-Aug-18	29-May-19
Wickes	DD-127	Twiggs	NYSB	23-Jan-18	28-Sep-18	28-Jul-19
Wickes	DD-128	Babbitt	NYSB	19-Feb-18	30-Sep-18	24-Oct-19
Wickes	DD-129	De Long	NYSB	21-Feb-18	29-Oct-18	20-Sep-19
Wickes	DD-130	Jacob Jones	NYSB	21-Feb-18	20-Nov-18	20-Oct-19
Wickes	DD-131	Buchanan	Bath	29-Jun-18	2-Jan-19	20-Jan-19
Wickes	DD-132	Aaron Ward	Bath	1-Aug-18	10-Apr-19	21-Apr-19
Wickes	DD-133	Hale	Bath	7-Oct-18	29-May-19	12-Jun-19
Wickes	DD-134	Crowinshield	Bath	5-Nov-18	24-Jul-19	6-Aug-19
Wickes	DD-135	Tillman	CharNY	29-Jul-18	7-Jul-19	30-Apr-21
Wickes	DD-136	Boggs	MINY	15-Nov-17	25-Apr-18	23-Sep-18
Wickes	DD-137	Kilty	MINY	15-Dec-17	25-Apr-18	17-Dec-18
Wickes	DD-138	Kennison	MINY	14-Feb-18	8-Jun-18	17-Dec-18
Wickes	DD-139	Ward	MINY	15-May-18	1-Jun-18	24-Jul-18
Wickes	DD-140	Claxton	MINY	25-Apr-18	14-Jan-19	13-Sep-19
Wickes	DD-141	Hamilton	MINY	8-Jun-18	15-Jan-19	7-Nov-19
Wickes	DD-142	Tarbell	Cramp	31-Dec-17	28-May-18	27-Nov-18
Wickes	DD-143	Yarnall	Cramp	12-Feb-18	19-Jun-18	29-Nov-18
Wickes	DD-144	Upshur	Cramp	19-Feb-18	4-Jul-18	23-Dec-18
Wickes	DD-145	Greer	Cramp	24-Feb-18	1-Aug-18	31-Dec-18
Wickes	DD-146	Elliot	Cramp	23-Feb-18	4-Jul-18	25-Jan-19
Wickes	DD-147	Roper	Cramp	19-Mar-18	17-Aug-18	15-Feb-19
Wickes	DD-148	Breckinridge	Cramp	11-Mar-18	17-Aug-18	27-Feb-19
Wickes	DD-149	Barney	Cramp	26-Mar-18	5-Sep-18	14-Mar-19
Wickes	DD-150	Blakeley	Cramp	26-Mar-18	19-Sep-18	8-May-19
Wickes	DD-151	Biddle	Cramp	22-Apr-18	3-Oct-18	22-Apr-19
Wickes	DD-152	Du Pont	Cramp	2-May-18	22-Oct-18	30-Apr-19
Wickes	DD-153	Bernadou	Cramp	4-Jun-18	7-Nov-18	19-May-19
Wickes	DD-154	Ellis	Cramp	8-Jul-18	30-Nov-18	7-Jun-19
Wickes	DD-155	Cole	Cramp	25-Jun-18	11-Jan-19	19-Jun-19
Wickes	DD-156	J. Fred Talbott	Cramp	8-Jul-18	14-Dec-18	30-Jun-19
Wickes	DD-157	Dickerson	NYSB	25-May-18	12-Mar-19	3-Sep-19
Wickes	DD-158	Leary	NYSB	6-Mar-18	18-Dec-18	5-Dec-19
Wickes	DD-159	Schenck	NYSB	26-Mar-18	23-Apr-19	30-Oct-19
Wickes	DD-160	Herbert	NYSB	4-Apr-18	8-May-19	21-Nov-19
Wickes	DD-161	Palmer	BethQ	29-May-18	18-Aug-18	22-Nov-18
Wickes	DD-162	Thatcher	BethQ	8-Jun-18	31-Aug-18	14-Jan-19
Wickes	DD-163	Walker	BethQ	18-Jun-18	14-Sep-18	31-Jan-19
Wickes	DD-164	Crosby	BethQ	23-Jun-18	28-Sep-18	24-Jan-19

Class	Number	Name	Shipyard	Laid Down	Launched	Commissioned
Wickes	DD-165	Meredith	BethQ	26-Jun-18	22-Sep-18	29-Jan-19
Wickes	DD-166	Bush	BethQ	4-Jul-18	27-Oct-18	19-Feb-19
Wickes	DD-167	Cowell	BethQ	15-Jul-18	23-Nov-18	17-Mar-19
Wickes	DD-168	Maddox	BethQ	20-Jul-18	27-Oct-18	10-Mar-19
Wickes	DD-169	Foote	BethQ	7-Aug-18	14-Dec-18	21-Mar-19
Wickes	DD-170	Kalk	BethQ	17-Aug-18	21-Dec-18	29-Mar-19
Wickes	DD-171	Burns	BethSF	15-Apr-18	4-Jul-18	7-Aug-19
Wickes	DD-172	Anthony	BethSF	18-Apr-18	10-Aug-18	19-Jun-19
Wickes	DD-173	Sproston	BethSF	20-Apr-18	10-Aug-18	12-Jul-19
Wickes	DD-174	Rizal	BethSF	26-Jun-18	21-Sep-18	28-May-19
Wickes	DD-175	Mackenzie	BethSF	4-Jul-18	29-Sep-18	25-Jul-19
Wickes	DD-176	Renshaw	BethSF	8-May-18	21-Sep-18	31-Jul-19
Wickes	DD-177	O'Bannon	BethSF	12-Nov-18	28-Feb-19	27-Aug-19
Wickes	DD-178	Hogan	BethSF	25-Nov-18	12-Apr-19	1-Oct-19
Wickes	DD-179	Howard	BethSF	9-Dec-18	26-Apr-19	28-Jan-20
Wickes	DD-180	Stansbury	BethSF	9-Dec-18	16-May-19	8-Jan-20
Wickes	DD-181	Hopewell	NN	19-Jan-18	8-Jun-18	21-Mar-19
Wickes	DD-182	Thomas	NN	23-Mar-18	4-Jul-18	25-Apr-19
Wickes	DD-183	Haraden	NN	30-Mar-18	4-Jul-18	7-Jun-19
Wickes	DD-184	Abbot	NN	5-Apr-18	4-Jul-18	19-Jul-19
Wickes	DD-185	Bagley (Doran)	NN	11-May-18	19-Oct-18	27-Aug-19
Clemson	DD-186	Clemson	NN	11-May-18	5-Sep-18	29-Dec-19
Clemson	DD-187	Dahlgren	NN	8-Jun-18	20-Nov-18	6-Jan-20
Clemson	DD-188	Goldsborough	NN	8-Jun-18	20-Nov-18	26-Jan-20
Clemson	DD-189	Semmes	NN	10-Jul-18	21-Dec-18	21-Feb-20
Clemson	DD-190	Satterlee	NN	10-Jul-18	21-Dec-18	23-Dec-19
Clemson	DD-191	Mason	NN	10-Jul-18	8-Mar-19	28-Feb-20
Clemson	DD-192	Graham	NN	7-Sep-18	22-Mar-19	13-Mar-20
Clemson	DD-193	Abel P. Upshur	NN	20-Aug-18	14-Feb-20	23-Nov-20
Clemson	DD-194	Hunt	NN	20-Aug-18	14-Feb-20	30-Sep-20
Clemson	DD-195	Welborn C. Wood	NN	24-Sep-18	6-Mar-20	14-Jan-21
Clemson	DD-196	George E. Badger	NN	24-Sep-18	6-Mar-20	28-Jul-20
Clemson	DD-197	Branch	NN	25-Oct-18	19-Apr-19	26-Jul-20
Clemson	DD-198	Herndon	NN	25-Nov-18	31-May-19	14-Sep-20
Clemson	DD-199	Dallas	NN	25-Nov-18	31-May-19	29-Oct-20
Clemson	DD-206	Chandler	Cramp	19-Aug-18	19-Mar-19	5-Sep-19
Clemson	DD-207	Southard	Cramp	18-Aug-18	31-Mar-19	24-Sep-19
Clemson	DD-208	Hovey	Cramp	7-Sep-18	26-Apr-19	2-Oct-19
Clemson	DD-209	Long	Cramp	23-Sep-18	26-Apr-19	20-Oct-19
Clemson	DD-210	Broome	Cramp	8-Oct-18	14-May-19	31-Oct-19
Clemson	DD-211	Alden	Cramp	24-Oct-18	7-Jun-19	24-Nov-19
Clemson	DD-212	Smith Thompson	Cramp	24-Mar-19	14-Jul-19	10-Dec-19
Clemson	DD-213	Barker	Cramp	30-Apr-19	11-Sep-19	27-Dec-19
Clemson	DD-214	Tracy	Cramp	3-Apr-19	12-Aug-19	9-Mar-20
Clemson	DD-215	Borie	Cramp	30-Apr-19	4-Oct-19	24-Mar-20
Clemson	DD-216	John D. Edwards	Cramp	21-May-19	18-Oct-19	6-Apr-20
Clemson	DD-217	Whipple	Cramp	12-Jun-19	6-Nov-19	23-Apr-20

Class	Number	Name	Shipyard	Laid Down	Launched	Commissioned
Clemson	DD-218	Parrott	Cramp	23-Jul-19	25-Nov-19	11-May-20
Clemson	DD-219	Edsall	Cramp	15-Sep-19	29-Jul-20	26-Nov-20
Clemson	DD-220	MacLeish	Cramp	19-Aug-19	18-Dec-19	2-Aug-20
Clemson	DD-221	Simpson	Cramp	9-Oct-19	28-Apr-20	3-Nov-20
Clemson	DD-222	Bulmer	Cramp	11-Aug-19	22-Jan-20	16-Aug-20
Clemson	DD-223	McCormick	Cramp	11-Aug-19	14-Feb-20	30-Aug-20
Clemson	DD-224	Stewart	Cramp	9-Sep-19	4-Mar-20	15-Sep-20
Clemson	DD-225	Pope	Cramp	9-Sep-19	23-Mar-20	27-Oct-20
Clemson	DD-226	Peary	Cramp	9-Sep-19	6-Apr-20	22-Oct-20
Clemson	DD-227	Pillsbury	Cramp	23-Oct-19	3-Aug-20	15-Dec-20
Clemson	DD-228	Ford (John D. Ford)	Cramp	11-Nov-19	2-Sep-20	30-Dec-20
Clemson	DD-229	Truxtun	Cramp	3-Dec-19	28-Sep-20	16-Feb-21
Clemson	DD-230	Paul Jones	Cramp	23-Dec-19	30-Sep-20	19-Apr-21
Clemson	DD-231	Hatfield	NYSB	10-Jun-18	17-Mar-19	16-Apr-20
Clemson	DD-232	Brooks	NYSB	11-Jun-18	24-Apr-19	18-Jun-20
Clemson	DD-233	Gilmer	NYSB	25-Jun-18	24-May-19	30-Apr-20
Clemson	DD-234	Fox	NYSB	25-Jun-18	12-Jun-19	17-May-20
Clemson	DD-235	Kane	NYSB	3-Jul-18	12-Aug-19	11-Jun-20
Clemson	DD-236	Humphreys	NYSB	31-Jul-18	28-Jul-19	21-Jul-20
Clemson	DD-237	McFarland	NYSB	31-Jul-18	30-Mar-20	30-Sep-20
Clemson	DD-238	James K. Paulding	NYSB	31-Jul-18	20-Apr-20	29-Nov-20
Clemson	DD-239	Overton	NYSB	30-Oct-18	10-Jul-19	30-Jun-20
Clemson	DD-240	Sturtevant	NYSB	23-Nov-18	29-Jul-20	21-Sep-20
Clemson	DD-241	Childs	NYSB	19-Mar-19	15-Sep-20	22-Oct-20
Clemson	DD-242	King	NYSB	28-Apr-19	14-Oct-20	16-Dec-20
Clemson	DD-243	Sands	NYSB	22-Mar-19	28-Oct-19	10-Nov-20
Clemson	DD-244	Williamson	NYSB	27-Mar-19	16-Oct-19	29-Oct-20
Clemson	DD-245	Reuben James	NYSB	2-Apr-19	4-Oct-19	24-Sep-20
Clemson	DD-246	Bainbridge	NYSB	27-Mar-19	12-Jun-20	9-Feb-21
Clemson	DD-247	Goff	NYSB	16-Jun-19	2-Jun-20	19-Jan-21
Clemson	DD-248	Barry	NYSB	26-Jul-19	28-Oct-20	28-Dec-20
Clemson	DD-249	Hopkins	NYSB	30-Jul-19	26-Jun-20	21-Mar-21
Clemson	DD-250	Lawrence	NYSB	14-Aug-19	10-Jul-20	18-Apr-21
Clemson	DD-251	Belknap	BethQ	3-Sep-18	14-Jan-19	28-Apr-19
Clemson	DD-252	McCook	BethQ	11-Sep-18	31-Jan-19	30-Apr-19
Clemson	DD-253	McCalla	BethQ	25-Sep-18	28-Mar-19	19-May-19
Clemson	DD-254	Rodgers	BethQ	25-Feb-18	26-Apr-19	22-Jul-19
Clemson	DD-255	Ingram	BethQ	15-Oct-18	28-Feb-19	28-Jun-19
Clemson	DD-256	Bancroft	BethQ	4-Nov-18	21-Mar-19	30-Jun-19
Clemson	DD-257	Welles	BethQ	13-Nov-18	8-May-19	2-Sep-19
Clemson	DD-258	Aulick	BethQ	3-Dec-18	11-Apr-19	26-Jul-19
Clemson	DD-259	Turner	BethQ	21-Dec-18	17-May-19	24-Sep-19
Clemson	DD-260	Gillis	BethQ	27-Dec-18	29-May-19	3-Sep-19
Clemson	DD-261	Delphy	BethSQ	20-Apr-18	18-Jul-18	30-Nov-18
Clemson	DD-262	McDermut	BethSQ	20-Apr-18	6-Jul-18	27-Mar-19
Clemson	DD-263	Laub	BethSQ	20-Apr-18	25-Aug-18	17-Mar-19
Clemson	DD-264	McLanahan	BethSQ	20-Apr-18	22-Sep-18	5-Apr-19

Class	Number	Name	Shipyard	Laid Down	Launched	Commissioned
Clemson	DD-265	Edwards	BethSQ	20-Apr-18	10-Oct-18	24-Apr-19
Clemson	DD-266	Greene (ex-Anthony)	BethSQ	3-Jun-18	2-Nov-18	9-May-19
Clemson	DD-267	Ballard	BethSQ	3-Jun-18	7-Dec-18	5-Jun-19
Clemson	DD-268	Shubrick	BethSQ	3-Jun-18	31-Dec-18	3-Jul-19
Clemson	DD-269	Bailey	BethSQ	3-Jun-18	5-Feb-19	27-Jun-19
Clemson	DD-270	Thornton	BethSQ	3-Jun-18	22-Mar-19	15-Jul-19
Clemson	DD-271	Morris	BethSQ	20-Jul-18	12-Apr-19	21-Jul-19
Clemson	DD-272	Tingey	BethSQ	8-Aug-18	24-Apr-19	25-Jul-19
Clemson	DD-273	Swasey	BethSQ	27-Aug-18	7-May-19	8-Aug-19
Clemson	DD-274	Meade	BethSQ	24-Sep-18	24-May-19	8-Sep-19
Clemson	DD-275	Sinclair	BethSQ	11-Oct-18	2-Jun-19	8-Oct-19
Clemson	DD-276	McCawley	BethSQ	2-Nov-18	14-Jun-19	22-Sep-19
Clemson	DD-277	Moody	BethSQ	9-Dec-18	28-Jun-19	10-Dec-19
Clemson	DD-278	Henshaw	BethSQ	3-Jan-19	28-Jun-19	10-Dec-19
Clemson	DD-279	Meyer	BethSQ	6-Feb-19	18-Jul-19	17-Dec-19
Clemson	DD-280	Doyen	BethSQ	24-Mar-19	26-Jul-19	17-Dec-19
Clemson	DD-281	Sharkey	BethSQ	14-Apr-19	12-Aug-19	28-Nov-19
Clemson	DD-282	Toucey	BethSQ	26-Apr-19	5-Sep-19	9-Dec-19
Clemson	DD-283	Breck	BethSQ	8-May-19	5-Sep-19	1-Dec-19
Clemson	DD-284	Isherwood	BethSQ	24-May-19	10-Sep-19	4-Dec-19
Clemson	DD-285	Case	BethSQ	3-Jun-19	21-Sep-19	8-Dec-19
Clemson	DD-286	Lardner	BethSQ	16-Jun-19	29-Sep-19	10-Dec-19
Clemson	DD-287	Putnam	BethSQ	30-Jun-19	30-Sep-19	18-Dec-19
Clemson	DD-288	Worden	BethSQ	30-Jun-19	24-Oct-19	24-Feb-20
Clemson	DD-289	Flusser	BethSQ	21-Jul-19	7-Nov-19	25-Feb-20
Clemson	DD-290	Dale	BethSQ	28-Jul-19	19-Nov-19	16-Feb-20
Clemson	DD-291	Converse	BethSQ	13-Aug-19	28-Nov-19	28-Apr-20
Clemson	DD-292	Reid	BethSQ	9-Sep-19	15-Oct-19	3-Dec-19
Clemson	DD-293	Billingsley	BethSQ	8-Sep-19	10-Dec-19	1-Mar-20
Clemson	DD-294	Charles Ausburn	BethSQ	11-Sep-19	18-Dec-19	23-Mar-20
Clemson	DD-295	Osborne	BethSQ	23-Sep-19	29-Dec-19	17-May-20
Clemson	DD-296	Chauncey	BethSF	17-Jun-18	29-Sep-18	25-Jun-19
Clemson	DD-297	Fuller	BethSF	4-Jul-18	5-Dec-18	28-Feb-20
Clemson	DD-298	Percival	BethSF	4-Jul-18	5-Dec-18	31-Mar-20
Clemson	DD-299	John Francis Burnes	BethSF	4-Jul-18	10-Nov-18	1-May-20
Clemson	DD-300	Farragut	BethSF	4-Jul-18	10-Nov-18	4-Jun-20
Clemson	DD-301	Somers	BethSF	4-Jul-18	21-Nov-18	23-Jun-20
Clemson	DD-302	Stoddert	BethSF	4-Jul-18	8-Jan-19	30-Jun-20
Clemson	DD-303	Reno	BethSF	4-Jul-18	22-Jan-19	23-Jul-20
Clemson	DD-304	Farquhar	BethSF	13-Aug-18	18-Jan-19	5-Aug-20
Clemson	DD-305	Thompson	BethSF	14-Aug-18	19-Jan-19	16-Aug-20
Clemson	DD-306	Kennedy	BethSF	25-Sep-18	15-Feb-19	28-Aug-20
Clemson	DD-307	Paul Hamilton	BethSF	25-Sep-18	21-Feb-19	24-Sep-20
Clemson	DD-308	William Jones	BethSF	2-Oct-18	9-Apr-19	30-Sep-20
Clemson	DD-309	Woodbury	BethSF	3-Oct-18	6-Feb-19	20-Oct-20
Clemson	DD-310	S.P. Lee	BethSF	31-Dec-18	22-Apr-19	30-Oct-20
Clemson	DD-311	Nicholas	BethSF	11-Jan-19	1-May-19	23-Nov-20

Class	Number	Name	Shipyard	Laid Down	Launched	Commissioned
Clemson	DD-312	Young	BethSF	28-Jan-19	8-May-19	29-Nov-20
Clemson	DD-313	Zeilin	BethSF	20-Feb-19	28-May-19	10-Dec-20
Clemson	DD-314	Yarborough	BethSF	27-Feb-19	20-Jun-19	31-Dec-20
Clemson	DD-315	La Vallette	BethSF	14-Apr-19	15-Jul-19	24-Dec-20
Clemson	DD-316	Sloat	BethSF	18-Jan-19	14-May-19	30-Dec-20
Clemson	DD-317	Wood	BethSF	23-Jan-19	28-May-19	28-Jan-21
Clemson	DD-318	Shirk	BethSF	13-Feb-19	20-Jun-19	5-Feb-21
Clemson	DD-319	Kidder	BethSF	5-Mar-19	10-Jul-19	7-Feb-21
Clemson	DD-320	Selfridge	BethSF	28-Apr-19	25-Jul-19	17-Feb-21
Clemson	DD-321	Marcus	BethSF	20-May-19	22-Aug-19	23-Feb-21
Clemson	DD-322	Mervine	BethSF	28-Apr-19	11-Aug-19	1-Mar-21
Clemson	DD-323	Chase	BethSF	5-May-19	2-Sep-19	10-Mar-21
Clemson	DD-324	Robert Smith	BethSF	13-May-19	19-Sep-19	17-Mar-21
Clemson	DD-325	Mullany	BethSF	3-Jun-19	9-Jul-20	29-Mar-21
Clemson	DD-326	Coghlan	BethSF	25-Jun-19	16-Jun-20	31-Mar-21
Clemson	DD-327	Preston	BethSF	19-Jul-19	7-Aug-20	13-Apr-21
Clemson	DD-328	Lamson	BethSF	13-Aug-19	1-Sep-20	19-Apr-21
Clemson	DD-329	Bruce	BethSF	30-Jul-19	20-May-20	29-Sep-20
Clemson	DD-330	Hull	BethSF	13-Sep-20	18-Feb-21	26-Apr-21
Clemson	DD-331	Macdonough	BethSF	24-May-20	15-Dec-20	30-Apr-21
Clemson	DD-332	Farenholt	BethSF	13-Sep-20	9-Mar-21	10-May-21
Clemson	DD-333	Sumner	BethSF	27-Aug-19	24-Nov-20	27-May-21
Clemson	DD-334	Corry	BethSF	15-Sep-20	28-Mar-21	25-May-21
Clemson	DD-335	Melvin	BethSF	15-Sep-20	11-Apr-21	31-May-21
Clemson	DD-336	Litchfield	MINY	15-Jan-19	12-Aug-19	12-May-20
Clemson	DD-337	Zane	MINY	15-Jan-19	12-Aug-19	15-Feb-21
Clemson	DD-338	Wasmuth	MINY	12-Aug-19	15-Sep-20	16-Dec-21
Clemson	DD-339	Trever	MINY	12-Aug-19	15-Sep-20	3-Aug-22
Clemson	DD-340	Perry	MINY	15-Sep-20	29-Oct-21	7-Aug-22
Clemson	DD-341	Decatur	MINY	15-Sep-20	29-Oct-21	9-Aug-22
Clemson	DD-342	Hulbert	NorNY	18-Nov-18	28-Jun-19	27-Oct-20
Clemson	DD-343	Noa	NorNY	18-Nov-18	28-Jun-19	15-Feb-21
Clemson	DD-344	William B. Preston	NorNY	18-Nov-18	9-Aug-19	23-Aug-20
Clemson	DD-345	Preble	Bath	12-Apr-19	8-Mar-20	19-Mar-20
Clemson	DD-346	Sicard	Bath	18-Jun-19	20-Apr-20	9-Jun-20
Clemson	DD-347	Pruitt	Bath	25-Jun-19	2-Aug-20	2-Sep-20

Eagle Boats

Number	Shipyard	Laid Down	Launched	Commissioned
PE-1	Ford Motor Co.	7-May-18	11-Jul-18	27-Oct-18
PE-2	Ford Motor Co.	10-May-18	19-Aug-18	7-Nov-18
PE-3	Ford Motor Co.	16-May-18	11-Sep-18	11-Nov-18
PE-4	Ford Motor Co.	21-May-18	15-Sep-18	14-Nov-18
PE-5	Ford Motor Co.	28-May-18	23-Sep-18	19-Nov-18
PE-6	Ford Motor Co.	3-Jun-18	16-Oct-18	21-Nov-18
PE-7	Ford Motor Co.	8-Jun-18	5-Oct-18	24-Nov-18
PE-8	Ford Motor Co.	10-Jun-18	11-Nov-18	31-Oct-19
PE-9	Ford Motor Co.	17-Jun-18	8-Nov-18	27-Oct-19
PE-10	Ford Motor Co.	6-Jul-18	9-Nov-18	31-Oct-19
PE-11	Ford Motor Co.	13-Jul-18	14-Nov-18	29-May-19
PE-12	Ford Motor Co.	13-Jul-18	12-Nov-18	6-Nov-19
PE-13	Ford Motor Co.	15-Jul-18	9-Jan-19	2-Apr-19
PE-14	Ford Motor Co.	20-Jul-18	23-Jan-19	17-Jun-19
PE-15	Ford Motor Co.	21-Jul-18	25-Jan-19	11-Jun-19
PE-16	Ford Motor Co.	22-Jul-18	11-Jan-19	5-Jun-19
PE-17	Ford Motor Co.	3-Aug-18	1-Feb-19	3-Jul-19
PE-18	Ford Motor Co.	5-Aug-18	10-Feb-19	7-Aug-19
PE-19	Ford Motor Co.	6-Aug-18	30-Jan-19	25-Jun-19
PE-20	Ford Motor Co.	26-Aug-18	15-Feb-19	28-Jul-19
PE-21	Ford Motor Co.	31-Aug-18	15-Feb-19	31-Jul-19
PE-22	Ford Motor Co.	5-Sep-18	10-Feb-19	17-Jul-19
PE-23	Ford Motor Co.	11-Sep-18	20-Feb-19	19-Jun-19
PE-24	Ford Motor Co.	13-Sep-18	24-Feb-19	12-Jul-19
PE-25	Ford Motor Co.	17-Sep-18	19-Feb-19	30-Jun-19
PE-26	Ford Motor Co.	25-Sep-18	1-Mar-19	1-Oct-19
PE-27	Ford Motor Co.	22-Oct-18	1-Mar-19	14-Jul-19
PE-28	Ford Motor Co.	23-Oct-18	1-Mar-19	28-Jul-19
PE-29	Ford Motor Co.	18-Nov-18	8-Mar-19	20-Aug-19
PE-30	Ford Motor Co.	19-Nov-18	8-Mar-19	14-Aug-19
PE-31	Ford Motor Co.	19-Nov-18	8-Mar-19	14-Aug-19
PE-32	Ford Motor Co.	30-Nov-18	15-Mar-19	4-Sep-19
PE-33	Ford Motor Co.	4-Dec-18	15-Mar-19	4-Sep-19
PE-34	Ford Motor Co.	8-Jan-19	15-Mar-19	3-Sep-19
PE-35	Ford Motor Co.	13-Jan-19	22-Mar-19	22-Aug-19
PE-36	Ford Motor Co.	22-Jan-19	22-Mar-19	20-Aug-19
PE-37	Ford Motor Co.	27-Jan-19	25-Mar-19	30-Sep-19
PE-38	Ford Motor Co.	31-Jan-19	29-Mar-19	30-Jul-19
PE-39	Ford Motor Co.	3-Feb-19	29-Mar-19	20-Sep-19
PE-40	Ford Motor Co.	7-Feb-19	5-Apr-19	1-Oct-19

Number	Shipyard	Laid Down	Launched	Commissioned
PE-42	Ford Motor Co.	13-Feb-19	17-May-19	3-Oct-19
PE-43	Ford Motor Co.	17-Feb-19	17-May-19	2-Oct-19
PE-41	Ford Motor Co.	20-Feb-19	5-Apr-19	26-Sep-19
PE-44	Ford Motor Co.	20-Feb-19	24-May-19	30-Sep-19
PE-45	Ford Motor Co.	20-Feb-19	17-May-19	2-Oct-19
PE-46	Ford Motor Co.	24-Feb-19	24-May-19	3-Oct-19
PE-47	Ford Motor Co.	3-Mar-19	19-Jun-19	4-Oct-19
PE-48	Ford Motor Co.	3-Mar-19	24-May-19	8-Oct-19
PE-49	Ford Motor Co.	4-Mar-19	14-Jun-19	10-Oct-19
PE-51	Ford Motor Co.	10-Mar-19	14-Jun-19	2-Oct-19
PE-50	Ford Motor Co.	10-Mar-19	18-Jul-19	6-Oct-19
PE-52	Ford Motor Co.	10-Mar-19	9-Jul-19	10-Oct-19
PE-54	Ford Motor Co.	17-Mar-19	17-Jul-19	10-Oct-19
PE-55	Ford Motor Co.	17-Mar-19	22-Jul-19	10-Oct-19
PE-53	Ford Motor Co.	17-Mar-19	13-Aug-19	20-Oct-19
PE-57	Ford Motor Co.	25-Mar-19	29-Jul-19	15-Oct-19
PE-58	Ford Motor Co.	25-Mar-19	2-Aug-19	20-Oct-19
PE-56	Ford Motor Co.	25-Mar-19	15-Aug-19	26-Oct-19
PE-59	Ford Motor Co.	31-Mar-19	12-Apr-19	19-Sep-19
PE-60	Ford Motor Co.	31-Mar-19	13-Aug-19	27-Oct-19

World War II Destroyers

Class	Number	Name	Shipyard	Laid Down	Launched	Commissioned
Bristol	DD-453	Bristol	Fed	2-Dec-40	25-Jul-41	21-Oct-41
Bristol	DD-454	Ellyson	Fed	2-Dec-40	25-Jul-41	28-Nov-41
Bristol	DD-455	Hambleton	Fed	16-Dec-40	26-Sep-41	22-Dec-41
Bristol	DD-456	Rodman	Fed	2-Dec-40	26-Sep-41	27-Jan-42
Bristol	DD-457	Emmons	Bath	14-Nov-40	23-Aug-41	5-Dec-41
Bristol	DD-458	Macomb	Bath	3-Sep-40	23-Sep-41	28-Jan-42
Bristol	DD-459	Laffey	BethSF	13-Jan-41	30-Oct-41	31-Mar-42
Bristol	DD-460	Woodworth	BethSF	13-Jan-41	30-Oct-41	30-Apr-42
Bristol	DD-461	Forrest	BosNY	6-Jan-41	14-Jun-41	13-Jan-42
Bristol	DD-462	Fitch	BosNY	6-Jan-41	14-Jun-41	3-Feb-42
Bristol	DD-463	Corry	CharNY	4-Sep-40	28-Jul-41	18-Dec-41
Bristol	DD-464	Hobson	CharNY	14-Nov-40	8-Sep-41	22-Jan-42
Bristol	DD-483	Aaron Ward	Fed	11-Feb-41	22-Nov-41	4-Mar-42
Bristol	DD-484	Buchanan	Fed	11-Feb-41	22-Nov-41	21-Mar-42
Bristol	DD-485	Duncan	Fed	31-Jul-41	20-Feb-42	16-Apr-42
Bristol	DD-486	Lansdowne	Fed	31-Jul-41	20-Feb-42	29-Apr-42
Bristol	DD-487	Lardner	Fed	15-Sep-41	20-Mar-42	13-May-42
Bristol	DD-488	McCalla	Fed	15-Sep-41	20-Mar-42	27-May-42
Bristol	DD-489	Mervine	Fed	3-Nov-41	3-May-42	17-Jun-42
Bristol	DD-490	Quick	Fed	3-Nov-41	3-May-42	3-Jul-42
Bristol	DD-491	Farenholt	BethSI	11-Dec-40	19-Nov-41	2-Apr-42
Bristol	DD-492	Bailey	BethSI	29-Jan-41	19-Dec-41	11-May-42
Bristol	DD-493	Carmick	Todd	29-May-41	8-Mar-42	28-Dec-42
Bristol	DD-494	Doyle	Todd	26-May-41	17-Mar-42	27-Jan-43
Bristol	DD-495	Endicott	Todd	1-May-41	5-Apr-42	25-Feb-43
Bristol	DD-496	McCook	Todd	1-May-41	20-Apr-42	15-Mar-43
Bristol	DD-497	Frankford	Todd	5-Jun-41	17-May-42	31-Mar-43
Bristol	DD-598	Bancroft	BethQ	1-May-41	31-Dec-41	30-Apr-42
Bristol	DD-599	Barton	BethQ	30-May-41	31-Jan-42	29-May-42
Bristol	DD-600	Boyle	BethQ	31-Dec-41	15-Jun-42	15-Aug-42
Bristol	DD-601	Champlin	BethQ	31-Jan-42	25-Jul-42	12-Sep-42
Bristol	DD-602	Meade	BethSI	25-Mar-41	15-Feb-42	22-Jun-42
Bristol	DD-603	Murphy	BethSI	19-May-41	29-Apr-42	23-Jul-42
Bristol	DD-604	Parker	BethSI	9-Jun-41	12-May-42	31-Aug-42
Bristol	DD-605	Caldwell	BethSF	24-Mar-41	15-Jan-42	10-Jun-42
Bristol	DD-606	Coghlan	BethSF	28-Mar-41	12-Feb-42	10-Jul-42
Bristol	DD-607	Frazier	BethSF	5-Jul-41	17-Mar-42	30-Jul-42
Bristol	DD-608	Gansevoort	BethSF	16-Jun-41	11-Apr-42	25-Aug-42
Bristol	DD-609	Gillespie	BethSF	16-Jun-41	8-May-42	18-Sep-42
Bristol	DD-610	Hobby	BethSF	30-Jun-41	4-Jun-42	18-Nov-42
Bristol	DD-611	Kalk	BethSF	30-Jun-41	18-Jul-42	17-Oct-42
Bristol	DD-612	Kendrick	BethSP	1-May-41	2-Apr-42	12-Sep-42
Bristol	DD-613	Laub	BethSP	1-May-41	28-Apr-42	24-Oct-42
Bristol	DD-614	Mackenzie	BethSP	29-May-41	27-Jun-42	21-Nov-42
Bristol	DD-615	McLanahan	BethSP	29-May-41	2-Sep-42	19-Dec-42
Bristol	DD-616	Nields	BethQ	15-Jun-42	1-Oct-42	15-Jan-43

Class	Number	Name	Shipyard	Laid Down	Launched	Commissioned
Bristol	DD-617	Ordronaux	BethQ	25-Jul-42	9-Nov-42	13-Feb-43
Bristol	DD-618	Davison	Fed	26-Feb-42	19-Jul-42	11-Sep-42
Bristol	DD-619	Edwards	Fed	26-Feb-42	19-Jul-42	18-Sep-42
Bristol	DD-620	Glennon	Fed	25-Mar-42	26-Aug-42	8-Oct-42
Bristol	DD-621	Jeffers	Fed	25-Mar-42	26-Aug-42	5-Nov-42
Bristol	DD-622	Maddox	Fed	7-May-42	15-Sep-42	31-Oct-42
Bristol	DD-623	Nelson	Fed	7-May-42	15-Sep-42	26-Nov-42
Bristol	DD-624	Baldwin	Todd	19-Jul-41	15-Jun-42	30-Apr-43
Bristol	DD-625	Harding	Todd	22-Jul-41	28-Jun-42	25-May-43
Bristol	DD-626	Satterlee	Todd	10-Sep-41	17-Jul-42	1-Jul-43
Bristol	DD-627	Thompson	Todd	22-Sep-41	15-Jul-42	10-Jul-43
Bristol	DD-628	Welles	Todd	27-Sep-41	7-Sep-42	16-Aug-43
Bristol	DD-632	Cowie	BosNY	18-Mar-41	27-Sep-41	1-Jun-42
Bristol	DD-633	Knight	BosNY	18-Mar-41	27-Sep-41	23-Jun-42
Bristol	DD-634	Doran	BosNY	14-Jun-41	10-Dec-41	4-Aug-42
Bristol	DD-635	Earle	BosNY	14-Jun-41	10-Dec-41	1-Sep-42
Bristol	DD-636	Butler	PHNY	16-Sep-41	12-Feb-42	15-Aug-42
Bristol	DD-637	Gherardi	PHNY	16-Sep-41	12-Feb-42	15-Sep-42
Bristol	DD-638	Herndon	NorNY	26-Aug-41	2-Feb-42	20-Dec-42
Bristol	DD-639	Shubrick	NorNY	17-Feb-42	18-Apr-42	7-Feb-43
Bristol	DD-640	Beatty	CharNY	1-May-41	20-Dec-41	7-May-42
Bristol	DD-641	Tillman	CharNY	1-May-41	20-Dec-41	4-Jun-42
Bristol	DD-645	Stevenson	Fed	23-Jul-42	11-Nov-42	15-Dec-42
Bristol	DD-646	Stockton	Fed	24-Jul-42	11-Nov-42	11-Jan-43
Bristol	DD-647	Thorn	Fed	15-Nov-42	28-Feb-43	1-Apr-43
Bristol	DD-648	Turner	Fed	15-Nov-42	28-Feb-43	15-Apr-43
Fletcher	DD-445	Fletcher	Fed	2-Oct-41	3-May-42	30-Jun-42
Fletcher	DD-446	Radford	Fed	2-Oct-41	3-May-42	22-Jul-42
Fletcher	DD-447	Jenkins	Fed	27-Nov-41	21-Jun-42	31-Jul-42
Fletcher	DD-448	La Vallette	Fed	27-Nov-41	21-Jun-42	12-Aug-42
Fletcher	DD-449	Nicholas	Bath	3-Mar-41	19-Feb-42	4-Jun-42
Fletcher	DD-450	O'Bannon	Bath	3-Mar-41	14-Mar-42	26-Jun-42
Fletcher	DD-451	Chevalier	Bath	30-Apr-41	11-Apr-42	20-Jul-42
Fletcher	DD-465	Saufley	Fed	27-Jan-42	19-Jul-42	29-Aug-42
Fletcher	DD-466	Waller	Fed	12-Feb-42	15-Aug-42	1-Oct-42
Fletcher	DD-467	Strong	Bath	30-Apr-41	17-May-42	7-Aug-42
Fletcher	DD-468	Taylor	Bath	28-Aug-41	7-Jun-42	28-Aug-42
Fletcher	DD-469	DeHaven	Bath	27-Sep-41	28-Jun-42	21-Sep-42
Fletcher	DD-470	Bache	BethSI	19-Nov-41	7-Jul-42	14-Nov-42
Fletcher	DD-471	Beale	BethSI	19-Dec-41	24-Aug-42	23-Dec-42
Fletcher	DD-472	Guest	BosNY	27-Sep-41	20-Feb-42	15-Dec-42
Fletcher	DD-473	Bennett	BosNY	10-Dec-41	16-Apr-42	9-Feb-43
Fletcher	DD-474	Fullam	BosNY	10-Dec-41	16-Apr-42	2-Mar-43
Fletcher	DD-475	Hudson	BosNY	20-Feb-42	3-Jun-42	13-Apr-43
Fletcher	DD-476	Hutchins	BosNY	27-Sep-41	20-Feb-42	17-Nov-42
Fletcher	DD-477	Pringle	CharNY	31-Jul-41	2-May-42	15-Sep-42
Fletcher	DD-478	Stanly	CharNY	15-Sep-41	12-May-42	15-Oct-42

Class	Number	Name	Shipyard	Laid Down	Launched	Commissioned
Fletcher	DD-479	Stevens	CharNY	30-Dec-41	24-Jun-42	1-Feb-43
Fletcher	DD-480	Halford	PSNY	3-Jun-41	29-Oct-42	10-Apr-43
Fletcher	DD-481	Leutze	PSNY	3-Jun-41	29-Oct-42	4-Mar-44
Fletcher	DD-498	Philip	Fed	7-May-42	13-Oct-42	21-Nov-42
Fletcher	DD-499	Renshaw	Fed	7-May-42	13-Oct-42	5-Dec-42
Fletcher	DD-500	Ringgold	Fed	25-Jun-42	11-Nov-42	30-Dec-42
Fletcher	DD-501	Schroeder	Fed	25-Jun-42	11-Nov-42	1-Jan-43
Fletcher	DD-502	Sigsbee	Fed	22-Jul-42	7-Dec-42	23-Jan-43
Fletcher	DD-507	Conway	Bath	5-Nov-41	16-Aug-42	9-Oct-42
Fletcher	DD-508	Cony	Bath	24-Dec-41	20-Aug-42	30-Oct-42
Fletcher	DD-509	Converse	Bath	23-Feb-42	30-Aug-42	20-Nov-42
Fletcher	DD-510	Eaton	Bath	17-Mar-42	20-Sep-42	4-Dec-42
Fletcher	DD-511	Foote	Bath	14-Apr-42	11-Oct-42	22-Dec-42
Fletcher	DD-512	Spence	Bath	18-May-42	27-Oct-42	8-Jan-43
Fletcher	DD-513	Terry	Bath	8-Jun-42	22-Nov-42	27-Jan-43
Fletcher	DD-514	Thatcher	Bath	29-Jun-42	6-Dec-42	10-Feb-43
Fletcher	DD-515	Anthony	Bath	17-Aug-42	20-Dec-42	26-Feb-43
Fletcher	DD-516	Wadsworth	Bath	18-Aug-42	10-Jan-43	16-Mar-43
Fletcher	DD-517	Walker	Bath	31-Aug-42	31-Jan-43	3-Apr-43
Fletcher	DD-518	Brownson	BethSI	15-Feb-42	24-Sep-42	3-Feb-43
Fletcher	DD-519	Daly	BethSI	29-Apr-42	24-Oct-42	10-Mar-43
Fletcher	DD-520	Isherwood	BethSI	12-May-42	24-Nov-42	12-Apr-43
Fletcher	DD-521	Kimberly	BethSI	27-Jul-42	4-Feb-43	22-May-43
Fletcher	DD-522	Luce	BethSI	24-Aug-42	6-Mar-43	21-Jun-43
Fletcher	DD-526	Abner Read	BethSF	30-Oct-41	18-Aug-42	5-Feb-43
Fletcher	DD-527	Ammen	BethSF	29-Nov-41	17-Sep-42	12-Mar-43
Fletcher	DD-528	Mullany	BethSF	15-Jan-42	10-Oct-42	10-May-43
Fletcher	DD-529	Bush	BethSF	12-Feb-42	27-Oct-42	10-May-43
Fletcher	DD-530	Trathen	BethSF	18-Jul-42	22-Oct-42	28-May-43
Fletcher	DD-531	Hazelwood	BethSF	11-Apr-42	20-Nov-42	18-Jun-43
Fletcher	DD-532	Heermann	BethSF	8-May-42	5-Dec-42	6-Jul-43
Fletcher	DD-533	Hoel	BethSF	4-Jun-42	19-Dec-42	29-Jul-43
Fletcher	DD-534	McCord	BethSF	17-Mar-42	10-Jan-43	19-Aug-43
Fletcher	DD-535	Miller	BethSF	18-Aug-42	15-Feb-43	31-Aug-43
Fletcher	DD-536	Owen	BethSF	17-Sep-42	21-Mar-43	20-Sep-43
Fletcher	DD-537	The Sullivans	BethSF	10-Oct-42	4-Apr-43	30-Sep-43
Fletcher	DD-538	Stephen Potter	BethSF	27-Oct-42	28-Apr-43	21-Oct-43
Fletcher	DD-539	Tingey	BethSF	22-Oct-42	28-May-43	25-Nov-43
Fletcher	DD-540	Twining	BethSF	20-Nov-42	11-Jul-43	1-Dec-43
Fletcher	DD-541	Yarnall	BethSF	5-Dec-42	25-Jul-43	30-Dec-43
Fletcher	DD-544	Boyd	BethSP	2-Apr-42	29-Oct-42	8-May-43
Fletcher	DD-545	Bradford	BethSP	28-Apr-42	12-Dec-42	12-Jun-43
Fletcher	DD-546	Brown	BethSP	27-Jun-42	21-Feb-43	10-Jul-43
Fletcher	DD-547	Cowell	BethSP	7-Sep-42	18-Mar-43	23-Aug-43
Fletcher	DD-550	Capps	Gulf	12-Jun-41	31-May-42	23-Jun-43
Fletcher	DD-551	David W. Taylor	Gulf	12-Jun-41	4-Jul-43	18-Sep-43
Fletcher	DD-552	Evans	Gulf	21-Jul-41	4-Oct-42	11-Dec-43

Class	Number	Name	Shipyard	Laid Down	Launched	Commissioned
Fletcher	DD-553	John D. Henley	Gulf	21-Jul-41	15-Nov-42	2-Feb-44
Fletcher	DD-554	Franks	Todd	8-Aug-42	7-Dec-42	30-Jul-43
Fletcher	DD-555	Haggard	Todd	27-Mar-42	9-Feb-43	31-Aug-43
Fletcher	DD-556	Hailey	Todd	11-Apr-42	9-Mar-43	30-Sep-43
Fletcher	DD-557	Johnston	Todd	6-May-42	25-Mar-43	27-Oct-43
Fletcher	DD-558	Laws	Todd	19-May-42	22-Apr-43	18-Nov-43
Fletcher	DD-559	Longshaw	Todd	16-Jun-42	4-Jun-43	4-Dec-43
Fletcher	DD-560	Morrison	Todd	30-Jun-42	4-Jul-43	18-Dec-43
Fletcher	DD-561	Prichett	Todd	20-Jul-42	31-Jul-43	15-Jan-44
Fletcher	DD-562	Robinson	Todd	12-Aug-42	28-Aug-43	31-Jan-44
Fletcher	DD-563	Ross	Todd	7-Sep-42	10-Sep-43	21-Feb-44
Fletcher	DD-564	Rowe	Todd	7-Dec-42	30-Sep-43	13-Mar-44
Fletcher	DD-565	Smalley	Todd	9-Feb-43	29-Oct-43	31-Mar-44
Fletcher	DD-566	Stoddard	Todd	10-Mar-43	19-Nov-43	15-Apr-44
Fletcher	DD-567	Watts	Todd	26-Mar-43	31-Dec-43	29-Apr-44
Fletcher	DD-568	Wren	Todd	24-Apr-43	29-Jan-44	20-May-44
Fletcher	DD-569	Aulick	Orange	14-May-41	2-Mar-42	27-Oct-42
Fletcher	DD-570	Charles Ausburne	Orange	14-May-41	16-Mar-42	24-Nov-42
Fletcher	DD-571	Claxton	Orange	25-Jun-41	1-Apr-42	8-Dec-42
Fletcher	DD-572	Dyson	Orange	25-Jun-41	15-Apr-42	30-Dec-42
Fletcher	DD-573	Harrison	Orange	25-Jul-41	7-May-42	25-Jan-43
Fletcher	DD-574	John Rodgers	Orange	25-Jul-41	7-May-42	9-Feb-43
Fletcher	DD-575	McKee	Orange	2-Mar-42	2-Aug-42	31-Mar-43
Fletcher	DD-576	Murray	Orange	16-Mar-42	16-Aug-42	20-Apr-43
Fletcher	DD-577	Sproston	Orange	1-Apr-42	31-Aug-42	19-May-43
Fletcher	DD-578	Wickes	Orange	15-Apr-42	13-Sep-42	16-Jun-43
Fletcher	DD-579	William D. Porter	Orange	7-May-42	27-Sep-42	6-Jul-43
Fletcher	DD-580	Young	Orange	7-May-42	11-Oct-42	31-Jul-43
Fletcher	DD-581	Charrette	BosNY	20-Feb-42	3-Jun-42	18-May-43
Fletcher	DD-582	Conner	BosNY	16-Apr-42	18-Jul-42	8-Jun-43
Fletcher	DD-583	Hall	BosNY	16-Apr-42	18-Jul-42	6-Jul-43
Fletcher	DD-584	Halligan	BosNY	9-Nov-42	19-Mar-43	19-Aug-43
Fletcher	DD-585	Haraden	BosNY	9-Nov-42	19-Mar-43	16-Sep-43
Fletcher	DD-586	Newcomb	BosNY	19-Mar-43	4-Jul-43	10-Nov-43
Fletcher	DD-587	Bell	CharNY	30-Dec-41	24-Jun-42	4-Mar-43
Fletcher	DD-588	Burns	CharNY	9-May-42	8-Aug-42	3-Apr-43
Fletcher	DD-589	Izard	CharNY	9-May-42	8-Aug-42	15-May-43
Fletcher	DD-590	Paul Hamilton	CharNY	20-Jan-43	7-Apr-43	25-Oct-43
Fletcher	DD-591	Twiggs	CharNY	20-Jan-43	7-Apr-43	4-Nov-43
Fletcher	DD-592	Howorth	PSNY	26-Nov-41	10-Jan-43	3-Apr-44
Fletcher	DD-593	Killen	PSNY	26-Nov-41	10-Jan-43	4-May-44
Fletcher	DD-594	Hart	PSNY	10-Aug-43	25-Sep-44	4-Nov-44
Fletcher	DD-595	Metcalfe	PSNY	10-Aug-43	25-Sep-44	18-Nov-44
Fletcher	DD-596	Shields	PSNY	10-Aug-43	25-Sep-44	8-Feb-45
Fletcher	DD-597	Wiley	PSNY	10-Aug-43	25-Sep-44	22-Feb-45
Fletcher	DD-629	Abbot	Bath	21-Sep-42	17-Feb-43	23-Apr-43
Fletcher	DD-630	Braine	Bath	12-Oct-42	7-Mar-43	23-Apr-43

Class	Number	Name	Shipyard	Laid Down	Launched	Commissioned
Fletcher	DD-631	Erben	Bath	28-Oct-42	21-Mar-43	28-May-43
Fletcher	DD-642	Hale	Bath	23-Nov-42	4-Apr-43	15-Jun-43
Fletcher	DD-643	Sigourney	Bath	7-Dec-42	24-Apr-43	29-Jun-43
Fletcher	DD-644	Stembel	Bath	21-Dec-42	8-May-43	16-Jul-43
Fletcher	DD-649	Albert W. Grant	CharNY	30-Dec-42	29-May-43	24-Nov-43
Fletcher	DD-650	Caperton	Bath	11-Jan-43	22-May-43	30-Jul-43
Fletcher	DD-651	Cogswell	Bath	1-Feb-43	5-Jun-43	17-Aug-43
Fletcher	DD-652	Ingersoll	Bath	18-Feb-43	28-Jun-43	31-Aug-43
Fletcher	DD-653	Knapp	Bath	8-Mar-43	10-Jul-43	10-Jul-43
Fletcher	DD-654	Bearss	Gulf	14-Jul-42	25-Jul-43	25-Jul-43
Fletcher	DD-655	John Hood	Gulf	12-Oct-42	25-Oct-43	7-Jun-44
Fletcher	DD-656	Van Valkenburgh	Gulf	15-Nov-42	19-Dec-43	2-Aug-44
Fletcher	DD-657	Charles J. Badger	BethSI	24-Sep-42	3-Apr-43	23-Jul-43
Fletcher	DD-658	Colahan	BethSI	24-Oct-42	3-May-43	23-Aug-43
Fletcher	DD-659	Dashiell	Fed	1-Oct-42	6-Feb-43	20-Mar-43
Fletcher	DD-660	Bullard	Fed	16-Oct-42	28-Feb-43	9-Apr-43
Fletcher	DD-661	Kidd	Fed	16-Oct-42	28-Feb-43	23-Apr-43
Fletcher	DD-662	Bennion	BosNY	19-Mar-43	4-Jul-43	14-Dec-43
Fletcher	DD-663	Heywood L. Edwards	BosNY	4-Jul-43	6-Oct-43	26-Jan-44
Fletcher	DD-664	Richard P. Leary	BosNY	4-Jul-43	6-Oct-43	23-Feb-44
Fletcher	DD-665	Bryant	CharNY	30-Dec-42	29-May-43	4-Dec-43
Fletcher	DD-666	Black	Fed	14-Nov-42	28-Mar-43	21-May-43
Fletcher	DD-667	Chauncey	Fed	14-Nov-42	28-Mar-43	31-May-43
Fletcher	DD-668	Clarence K. Bronson	Fed	9-Dec-42	18-Apr-43	11-Jun-43
Fletcher	DD-669	Cotten	Fed	8-Feb-43	12-Jun-43	24-Jul-43
Fletcher	DD-670	Dortch	Fed	2-Mar-43	20-Jun-43	7-Aug-43
Fletcher	DD-671	Gatling	Fed	3-Mar-43	20-Jun-43	19-Aug-43
Fletcher	DD-672	Healy	Fed	4-Mar-43	4-Jul-43	3-Sep-43
Fletcher	DD-673	Hickox	Fed	12-Mar-43	4-Jul-43	10-Sep-43
Fletcher	DD-674	Hunt	Fed	31-Mar-43	1-Aug-43	22-Sep-43
Fletcher	DD-675	Lewis Hancock	Fed	31-Mar-43	1-Aug-43	29-Sep-43
Fletcher	DD-676	Marshall	Fed	19-Apr-43	29-Aug-43	16-Oct-43
Fletcher	DD-677	McDermut	Fed	14-Jun-43	17-Oct-43	19-Nov-43
Fletcher	DD-678	McGowan	Fed	30-Jun-43	14-Nov-43	20-Dec-43
Fletcher	DD-679	McNair	Fed	30-Jun-43	14-Nov-43	30-Dec-43
Fletcher	DD-680	Melvin	Fed	6-Jul-43	17-Oct-43	24-Nov-43
Fletcher	DD-681	Hopewell	BethSP	29-Oct-42	2-May-43	30-Sep-43
Fletcher	DD-682	Porterfield	BethSP	12-Dec-42	13-Jun-43	30-Oct-43
Fletcher	DD-683	Stockham	BethSF	19-Dec-42	25-Jun-43	11-Feb-44
Fletcher	DD-684	Wedderburn	BethSF	10-Jan-43	1-Aug-43	9-Mar-44
Fletcher	DD-685	Picking	BethSI	24-Nov-42	1-Jun-43	21-Sep-43
Fletcher	DD-686	Halsey Powell	BethSI	4-Feb-43	30-Jun-43	25-Oct-43
Fletcher	DD-687	Uhlmann	BethSI	6-Mar-43	30-Jul-43	22-Nov-43
Fletcher	DD-688	Remey	Bath	22-Mar-43	25-Jul-43	30-Sep-43
Fletcher	DD-689	Wadleigh	Bath	5-Apr-43	7-Aug-43	19-Oct-43
Fletcher	DD-690	Norman Scott	Bath	26-Apr-43	28-Aug-43	5-Nov-43
Fletcher	DD-691	Mertz	Bath	10-May-43	11-Sep-43	19-Nov-43

Class	Number	Name	Shipyard	Laid Down	Launched	Commissioned
Fletcher	DD-792	Callaghan	BethSP	21-Feb-43	1-Aug-43	27-Nov-43
Fletcher	DD-793	Cassin Young	BethSP	18-Mar-43	12-Sep-43	31-Dec-43
Fletcher	DD-794	Irwin	BethSP	2-May-43	31-Oct-43	14-Feb-44
Fletcher	DD-795	Preston	BethSP	13-Jun-43	12-Dec-43	20-Mar-44
Fletcher	DD-796	Benham	BethSI	3-Apr-43	30-Aug-43	20-Dec-43
Fletcher	DD-797	Cushing	BethSI	3-May-43	30-Sep-43	17-Jan-44
Fletcher	DD-798	Monssen	BethSI	1-Jun-43	30-Oct-43	14-Feb-44
Fletcher	DD-799	Jarvis	Todd	7-Jun-43	14-Feb-44	3-Jun-44
Fletcher	DD-800	Porter	Todd	6-Jul-43	13-Mar-44	24-Jun-44
Fletcher	DD-801	Colhoun	Todd	3-Aug-43	10-Apr-44	8-Jul-44
Fletcher	DD-802	Gregory	Todd	31-Aug-43	8-May-44	29-Jul-44
Fletcher	DD-803	Little	Todd	13-Sep-43	22-May-44	19-Aug-44
Fletcher	DD-804	Rooks	Todd	27-Oct-43	6-Jun-44	2-Sep-44
Sumner	DD-692	Allen M. Sumner	Fed	7-Jul-43	15-Dec-43	26-Jan-44
Sumner	DD-693	Moale	Fed	5-Aug-43	16-Jan-44	28-Feb-44
Sumner	DD-694	Ingraham	Fed	4-Aug-43	16-Jan-44	10-Mar-44
Sumner	DD-695	Cooper	Fed	30-Aug-43	9-Feb-44	27-Mar-44
Sumner	DD-696	English	Fed	19-Oct-43	27-Feb-44	4-May-44
Sumner	DD-697	Charles S. Sperry	Fed	19-Oct-43	13-Mar-44	17-May-44
Sumner	DD-698	Ault	Fed	15-Nov-43	26-Mar-44	31-May-44
Sumner	DD-699	Waldron	Fed	16-Nov-43	26-Mar-44	8-Jun-44
Sumner	DD-700	Haynsworth	Fed	16-Dec-43	15-Apr-44	22-Jun-44
Sumner	DD-701	John W. Weeks	Fed	17-Jan-44	21-May-44	21-Jul-44
Sumner	DD-702	Hank	Fed	17-Jan-44	21-May-44	28-Aug-44
Sumner	DD-703	Wallace L. Lind	Fed	14-Feb-44	14-Jun-44	8-Sep-44
Sumner	DD-704	Borie	Fed	29-Feb-44	4-Jul-44	21-Sep-44
Sumner	DD-705	Compton	Fed	29-Mar-44	17-Sep-44	4-Nov-44
Sumner	DD-706	Gainard	Fed	29-Mar-44	17-Sep-44	23-Nov-44
Sumner	DD-707	Soley	Fed	18-Apr-44	8-Sep-44	8-Dec-44
Sumner	DD-708	Harlan R. Dickson	Fed	23-May-44	17-Dec-44	15-Feb-45
Sumner	DD-709	Hugh Purvis	Fed	23-May-44	17-Dec-44	1-Mar-45
Sumner	DD-722	Barton	Bath	24-May-43	10-Oct-43	30-Dec-43
Sumner	DD-723	Walke	Bath	7-Jun-43	27-Oct-43	21-Jan-44
Sumner	DD-724	Laffey	Bath	28-Jun-43	21-Nov-43	8-Feb-44
Sumner	DD-725	O'Brien	Bath	12-Jul-43	8-Dec-43	25-Jan-44
Sumner	DD-726	Meredith	Bath	26-Jul-43	21-Dec-43	14-Mar-44
Sumner	DD-727	De Haven	Bath	9-Aug-43	9-Jan-44	31-Mar-44
Sumner	DD-728	Mansfield	Bath	28-Aug-43	29-Jan-44	14-Apr-44
Sumner	DD-729	Lyman K. Swenson	Bath	11-Sep-43	12-Feb-44	2-May-44
Sumner	DD-730	Collett	Bath	11-Oct-43	5-Mar-44	16-May-44
Sumner	DD-731	Maddox	Bath	28-Oct-43	19-Mar-44	2-Jun-44
Sumner	DD-732	Hyman	Bath	22-Nov-43	8-Apr-44	16-Jun-44
Sumner	DD-733	Mannert L. Abele	Bath	9-Dec-43	23-Apr-44	4-Jul-44
Sumner	DD-734	Purdy	Bath	22-Dec-43	7-May-44	18-Jul-44
Sumner	DD-735	Robert H. Smith	Bath	10-Jan-44	25-May-44	4-Aug-44
Sumner	DD-736	Thomas E. Fraser	Bath	31-Jan-43	10-Jun-44	23-Aug-44
Sumner	DD-737	Shannon	Bath	14-Feb-44	24-Jun-44	8-Sep-44

Class	Number	Name	Shipyard	Laid Down	Launched	Commissioned
Sumner	DD-738	Harry F. Bauer	Bath	6-Mar-44	9-Jul-44	22-Sep-44
Sumner	DD-739	Adams	Bath	20-Mar-44	23-Jul-44	10-Aug-44
Sumner	DD-740	Tolman	Bath	10-Apr-44	13-Aug-44	27-Oct-44
Sumner	DD-741	Drexler	Bath	24-Apr-44	3-Sep-44	14-Nov-44
Sumner	DD-744	Blue	BethSI	30-Jun-43	28-Nov-43	20-Mar-44
Sumner	DD-745	Brush	BethSI	30-Jul-43	28-Dec-43	17-Apr-44
Sumner	DD-746	Taussig	BethSI	30-Aug-43	25-Jan-44	20-May-44
Sumner	DD-747	Samuel N. Moore	BethSI	30-Sep-43	23-Feb-44	24-Jun-44
Sumner	DD-748	Harry E. Hubbard	BethSI	30-Oct-43	24-Mar-44	22-Jul-44
Sumner	DD-749	Henry A. Wiley	BethSI	28-Nov-43	21-Apr-44	31-Aug-44
Sumner	DD-750	Shea	BethSI	28-Dec-43	20-May-44	30-Sep-44
Sumner	DD-751	J. William Ditter	BethSI	25-Jan-44	4-Jul-44	28-Oct-44
Sumner	DD-752	Alfred A. Cunningham	BethSI	23-Feb-44	3-Aug-44	23-Nov-44
Sumner	DD-753	John R. Pierce	BethSI	24-Mar-44	1-Sep-44	30-Dec-44
Sumner	DD-754	Frank E. Evans	BethSI	21-Apr-44	3-Oct-44	3-Feb-45
Sumner	DD-755	John A. Bole	BethSI	20-May-44	1-Nov-44	3-Mar-45
Sumner	DD-756	Beatty	BethSI	4-Jul-44	30-Nov-44	31-Mar-45
Sumner	DD-757	Putnam	BethSF	11-Jul-43	26-Mar-44	12-Oct-44
Sumner	DD-758	Strong	BethSF	25-Jul-43	23-Apr-44	8-Mar-45
Sumner	DD-759	Lofberg	BethSF	11-Apr-43	12-Aug-44	26-Apr-45
Sumner	DD-760	John W. Thomason	BethSF	21-Nov-43	30-Sep-44	11-Oct-45
Sumner	DD-761	Buck	BethSF	1-Feb-44	11-Mar-45	28-Jun-46
Sumner	DD-762	Henley	BethSF	8-Feb-44	8-Apr-45	8-Oct-46
Sumner	DD-770	Lowry	BethSP	1-Aug-43	6-Feb-44	23-Jul-44
Sumner	DD-771	Lindsey	BethSP	12-Sep-43	5-Mar-44	20-Aug-44
Sumner	DD-772	Gwin	BethSP	31-Oct-43	9-Apr-44	30-Sep-44
Sumner	DD-773	Aaron Ward	BethSP	12-Dec-43	5-May-44	28-Oct-44
Sumner	DD-774	Hugh W. Hadley	BethSP	6-Feb-44	16-Jul-44	25-Nov-44
Sumner	DD-775	Willard Keith	BethSP	5-Mar-44	29-Aug-44	27-Dec-44
Sumner	DD-776	James C. Owens	BethSP	9-Apr-44	1-Oct-44	17-Feb-45
Sumner	DD-777	Zellars	Todd	24-Dec-43	19-Jul-44	25-Oct-44
Sumner	DD-778	Massey	Todd	14-Jan-44	19-Aug-44	24-Nov-44
Sumner	DD-779	Douglas H. Fox	Todd	31-Jan-44	30-Sep-44	26-Dec-44
Sumner	DD-780	Stormes	Todd	25-Jul-43	4-Nov-44	27-Jan-45
Sumner	DD-781	Robert K. Huntington	Todd	29-Feb-44	5-Dec-44	3-Mar-45
Sumner	DD-857	Bristol	BethSP	5-May-44	29-Oct-44	17-Mar-45
Gearing	DD-710	Gearing	Fed	10-Aug-44	18-Feb-45	3-May-45
Gearing	DD-711	Eugene A. Greene	Fed	17-Aug-44	18-Mar-45	8-Jun-45
Gearing	DD-712	Gyatt	Fed	7-Sep-44	15-Apr-45	2-Jul-45
Gearing	DD-713	Kenneth D. Bailey	Fed	21-Sep-44	17-Jun-45	31-Jul-45
Gearing	DD-714	William R. Rush	Fed	19-Oct-44	8-Jul-45	21-Sep-45
Gearing	DD-715	William M. Wood	Fed	22-Nov-44	29-Jul-45	24-Nov-45
Gearing	DD-716	Wiltsie	Fed	13-Mar-45	31-Aug-45	12-Jan-46
Gearing	DD-717	Theo. E. Chandler	Fed	23-Apr-45	20-Oct-45	22-Mar-46
Gearing	DD-718	Hamner	Fed	25-Apr-45	24-Nov-45	12-Jul-46
Gearing	DD-719	Epperson	Fed	20-Jun-45	22-Dec-45	19-Mar-49
Gearing	DD-742	Frank Knox	Bath	8-May-44	17-Sep-44	11-Dec-44

Emergency Production Historical Study

Class	Number	Name	Shipyard	Laid Down	Launched	Commissioned
Gearing	DD-743	Southerland	Bath	27-May-44	5-Oct-44	22-Dec-44
Gearing	DD-763	William C. Lawe	BethSF	12-Mar-44	21-May-45	18-Dec-46
Gearing	DD-764	Lloyd Thomas	BethSF	26-Mar-44	5-Oct-45	21-Mar-47
Gearing	DD-765	Keppler	BethSF	23-Apr-44	24-Jun-46	23-May-47
Gearing	DD-782	Rowan	Todd	25-Mar-44	29-Dec-44	31-Mar-45
Gearing	DD-783	Gurke	Todd	1-Jul-44	15-Feb-45	12-May-45
Gearing	DD-784	McKean	Todd	15-Sep-44	31-Mar-45	9-Jun-45
Gearing	DD-785	Henderson	Todd	27-Oct-44	28-May-45	4-Aug-45
Gearing	DD-786	R.B. Anderson	Todd	1-Dec-44	7-Jul-45	26-Oct-45
Gearing	DD-787	James E. Kyes	Todd	27-Dec-44	4-Aug-45	8-Feb-46
Gearing	DD-788	Hollister	Todd	18-Jan-45	9-Oct-45	26-Mar-46
Gearing	DD-789	Eversole	Todd	21-Mar-45	8-Jan-46	10-May-46
Gearing	DD-790	Shelton	Todd	31-May-45	8-Mar-46	21-Jun-46
Gearing	DD-805	Chevalier	Bath	12-Jul-44	29-Oct-44	9-Jan-45
Gearing	DD-806	Higbee	Bath	26-Jun-44	12-Nov-44	27-Jan-45
Gearing	DD-807	Benner	Bath	10-Jul-44	30-Nov-44	13-Feb-45
Gearing	DD-808	Dennis J. Buckley	Bath	24-Jul-44	20-Dec-44	2-Mar-45
Gearing	DD-817	Corry	Orange	5-Apr-45	28-Jul-45	27-Feb-46
Gearing	DD-818	New	Orange	14-Apr-45	18-Aug-45	5-Apr-46
Gearing	DD-819	Holder	Orange	23-Apr-45	25-Aug-45	18-May-46
Gearing	DD-820	Rich	Orange	16-May-45	5-Oct-45	3-Jul-46
Gearing	DD-821	Johnston	Orange	26-Mar-45	10-Oct-45	23-Aug-46
Gearing	DD-822	Robert H. McCard	Orange	20-Jun-45	9-Nov-45	26-Oct-46
Gearing	DD-823	Samuel B. Roberts	Orange	27-Jun-45	30-Nov-45	20-Dec-46
Gearing	DD-824	Basilone	Orange	7-Jul-45	21-Dec-45	26-Jul-49
Gearing	DD-825	Carpenter	Orange	30-Jul-45	28-Dec-45	15-Dec-49
Gearing	DD-826	Agerholm	Bath	10-Sep-45	30-Mar-46	20-Jun-46
Gearing	DD-827	Robert A. Owens	Bath	29-Oct-45	15-Jul-46	5-Nov-49
Gearing	DD-828	Timmerman	Bath	1-Oct-45	19-May-51	26-Sep-52
Gearing	DD-829	Myles C. Fox	Bath	14-Aug-44	13-Jan-45	20-Mar-45
Gearing	DD-830	Everett F. Larson	Bath	4-Sep-44	28-Jan-45	6-Apr-45
Gearing	DD-831	Goodrich	Bath	18-Sep-44	25-Feb-45	24-Apr-45
Gearing	DD-832	Hanson	Bath	7-Oct-44	11-Mar-45	11-May-45
Gearing	DD-833	Herbert J. Thomas	Bath	30-Oct-44	25-Mar-45	29-May-45
Gearing	DD-834	Turner	Bath	13-Nov-44	8-Apr-45	12-Jun-45
Gearing	DD-835	Charles P. Cecil	Bath	2-Dec-44	22-Apr-45	29-Jun-45
Gearing	DD-836	George K. MacKenzie	Bath	21-Dec-44	13-May-45	13-Jul-45
Gearing	DD-837	Sarsfield	Bath	15-Jan-45	27-May-45	31-Jul-45
Gearing	DD-838	Ernest G. Small	Bath	30-Jan-45	9-Jun-45	21-Aug-45
Gearing	DD-839	Power	Bath	26-Feb-45	30-Jun-45	13-Sep-45
Gearing	DD-840	Glennon	Bath	12-Mar-45	14-Jul-45	4-Oct-45
Gearing	DD-841	Noa	Bath	26-Mar-45	30-Jul-45	2-Nov-45
Gearing	DD-842	Fiske	Bath	9-Apr-45	8-Sep-45	28-Nov-45
Gearing	DD-843	Warrington	Bath	23-Apr-45	27-Sep-45	20-Dec-45
Gearing	DD-844	Perry	Bath	14-May-45	25-Nov-45	17-Jan-46
Gearing	DD-845	Bausell	Bath	28-May-45	19-Nov-45	7-Feb-46
Gearing	DD-846	Ozbourn	Bath	16-Jun-45	22-Dec-45	5-Mar-46

Class	Number	Name	Shipyard	Laid Down	Launched	Commissioned
Gearing	DD-847	Robert L. Wilson	Bath	2-Jul-45	5-Jan-46	25-Apr-46
Gearing	DD-848	Witek	Bath	16-Jul-45	2-Feb-46	25-Apr-46
Gearing	DD-849	Richard E. Kraus	Bath	31-Jul-45	2-Mar-46	23-May-46
Gearing	DD-850	J.P. Kennedy, Jr.	BethQ	2-Apr-45	26-Jul-45	15-Dec-45
Gearing	DD-851	Rupertus	BethQ	2-May-45	21-Sep-45	8-Mar-46
Gearing	DD-852	Leonard F. Mason	BethQ	6-Aug-45	4-Jan-46	28-Jun-46
Gearing	DD-853	Charles H. Roan	BethQ	27-Sep-45	15-Mar-46	2-Sep-46
Gearing	DD-858	Fred T. Berry	BethSP	16-Jul-44	28-Jan-45	12-May-45
Gearing	DD-859	Norris	BethSP	29-Aug-44	25-Feb-45	9-Jun-45
Gearing	DD-860	McCaffery	BethSP	1-Oct-44	4-Apr-45	26-Jul-45
Gearing	DD-861	Harwood	BethSP	29-Oct-44	24-May-45	28-Sep-45
Gearing	DD-862	Vogelsgesang	BethSI	3-Aug-44	15-Jan-45	28-Apr-45
Gearing	DD-863	Steinaker	BethSI	1-Sep-44	13-Feb-45	26-May-45
Gearing	DD-864	Harold J. Ellison	BethSI	3-Oct-44	14-Mar-45	23-Jun-45
Gearing	DD-865	Charles R. Ware	BethSI	1-Nov-44	12-Apr-45	21-Jul-45
Gearing	DD-866	Cone	BethSI	30-Nov-44	10-May-45	18-Aug-45
Gearing	DD-867	Stribling	BethSI	15-Jan-45	8-Jun-45	29-Sep-45
Gearing	DD-868	Brownson	BethSI	13-Feb-45	7-Jul-45	17-Nov-45
Gearing	DD-869	Arnold J. Isbell	BethSI	14-Mar-45	6-Aug-45	5-Apr-46
Gearing	DD-870	Fechteler	BethSI	12-Apr-45	19-Sep-45	2-Mar-46
Gearing	DD-871	Damato	BethSI	10-May-45	21-Nov-45	27-Apr-46
Gearing	DD-872	Forrest Royal	BethSI	8-Jun-45	17-Jan-46	29-Jun-46
Gearing	DD-873	Hawkins	Orange	14-May-44	7-Oct-44	10-Feb-45
Gearing	DD-874	Duncan	Orange	22-May-44	27-Oct-44	25-Feb-45
Gearing	DD-875	Henry W. Tucker	Orange	29-May-44	8-Nov-44	12-Mar-45
Gearing	DD-876	Rodgers	Orange	3-Jun-44	20-Nov-44	26-Mar-45
Gearing	DD-877	Perkins	Orange	19-Jun-44	7-Dec-44	4-Apr-45
Gearing	DD-878	Vesole	Orange	3-Jul-44	29-Dec-44	23-Apr-45
Gearing	DD-879	Leary	Orange	11-Aug-44	20-Jan-45	7-May-45
Gearing	DD-880	Dyess	Orange	17-Aug-44	26-Jan-45	21-May-45
Gearing	DD-881	Bordelon	Orange	9-Sep-44	3-Mar-45	5-Jun-45
Gearing	DD-882	Furse	Orange	23-Sep-44	9-Mar-45	10-Jul-45
Gearing	DD-883	Newman K. Perry	Orange	10-Oct-44	17-Mar-45	26-Jul-45
Gearing	DD-884	Floyd B. Parks	Orange	30-Oct-44	31-Mar-45	31-Aug-45
Gearing	DD-885	John R. Craig	Orange	17-Nov-44	14-Apr-45	20-Aug-45
Gearing	DD-886	Orleck	Orange	28-Nov-44	12-May-45	15-Sep-45
Gearing	DD-887	Brinkley Bass	Orange	20-Dec-44	26-May-45	1-Oct-45
Gearing	DD-888	Stickell	Orange	5-Jan-45	16-Jun-45	31-Oct-45
Gearing	DD-889	O'Hare	Orange	27-Jan-45	22-Jun-45	29-Nov-45
Gearing	DD-890	Meredith	Orange	27-Jan-45	28-Jun-45	31-Dec-45

World War II Destroyer Escorts

Class	Number	Name	Shipyard	Laid Down	Launched	Commissioned
Evarts	DE-1	Bayntum	BosNY	5-Apr-42	27-Jun-42	20-Jan-43
Evarts	DE-2	Bazely	BosNY	5-Apr-42	27-Jun-42	18-Feb-43
Evarts	DE-3	Berry	BosNY	22-Sep-42	23-Nov-42	15-Mar-43
Evarts	DE-4	Blackwood	BosNY	22-Sep-42	23-Nov-42	27-Mar-43
Evarts	DE-5	Evarts	BosNY	17-Oct-42	7-Dec-42	15-Apr-43
Evarts	DE-6	Wyfells	BosNY	17-Oct-42	7-Dec-42	21-Apr-43
Evarts	DE-7	Griswold	BosNY	27-Nov-42	28-Apr-43	28-Apr-43
Evarts	DE-8	Steele	BosNY	27-Nov-42	9-Jan-43	4-May-43
Evarts	DE-9	Carlson	BosNY	27-Nov-42	9-Jan-43	10-May-43
Evarts	DE-10	Bebas	BosNY	27-Nov-42	9-Jan-43	15-May-43
Evarts	DE-11	Crouter	BosNY	8-Dec-42	26-Jan-43	25-May-43
Evarts	DE-12	Burges	BosNY	8-Dec-42	26-Jan-43	2-Jun-43
Evarts	DE-13	Brennan	MINY	28-Feb-42	22-Aug-42	20-Jan-43
Evarts	DE-14	Doherty	MINY	28-Feb-42	24-Aug-42	6-Feb-43
Evarts	DE-15	Austin	MINY	14-Mar-42	25-Sep-42	13-Feb-43
Evarts	DE-16	Edgar G. Chase	MINY	14-Mar-42	26-Sep-42	20-Mar-43
Evarts	DE-17	Edward C. Daly	MINY	1-Apr-42	21-Oct-42	3-Apr-43
Evarts	DE-18	Gilmore	MINY	1-Apr-42	22-Oct-42	17-Apr-43
Evarts	DE-19	Burden R. Hastings	MINY	15-Apr-42	20-Nov-42	1-May-43
Evarts	DE-20	Le Hardy	MINY	15-Apr-42	21-Nov-42	15-May-43
Evarts	DE-21	Harold C. Thomas	MINY	30-Apr-42	18-Dec-42	31-May-43
Evarts	DE-22	Wileman	MINY	30-Apr-42	19-Dec-42	11-Jun-43
Evarts	DE-23	Charles R. Greer	MINY	7-Sep-42	18-Jan-43	25-Jun-43
Evarts	DE-24	Whitman	MINY	7-Sep-42	19-Jan-43	3-Jul-43
Evarts	DE-25	Wintle	MINY	1-Oct-42	18-Feb-43	10-Jul-43
Evarts	DE-26	Dempsey	MINY	1-Oct-42	19-Feb-43	24-Jul-43
Evarts	DE-27	Duffy	MINY	29-Oct-42	16-Apr-43	5-Aug-43
Evarts	DE-28	Emery	MINY	29-Nov-42	17-Apr-43	14-Aug-43
Evarts	DE-29	Stadtfield	MINY	26-Nov-42	17-Apr-43	26-Aug-43
Evarts	DE-30	Martin	MINY	26-Nov-42	18-Apr-43	4-Sep-43
Evarts	DE-31	Sederstrom	MINY	24-Dec-42	15-Jun-43	11-Sep-43
Evarts	DE-32	Fleming	MINY	24-Dec-42	16-Jun-43	18-Sep-43
Evarts	DE-33	Tisdale	MINY	23-Jan-43	28-Jun-43	11-Oct-43
Evarts	DE-34	Eisele	MINY	23-Jan-43	29-Jun-43	18-Oct-43
Evarts	DE-35	Fair	MINY	24-Feb-43	27-Jul-43	23-Oct-43
Evarts	DE-36	Manlove	MINY	24-Feb-43	28-Jul-43	8-Nov-43
Evarts	DE-37	Greiner	PSNY	7-Sep-42	20-May-43	18-Aug-43
Evarts	DE-38	Wyman	PSNY	7-Sep-42	3-Jun-43	1-Sep-43
Evarts	DE-39	Lovering	PSNY	7-Sep-42	18-Jun-43	17-Sep-43

Evarts	DE-40	Sanders	PSNY	7-Sep-42	18-Jun-43	1-Oct-43
Evarts	DE-41	Brackett	PSNY	12-Jan-43	1-Aug-43	18-Oct-43
Evarts	DE-42	Reynolds	PSNY	12-Jan-43	1-Aug-43	1-Nov-43
Evarts	DE-43	Mitchell	PSNY	12-Jan-43	1-Aug-43	17-Nov-43
Evarts	DE-44	Donaldson	PSNY	12-Jan-43	1-Aug-43	1-Dec-43
Evarts	DE-45	Andres	PHNY	12-Feb-42	24-Jul-42	15-Mar-43
Evarts	DE-46	Drury	PHNY	12-Feb-42	24-Jul-42	4-Dec-43
Evarts	DE-47	Decker	PHNY	1-Apr-42	24-Jul-42	3-May-43
Evarts	DE-48	Dobler	PHNY	1-Apr-42	24-Jul-42	17-May-43
Evarts	DE-49	Doneff	PHNY	1-Apr-42	24-Jul-42	10-Jun-43
Evarts	DE-256	Sied	BosNY	10-Jan-43	22-Feb-43	11-Jun-43
Evarts	DE-257	Smartt	BosNY	10-Jan-43	22-Feb-43	18-Jun-43
Evarts	DE-258	Walter S. Brown	BosNY	10-Jan-43	22-Feb-43	25-Jun-43
Evarts	DE-259	William C. Miller	BosNY	10-Jan-43	22-Feb-43	2-Jul-43
Evarts	DE-260	Cabana	BosNY	27-Jan-43	10-Mar-43	9-Jul-43
Evarts	DE-261	Dionne	BosNY	27-Jan-43	10-Mar-43	16-Jul-43
Evarts	DE-262	Canfield	BosNY	23-Feb-43	6-Apr-43	22-Jul-43
Evarts	DE-263	Deede	BosNY	23-Feb-43	6-Apr-43	29-Jul-43
Evarts	DE-264	Elden	BosNY	23-Feb-43	6-Apr-43	4-Aug-43
Evarts	DE-265	Cloues	BosNY	23-Feb-43	6-Apr-43	10-Aug-43
Evarts	DE-266	Capel	BosNY	11-Mar-43	22-Apr-43	16-Aug-43
Evarts	DE-267	Cooke	BosNY	11-Mar-43	22-Apr-43	16-Aug-43
Evarts	DE-268	Dacres	BosNY	7-Apr-43	14-Apr-43	28-Aug-43
Evarts	DE-269	Domett	BosNY	7-Apr-43	2-Sep-43	3-Sep-43
Evarts	DE-270	Foley	BosNY	7-Apr-43	19-May-43	8-Sep-43
Evarts	DE-271	Garlies	BosNY	7-Apr-43	19-May-43	13-Sep-43
Evarts	DE-272	Gould	BosNY	23-Apr-43	4-Jun-43	18-Sep-43
Evarts	DE-273	Grindall	BosNY	23-Apr-43	4-Jun-43	23-Sep-43
Evarts	DE-274	Gardiner	BosNY	20-May-43	8-Jul-43	28-Sep-43
Evarts	DE-275	Goodall	BosNY	20-May-43	8-Jul-43	4-Oct-43
Evarts	DE-276	Goodson	BosNY	20-May-43	8-Jul-43	9-Oct-43
Evarts	DE-277	Gore	BosNY	20-May-43	8-Jul-43	14-Oct-43
Evarts	DE-278	Keats	BosNY	5-Jun-43	17-Jul-43	19-Oct-43
Evarts	DE-279	Kempthorne	BosNY	5-Jun-43	17-Jul-43	23-Oct-43
Evarts	DE-280	Kingsmill	BosNY	9-Jul-43	13-Aug-43	29-Oct-43
Evarts	DE-301	Lake	MINY	22-Apr-43	18-Aug-43	5-Feb-44
Evarts	DE-302	Lyman	MINY	22-Apr-43	19-Aug-43	19-Feb-44
Evarts	DE-303	Crowley	MINY	24-May-43	22-Sep-43	25-Mar-44
Evarts	DE-304	Rall	MINY	24-May-43	23-Sep-43	8-Apr-44
Evarts	DE-305	Halloran	MINY	21-Jun-43	14-Feb-44	27-May-44
Evarts	DE-306	Connolly	MINY	30-Jun-43	15-Jan-44	8-Jul-44
Evarts	DE-307	Finnegan	MINY	5-Jul-43	22-Feb-44	19-Aug-44

Evarts	DE-516	Lawford	BosNY	9-Jul-43	13-Aug-43	3-Nov-43
Evarts	DE-517	Louis	BosNY	9-Jul-43	13-Aug-43	9-Nov-43
Evarts	DE-518	Lawson	BosNY	9-Jul-43	13-Aug-43	15-Nov-43
Evarts	DE-519	Paisley	BosNY	18-Jul-43	30-Aug-43	20-Nov-43
Evarts	DE-520	Loring	BosNY	18-Jul-43	30-Aug-43	27-Nov-43
Evarts	DE-521	Hoste	BosNY	14-Aug-43	24-Sep-43	3-Dec-43
Evarts	DE-522	Moorson	BosNY	14-Aug-43	24-Sep-43	16-Dec-43
Evarts	DE-523	Manners	BosNY	14-Aug-43	24-Sep-43	6-Dec-43
Evarts	DE-524	Mounsey	BosNY	14-Aug-43	24-Sep-43	23-Dec-43
Evarts	DE-525	Inglis	BosNY	25-Sep-43	2-Nov-43	29-Dec-43
Evarts	DE-526	Inman	BosNY	25-Sep-43	2-Nov-43	13-Jan-44
Evarts	DE-527	O'Toole	BosNY	25-Sep-43	2-Nov-43	22-Jan-44
Evarts	DE-528	John J. Powers	BosNY	25-Sep-43	2-Nov-43	29-Feb-44
Evarts	DE-529	Mason	BosNY	14-Oct-43	17-Nov-43	20-Mar-44
Evarts	DE-530	John M. Bermingham	BosNY	14-Oct-43	17-Nov-43	8-Apr-44
Evarts	DE-50	Engstrom	PHNY	1-Apr-42	24-Jul-42	21-Jun-43
Buckley	DE-51	Buckley	BethHi	21-Jul-42	9-Jan-43	30-Apr-43
Buckley	DE-52	Bentinick	BethHi	29-Jun-42	22-Aug-42	19-May-43
Buckley	DE-53	Charles Lawrence	BethHi	1-Aug-42	16-Feb-43	31-May-43
Buckley	DE-54	Daniel T. Griffin	BethHi	7-Sep-42	25-Feb-43	9-Jun-43
Buckley	DE-55	Byard	BethHi	15-Oct-42	13-Mar-43	18-Jun-43
Buckley	DE-56	Donnell	BethHi	27-Nov-42	13-Mar-43	26-Jun-43
Buckley	DE-57	Fogg	BethHi	4-Dec-42	20-Mar-43	7-Jul-43
Buckley	DE-58	Calder	BethHi	11-Dec-42	27-Mar-43	15-Jul-43
Buckley	DE-59	Foss	BethHi	31-Dec-42	10-Apr-43	23-Jul-43
Buckley	DE-60	Gantner	BethHi	31-Dec-42	17-Apr-43	23-Jul-43
Buckley	DE-61	Duckworth	BethHi	16-Jan-43	1-May-43	4-Aug-43
Buckley	DE-62	George W. Ingram	BethHi	6-Feb-43	8-May-43	11-Aug-43
Buckley	DE-63	Ira Jeffery	BethHi	13-Feb-43	15-May-43	15-Aug-43
Buckley	DE-64	Duff	BethHi	22-Feb-43	29-May-43	23-Aug-43
Buckley	DE-65	Lee Fox	BethHi	1-Mar-43	29-May-43	30-Aug-43
Buckley	DE-66	Amesbury	BethHi	8-Mar-43	5-Jun-43	31-Aug-43
Buckley	DE-67	Essington	BethHi	15-Mar-43	19-Jun-43	7-Sep-43
Buckley	DE-68	Bates	BethHi	29-Mar-43	6-Jun-43	12-Sep-43
Buckley	DE-69	Blessman	BethHi	22-Mar-43	19-Jun-43	19-Sep-43
Buckley	DE-70	Joseph F. Campbell	BethHi	29-Mar-43	26-Jun-43	23-Sep-43
Buckley	DE-71	Affleck	BethHi	05-Apr-43	30-Jun-43	29-Sep-43
Buckley	DE-72	Aylmer	BethHi	12-Apr-43	10-Jul-43	20-Sep-43
Buckley	DE-73	Balfour	BethHi	19-Apr-43	10-Jul-43	07-Oct-43
Buckley	DE-74	Bentley	BethHi	26-Apr-43	17-Jul-43	13-Oct-43
Buckley	DE-75	Bickerton	BethHi	03-May-43	24-Jul-43	17-Oct-43

Buckley	DE-76	Bligh	BethHi	10-May-43	31-Jul-43	22-Oct-43
Buckley	DE-77	Braithwaite	BethHi	10-May-43	31-Jul-43	13-Nov-43
Buckley	DE-78	Bullen	BethHi	17-May-43	7-Aug-43	25-Oct-43
Buckley	DE-79	Bryon	BethHi	24-May-43	14-Aug-43	30-Oct-43
Buckley	DE-80	Conn	BethHi	02-Jun-43	21-Aug-43	31-Oct-43
Buckley	DE-81	Cotton	BethHi	02-Jun-43	21-Aug-43	08-Nov-43
Buckley	DE-82	Cranstoun	BethHi	09-Jun-43	28-Aug-43	13-Nov-43
Buckley	DE-83	Cubitt	BethHi	09-Jun-43	11-Sep-43	17-Nov-43
Buckley	DE-84	Curzon	BethHi	23-Jun-43	18-Sep-43	20-Nov-43
Buckley	DE-85	Dakins	BethHi	23-Jun-43	18-Sep-43	23-Nov-43
Buckley	DE-86	Deane	BethHi	30-Jun-43	25-Sep-43	26-Nov-43
Buckley	DE-87	Ekins	BethHi	05-Jul-43	2-Oct-43	29-Nov-43
Buckley	DE-88	Fitzroy	BethHi	24-Aug-43	1-Sep-43	16-Oct-43
Buckley	DE-89	Redmill	BethHi	14-Jul-43	2-Oct-43	30-Nov-43
Buckley	DE-90	Retalick	BethHi	21-Jul-43	9-Oct-43	08-Dec-43
Buckley	DE-91	Halsted	BethHi	10-Jul-43	14-Oct-43	03-Nov-43
Buckley	DE-92	Riou	BethHi	04-Aug-43	23-Oct-43	14-Dec-43
Buckley	DE-93	Rutherford	BethHi	04-Aug-43	23-Oct-43	16-Dec-43
Buckley	DE-94	Cosby	BethHi	11-Aug-43	30-Oct-43	20-Dec-43
Buckley	DE-95	Rowley	BethHi	18-Aug-43	30-Oct-43	22-Dec-43
Buckley	DE-96	Rupert	BethHi	25-Aug-43	31-Oct-43	24-Dec-43
Buckley	DE-97	Stockham	BethHi	25-Aug-43	31-Oct-43	28-Dec-43
Buckley	DE-98	Seymour	BethHi	01-Sep-43	1-Nov-43	23-Dec-43
Buckley	DE-153	Reuben James	NorNY	7-Sep-42	6-Feb-43	1-Apr-43
Buckley	DE-154	Sims	NorNY	7-Sep-42	6-Feb-43	24-Apr-43
Buckley	DE-155	Hopping	NorNY	15-Dec-42	10-Mar-43	21-May-43
Buckley	DE-156	Reeves	NorNY	7-Feb-43	22-Apr-43	9-Jun-43
Buckley	DE-157	Fechteler	NorNY	7-Feb-43	22-Apr-43	1-Jul-43
Buckley	DE-158	Chase	NorNY	16-Mar-43	24-Apr-43	18-Jul-43
Buckley	DE-159	Laning	NorNY	23-Apr-43	4-Jul-43	1-Aug-43
Buckley	DE-160	Loy	NorNY	23-Apr-43	4-Jul-43	12-Sep-43
Buckley	DE-161	Barber	NorNY	27-Apr-43	20-May-43	10-Oct-43
Buckley	DE-198	Lovelace	NorNY	22-May-43	4-Jul-43	7-Nov-43
Buckley	DE-199	Manning	CharNY	15-Feb-43	1-Jun-43	1-Oct-43
Buckley	DE-200	Neuendorf	CharNY	15-Feb-43	1-Jun-43	18-Oct-43
Buckley	DE-201	James E. Craig	CharNY	15-Apr-43	22-Jul-43	1-Nov-43
Buckley	DE-202	Eichenberger	CharNY	15-Apr-43	22-Jul-43	17-Nov-43
Buckley	DE-203	Thomason	CharNY	5-Jun-43	23-Aug-43	10-Dec-43
Buckley	DE-204	Jordan	CharNY	5-Jun-43	23-Aug-43	17-Dec-43
Buckley	DE-205	Newman	CharNY	8-Jun-43	9-Aug-43	26-Nov-43
Buckley	DE-206	Liddle	CharNY	8-Jun-43	9-Aug-43	6-Dec-43
Buckley	DE-207	Kephart	CharNY	12-May-43	6-Sep-43	7-Jan-44

Buckley	DE-208	Cofer	CharNY	12-May-43	6-Sep-43	19-Jan-44
Buckley	DE-209	Lloyd	CharNY	26-Jul-43	23-Oct-43	11-Feb-44
Buckley	DE-210	Otter	CharNY	26-Jul-43	23-Oct-43	21-Feb-44
Buckley	DE-211	Joseph C. Hubbard	CharNY	11-Aug-43	11-Nov-43	6-Mar-44
Buckley	DE-212	Hayter	CharNY	11-Aug-43	11-Nov-43	16-Mar-44
Buckley	DE-213	William T. Powell	CharNY	26-Aug-43	27-Nov-43	28-Mar-44
Buckley	DE-214	Scott	PHNY	1-Jan-43	3-Apr-43	20-Jul-43
Buckley	DE-215	Burke	PHNY	1-Jan-43	3-Apr-43	20-Aug-43
Buckley	DE-216	Enright	PHNY	22-Feb-43	29-May-43	21-Sep-43
Buckley	DE-217	Coolbaugh	PHNY	22-Feb-43	29-May-43	15-Oct-43
Buckley	DE-218	Darby	PHNY	22-Feb-43	29-May-43	15-Nov-43
Buckley	DE-219	J. Douglas Blackwood	PHNY	22-Feb-43	29-May-43	15-Dec-43
Buckley	DE-220	Francis M. Robinson	PHNY	22-Feb-43	1-May-43	15-Jan-44
Buckley	DE-221	Solar	PHNY	22-Feb-43	29-May-43	15-Feb-44
Buckley	DE-222	Fowler	PHNY	5-Apr-43	3-Jul-43	15-Mar-44
Buckley	DE-223	Spangenberg	PHNY	5-Apr-43	3-Jul-43	15-Apr-44
Buckley	DE-563	Spragge	BethHi	15-Sep-43	16-Oct-43	14-Jan-44
Buckley	DE-564	Stayner	BethHi	22-Sep-43	6-Nov-43	30-Dec-43
Buckley	DE-565	Thornborough	BethHi	22-Sep-43	13-Nov-43	31-Dec-43
Buckley	DE-566	Trollope	BethHi	29-Sep-43	20-Nov-43	10-Jan-44
Buckley	DE-567	Tyler	BethHi	6-Oct-43	20-Nov-43	14-Jan-44
Buckley	DE-568	Torrington	BethHi	22-Sep-43	27-Nov-43	18-Jan-44
Buckley	DE-569	Narbrough	BethHi	6-Oct-43	27-Nov-43	21-Jan-44
Buckley	DE-570	Waldegrave	BethHi	16-Oct-43	4-Dec-43	25-Jan-44
Buckley	DE-571	Whitaker	BethHi	20-Oct-43	12-Dec-43	28-Jan-44
Buckley	DE-572	Holmes	BethHi	27-Oct-43	18-Dec-43	31-Jan-44
Buckley	DE-573	Hargood	BethHi	27-Oct-43	18-Dec-43	7-Feb-44
Buckley	DE-574	Hotham	BethHi	5-Nov-43	21-Dec-43	8-Feb-44
Buckley	DE-575	Ahrens	BethHi	5-Nov-43	21-Dec-43	12-Feb-44
Buckley	DE-576	Barr	BethHi	5-Nov-43	28-Dec-43	15-Feb-44
Buckley	DE-577	Alexander J. Luke	BethHi	5-Nov-43	28-Dec-43	19-Feb-44
Buckley	DE-578	Robert J. Paine	BethHi	5-Nov-43	30-Dec-43	26-Feb-44
Buckley	DE-633	Foreman	BethSF	9-Apr-43	1-Aug-43	22-Oct-43
Buckley	DE-634	Whitehurst	BethSF	21-Mar-43	5-Sep-43	19-Nov-43
Buckley	DE-635	England	BethSF	4-Apr-43	26-Sep-43	10-Dec-43
Buckley	DE-636	Witter	BethSF	28-Apr-43	17-Oct-43	29-Dec-43
Buckley	DE-637	Bowers	BethSF	28-May-43	31-Oct-43	27-Jan-44
Buckley	DE-638	Willmarth	BethSF	25-Jun-43	21-Nov-43	13-Mar-44
Buckley	DE-639	Gendreau	BethSF	1-Aug-43	12-Dec-43	17-Mar-44
Buckley	DE-640	Fieberling	BethSF	19-Mar-44	2-Apr-44	11-Apr-44

Buckley	DE-641	William C. Cole	BethSF	5-Sep-43	29-Dec-43	12-May-44
Buckley	DE-642	Paul G. Baker	BethSF	26-Sep-43	12-Mar-44	25-May-44
Buckley	DE-643	Damon M. Cummings	BethSF	17-Oct-43	18-Apr-44	29-Jun-44
Buckley	DE-644	Vammen	BethSF	1-Aug-43	21-May-44	27-Jul-44
Buckley	DE-665	Jenks	DravoP	12-May-43	11-Sep-43	19-Jan-44
Buckley	DE-666	Durik	DravoP	22-Jun-43	9-Oct-43	24-Mar-44
Buckley	DE-667	Wiseman	DravoP	26-Jul-43	6-Nov-43	4-Apr-44
Buckley	DE-675	Weber	BethQ	22-Feb-43	1-May-43	30-Jun-43
Buckley	DE-676	Schmitt	BethQ	22-Feb-43	29-May-43	24-Jul-43
Buckley	DE-677	Frament	BethQ	1-May-43	28-Jun-43	15-Aug-43
Buckley	DE-678	Harmon	BethQ	31-May-43	25-Jul-43	31-Aug-43
Buckley	DE-679	Greenwood	BethQ	29-Jun-43	21-Aug-43	25-Sep-43
Buckley	DE-680	Loeser	BethQ	27-Jul-43	11-Sep-43	10-Oct-43
Buckley	DE-681	Gillette	BethQ	24-Aug-43	25-Sep-43	27-Oct-43
Buckley	DE-682	Underhill	BethQ	16-Sep-43	15-Oct-43	15-Nov-43
Buckley	DE-683	Henry R. Kenyon	BethQ	29-Sep-43	30-Oct-43	30-Nov-43
Buckley	DE-693	Bull	Defoe	15-Dec-42	25-Mar-43	12-Aug-43
Buckley	DE-694	Bunch	Defoe	22-Feb-43	29-May-43	21-Aug-43
Buckley	DE-695	Rich	Defoe	27-Mar-43	22-Jun-43	1-Oct-43
Buckley	DE-696	Spangler	Defoe	28-Apr-43	15-Jul-43	31-Oct-43
Buckley	DE-697	George	Defoe	22-May-43	4-Aug-43	20-Nov-43
Buckley	DE-698	Raby	Defoe	7-Jun-43	4-Sep-43	7-Dec-43
Buckley	DE-699	Marsh	Defoe	23-Jun-43	25-Sep-43	12-Jan-44
Buckley	DE-700	Currier	Defoe	21-Jul-43	14-Oct-43	1-Feb-44
Buckley	DE-701	Osmus	Defoe	17-Aug-43	4-Nov-43	23-Feb-44
Buckley	DE-702	Earl V. Johnson	Defoe	7-Sep-43	24-Nov-43	18-Mar-44
Buckley	DE-703	Holton	Defoe	28-Sep-43	15-Dec-43	1-May-44
Buckley	DE-704	Cronin	Defoe	19-Oct-43	5-Jan-44	5-May-44
Buckley	DE-705	Frybarger	Defoe	8-Nov-43	25-Jan-44	18-May-44
Buckley	DE-789	Tatum	Orange	22-Apr-43	7-Aug-43	22-Nov-43
Buckley	DE-790	Borum	Orange	28-Apr-43	14-Aug-43	30-Nov-43
Buckley	DE-791	Maloy	Orange	10-May-43	18-Aug-43	13-Dec-43
Buckley	DE-792	Haines	Orange	17-May-43	26-Aug-43	27-Dec-43
Buckley	DE-793	Runels	Orange	7-Jun-43	4-Sep-43	3-Jan-44
Buckley	DE-794	Hollis	Orange	5-Jul-43	11-Sep-43	24-Jan-44
Buckley	DE-795	Gunason	Orange	9-Sep-43	16-Oct-43	1-Feb-44
Buckley	DE-796	Major	Orange	16-Aug-43	23-Oct-43	12-Feb-44
Buckley	DE-797	Weeden	Orange	18-Aug-43	27-Oct-43	19-Feb-44
Buckley	DE-798	Varian	Orange	27-Aug-43	6-Nov-43	29-Feb-44
Buckley	DE-799	Scroggins	Orange	4-Sep-43	6-Nov-43	30-Mar-44
Buckley	DE-800	Jack W. Wilke	Orange	18-Oct-43	18-Dec-43	7-Mar-44
Cannon	DE-100	Christopher	Dravo	7-Dec-42	19-Jun-43	23-Oct-43

Cannon	DE-101	Alger	Dravo	2-Jan-43	8-Jul-43	12-Nov-43
Cannon	DE-102	Thomas	Dravo	16-Jan-43	31-Jul-43	21-Nov-43
Cannon	DE-103	Bostwick	Dravo	6-Feb-43	30-Aug-43	1-Dec-43
Cannon	DE-104	Breeman	Dravo	20-Mar-43	4-Sep-43	12-Dec-43
Cannon	DE-105	Burrows	Dravo	24-Mar-43	2-Oct-43	19-Dec-43
Cannon	DE-106	Senegalais	Dravo	24-Apr-43	1-Nov-43	02-Jan-44
Cannon	DE-107	Algerien	Dravo	13-May-43	7-Nov-43	23-Jan-44
Cannon	DE-108	Tunisien	Dravo	23-Jun-43	7-Dec-43	11-Feb-44
Cannon	DE-109	Marocain	Dravo	07-Sep-43	1-Jan-44	23-Feb-44
Cannon	DE-110	Hova	Dravo	25-Sep-43	22-Jan-44	18-Mar-44
Cannon	DE-111	Somali	Dravo	23-Oct-43	2-Feb-44	09-Apr-44
Cannon	DE-112	Carter	Dravo	19-Nov-43	29-Feb-44	3-May-44
Cannon	DE-113	Clarence L. Evans	Dravo	23-Dec-43	22-Mar-44	25-Jun-44
Cannon	DE-162	Levy	FedN	19-Oct-42	26-Mar-43	13-May-43
Cannon	DE-163	McConnell	FedN	19-Oct-42	28-Mar-43	28-May-43
Cannon	DE-164	Osterhaus	FedN	11-Nov-42	8-Apr-43	12-Jun-43
Cannon	DE-165	Parks	FedN	11-Nov-42	8-Apr-43	23-Jun-43
Cannon	DE-166	Baron	FedN	30-Nov-42	9-May-43	5-Jul-43
Cannon	DE-167	Acree	FedN	30-Nov-42	9-May-43	19-Jul-43
Cannon	DE-168	Amick	FedN	30-Nov-42	27-May-43	26-Jul-43
Cannon	DE-169	Atherton	NorNY	14-Jan-43	27-May-43	29-Aug-43
Cannon	DE-170	Booth	NorNY	30-Jan-43	21-Jun-43	19-Sep-43
Cannon	DE-171	Carroll	NorNY	30-Jan-43	21-Jun-43	24-Oct-43
Cannon	DE-172	Cooner	FedN	22-Feb-43	23-Jul-43	21-Aug-43
Cannon	DE-173	Eldridge	FedN	22-Feb-43	25-Jul-43	27-Aug-43
Cannon	DE-174	Marts	FedN	26-Apr-43	8-Aug-43	3-Sep-43
Cannon	DE-175	Pennewill	FedN	26-Apr-43	8-Aug-43	15-Sep-43
Cannon	DE-176	Micka	FedN	3-May-43	22-Aug-43	23-Sep-44
Cannon	DE-177	Reybold	FedN	3-May-43	22-Aug-43	29-Sep-43
Cannon	DE-178	Herzog	FedN	17-May-43	5-Sep-43	6-Oct-43
Cannon	DE-179	McAnn	FedN	17-May-43	5-Sep-43	11-Oct-43
Cannon	DE-180	Trumpeter	FedN	7-Jun-43	19-Sep-43	16-Oct-43
Cannon	DE-181	Straub	FedN	7-Jun-43	19-Sep-43	25-Oct-43
Cannon	DE-182	Gustafson	FedN	5-Jul-43	3-Oct-43	1-Nov-43
Cannon	DE-183	Samuel S. Miles	FedN	5-Jul-43	3-Oct-43	4-Nov-43
Cannon	DE-184	Wesson	FedN	29-Jul-43	17-Oct-43	11-Nov-43
Cannon	DE-185	Riddle	FedN	29-Jul-43	17-Oct-43	17-Nov-43
Cannon	DE-186	Swearer	FedN	12-Aug-43	31-Oct-43	24-Nov-43
Cannon	DE-187	Stern	FedN	12-Aug-43	31-Oct-43	1-Dec-43
Cannon	DE-188	O'Neill	FedN	26-Aug-43	14-Nov-43	6-Dec-43
Cannon	DE-189	Bronstein	FedN	26-Aug-43	14-Nov-43	13-Dec-43
Cannon	DE-190	Baker	FedN	9-Sep-43	28-Nov-43	23-Dec-43

Cannon	DE-191	Coffman	FedN	9-Sep-43	28-Nov-43	27-Dec-43
Cannon	DE-192	Eisner	FedN	23-Sep-43	12-Dec-43	1-Jan-44
Cannon	DE-193	Garlield Thomas	FedN	23-Sep-43	12-Dec-43	24-Jan-44
Cannon	DE-194	Wingfield	FedN	7-Oct-43	30-Dec-43	28-Jan-44
Cannon	DE-195	Thornhill	FedN	7-Oct-43	20-Dec-43	1-Feb-44
Cannon	DE-196	Rinehart	FedN	21-Oct-43	9-Jan-44	12-Feb-44
Cannon	DE-197	Roche	FedN	21-Oct-43	9-Jan-44	21-Feb-44
Cannon	DE-739	Bangust	WPS	11-Feb-43	6-Jun-43	30-Oct-43
Cannon	DE-740	Waterman	WPS	24-Feb-43	20-Jun-43	30-Nov-43
Cannon	DE-741	Weaver	WPS	13-Mar-43	4-Jul-43	31-Dec-43
Cannon	DE-742	Hilbert	WPS	23-Mar-43	18-Jul-43	4-Feb-44
Cannon	DE-743	Lamons	WPS	10-Apr-43	1-Aug-43	29-Feb-44
Cannon	DE-744	Kyne	WPS	16-Apr-43	15-Aug-43	4-Apr-44
Cannon	DE-745	Snyder	WPS	28-Apr-43	29-Aug-43	5-May-44
Cannon	DE-746	Hemminger	WPS	8-May-43	12-Sep-43	30-May-44
Cannon	DE-747	Bright	WPS	9-Jun-43	26-Sep-43	30-Jun-44
Cannon	DE-748	Tills	WPS	23-Jun-43	3-Oct-43	8-Aug-44
Cannon	DE-749	Roberts	WPS	7-Jul-43	14-Nov-43	2-Sep-44
Cannon	DE-750	McClelland	WPS	21-Jul-43	28-Nov-43	19-Sep-44
Cannon	DE-763	Cates	Tampa	1-Mar-43	10-Oct-43	15-Dec-43
Cannon	DE-764	Gandy	Tampa	1-Mar-43	12-Dec-43	7-Feb-44
Cannon	DE-765	Earl K. Olsen	Tampa	9-Mar-43	13-Feb-44	10-Apr-44
Cannon	DE-766	Slater	Tampa	9-Mar-43	13-Feb-44	1-May-44
Cannon	DE-767	Oswald	Tampa	1-Apr-43	25-Apr-44	12-Jun-44
Cannon	DE-768	Ebert	Tampa	1-Apr-43	11-May-44	12-Jul-44
Cannon	DE-769	Neal A. Scott	Tampa	1-Jun-43	4-Jun-44	31-Jul-44
Cannon	DE-770	Muir	Tampa	1-Jun-43	4-Jun-44	30-Aug-44
Cannon	DE-771	Sutton	Tampa	23-Aug-43	6-Aug-44	12-Dec-44
Cannon	DE-99	Cannon	Dravo	14-Nov-42	25-May-43	26-Sep-43
Edsall	DE-129	Edsall	Orange	2-Jul-42	1-Nov-42	10-Apr-43
Edsall	DE-130	Jacob Jones	Orange	26-Jun-42	1-Nov-42	29-Apr-43
Edsall	DE-131	Hammann	Orange	10-Jul-42	13-Dec-42	17-May-43
Edsall	DE-132	Robert E. Peary	Orange	30-Jun-42	3-Jan-43	31-May-43
Edsall	DE-133	Pillsbury	Orange	18-Jul-42	10-Jan-43	7-Jun-43
Edsall	DE-134	Pope	Orange	14-Jul-42	12-Jan-43	25-Jun-43
Edsall	DE-135	Flaherty	Orange	7-Nov-42	17-Jan-43	26-Jun-43
Edsall	DE-136	Frederick C. Davis	Orange	9-Nov-42	24-Jan-43	14-Jul-43
Edsall	DE-137	Herbert C. Jones	Orange	30-Nov-42	19-Jan-43	21-Jul-43
Edsall	DE-138	Douglas L. Howard	Orange	8-Dec-42	24-Jan-43	29-Jul-43
Edsall	DE-139	Farquhar	Orange	14-Dec-42	13-Feb-43	5-Aug-43
Edsall	DE-140	J.R.Y. Blakely	Orange	16-Dec-42	7-Mar-43	16-Aug-43
Edsall	DE-141	Hill	Orange	21-Dec-42	28-Feb-43	16-Aug-43

Edsall	DE-142	Fessenden	Orange	4-Jan-43	9-Mar-43	25-Aug-43
Edsall	DE-143	Fiske	Orange	4-Jan-43	14-Mar-43	25-Aug-43
Edsall	DE-144	Frost	Orange	13-Jan-43	21-Mar-43	30-Aug-43
Edsall	DE-145	Huse	Orange	11-Jan-43	23-Apr-43	30-Aug-43
Edsall	DE-146	Inch	Orange	19-Jan-43	4-Apr-43	8-Sep-43
Edsall	DE-147	Blair	Orange	19-Jan-43	6-Apr-43	13-Sep-43
Edsall	DE-148	Brough	Orange	22-Jan-43	10-Apr-43	18-Sep-43
Edsall	DE-149	Chatelaine	Orange	25-Jan-43	21-Apr-43	22-Sep-43
Edsall	DE-150	Neunzer	Orange	29-Jan-43	27-Apr-43	27-Sep-43
Edsall	DE-151	Poole	Orange	13-Feb-43	8-May-43	29-Sep-43
Edsall	DE-152	Peterson	Orange	28-Feb-43	15-May-43	29-Sep-43
Edsall	DE-238	Stewart	Brown	15-Jul-42	22-Nov-42	31-May-43
Edsall	DE-239	Sturtevant	Brown	15-Jul-42	3-Dec-42	16-Jun-43
Edsall	DE-240	Moore	Brown	20-Jul-42	20-Dec-42	1-Jul-43
Edsall	DE-241	Keith	Brown	4-Aug-42	21-Dec-42	19-Jul-43
Edsall	DE-242	Tomich	Brown	15-Sep-42	28-Dec-42	27-Jul-43
Edsall	DE-243	J. Richard Ward	Brown	30-Sep-42	6-Jan-43	5-Jul-43
Edsall	DE-244	Otterstetter	Brown	9-Nov-42	19-Jan-43	6-Aug-43
Edsall	DE-245	Sloat	Brown	22-Nov-42	21-Jan-43	16-Aug-43
Edsall	DE-246	Snowden	Brown	7-Dec-42	19-Feb-43	23-Aug-43
Edsall	DE-247	Stanton	Brown	7-Dec-42	21-Feb-43	7-Aug-43
Edsall	DE-248	Swasey	Brown	30-Dec-42	18-Mar-43	31-Aug-43
Edsall	DE-249	Marchand	Brown	3-Dec-42	30-Mar-43	8-Sep-43
Edsall	DE-250	Hurst	Brown	27-Jan-43	1-Apr-43	30-Aug-43
Edsall	DE-251	Camp	Brown	27-Jan-43	16-Apr-43	16-Sep-43
Edsall	DE-252	Howard D. Crow	Brown	6-Feb-43	16-Apr-43	27-Sep-43
Edsall	DE-253	Pettit	Brown	6-Feb-43	28-Apr-43	23-Sep-43
Edsall	DE-254	Ricketts	Brown	16-Mar-43	10-May-43	5-Oct-43
Edsall	DE-255	Sellstrom	Brown	16-Mar-43	12-May-43	12-Oct-43
Edsall	DE-316	Harveson	Orange	9-Mar-43	22-May-43	12-Oct-43
Edsall	DE-317	Joyce	Orange	8-Mar-43	26-May-43	30-Sep-43
Edsall	DE-318	Kirkpatrick	Orange	15-Mar-43	5-Jun-43	23-Oct-43
Edsall	DE-319	Leopold	Orange	24-Mar-43	12-Jun-43	18-Oct-43
Edsall	DE-320	Menges	Orange	22-Mar-43	15-Jun-43	26-Oct-43
Edsall	DE-321	Mosley	Orange	6-Apr-43	26-Jun-43	30-Oct-43
Edsall	DE-322	Newell	Orange	5-Apr-43	29-Jun-43	30-Oct-43
Edsall	DE-323	Pride	Orange	12-Apr-43	3-Jul-43	13-Nov-43
Edsall	DE-324	Falgout	Orange	26-May-43	24-Jul-43	15-Nov-43
Edsall	DE-325	Lowe	Orange	24-May-43	28-Jul-43	22-Nov-43
Edsall	DE-326	Gary	Orange	15-Jun-43	21-Aug-43	27-Nov-43
Edsall	DE-327	Brister	Orange	14-Jun-43	24-Aug-43	30-Nov-43
Edsall	DE-328	Finch	Orange	29-Jun-43	28-Aug-43	13-Dec-43

Edsall	DE-329	Kretchmer	Orange	28-Jun-43	31-Aug-43	13-Dec-43
Edsall	DE-330	O'Reilly	Orange	29-Jul-43	14-Nov-43	28-Dec-43
Edsall	DE-331	Koiner	Orange	26-Jul-43	5-Sep-43	27-Dec-43
Edsall	DE-332	Price	Orange	24-Aug-43	30-Oct-43	12-Jan-44
Edsall	DE-333	Strickland	Orange	23-Aug-43	2-Nov-43	10-Jan-44
Edsall	DE-334	Forster	Orange	31-Aug-43	13-Nov-43	25-Jan-44
Edsall	DE-335	Daniel	Orange	30-Aug-43	16-Nov-43	24-Jan-44
Edsall	DE-336	Roy O. Hale	Orange	13-Sep-43	20-Nov-43	3-Feb-44
Edsall	DE-337	Dale W. Peterson	Orange	25-Oct-43	22-Dec-43	17-Feb-44
Edsall	DE-338	Martin H. Ray	Orange	27-Oct-43	23-Dec-43	28-Feb-44
Edsall	DE-382	Ramsden	Brown	26-Mar-43	24-May-43	19-Oct-43
Edsall	DE-383	Mills	Brown	26-Mar-43	26-May-43	12-Oct-43
Edsall	DE-384	Rhodes	Brown	19-Apr-43	29-Jun-43	25-Oct-43
Edsall	DE-385	Richey	Brown	19-Apr-43	30-Jun-43	30-Oct-43
Edsall	DE-386	Savage	Brown	30-Apr-43	15-Jul-43	29-Oct-43
Edsall	DE-387	Vance	Brown	30-Apr-43	16-Jul-43	1-Nov-43
Edsall	DE-388	Lansing	Brown	15-May-43	2-Aug-43	10-Nov-43
Edsall	DE-389	Durant	Brown	15-May-43	1-Aug-43	16-Nov-43
Edsall	DE-390	Calcaterra	Brown	28-May-43	16-Aug-43	17-Nov-43
Edsall	DE-391	Chambers	Brown	28-May-43	17-Aug-43	22-Nov-43
Edsall	DE-392	Merrill	Brown	1-Jul-43	29-Aug-43	27-Nov-43
Edsall	DE-393	Haverfield	Brown	1-Jul-43	30-Aug-43	29-Nov-43
Edsall	DE-394	Swenning	Brown	17-Jul-43	13-Sep-43	1-Dec-43
Edsall	DE-395	Willis	Brown	17-Jul-43	14-Sep-43	10-Dec-43
Edsall	DE-396	Janssen	Brown	4-Aug-43	10-Oct-43	18-Dec-43
Edsall	DE-397	Wilhoite	Brown	4-Aug-43	5-Oct-43	16-Dec-43
Edsall	DE-398	Cockrill	Brown	31-Aug-43	29-Oct-43	24-Dec-43
Edsall	DE-399	Stockdale	Brown	31-Aug-43	30-Oct-43	31-Dec-43
Edsall	DE-400	Hissem	Brown	6-Oct-43	26-Oct-43	13-Jan-44
Edsall	DE-401	Holder	Brown	6-Oct-43	27-Nov-43	18-Jan-44
Rudderow	DE-224	Rudderow	PHNY	15-Jul-43	14-Oct-43	15-May-44
Rudderow	DE-225	Day	PHNY	15-Jul-43	14-Oct-43	10-Jun-44
Rudderow	DE-230	Chaffee	CharNY	26-Aug-43	27-Nov-43	9-May-44
Rudderow	DE-231	Hodges	CharNY	9-Sep-43	9-Dec-43	27-May-44
Rudderow	DE-579	Riley	BethHi	20-Oct-43	29-Dec-43	13-Mar-44
Rudderow	DE-580	Leslie L.B. Knox	BethHi	7-Nov-43	8-Jan-44	22-Mar-44
Rudderow	DE-581	McNulty	BethHi	17-Nov-43	8-Jan-44	31-Mar-44
Rudderow	DE-582	Metivier	BethHi	24-Nov-43	12-Jan-44	7-Apr-44
Rudderow	DE-583	George A. Johnson	BethHi	24-Nov-43	12-Jan-44	15-Apr-44
Rudderow	DE-584	Charles J. Kimmel	BethHi	1-Dec-43	15-Jan-44	20-Apr-44
Rudderow	DE-585	Daniel A. Joy	BethHi	1-Dec-43	15-Jan-44	28-Apr-44
Rudderow	DE-586	Lough	BethHi	8-Dec-43	22-Jan-44	2-May-44

Rudderow	DE-587	Thomas F. Nickel	BethHi	15-Dec-43	22-Jan-44	9-Jun-44
Rudderow	DE-588	Peiffer	BethHi	21-Dec-43	26-Jan-44	15-Jun-44
Rudderow	DE-589	Tinsman	BethHi	21-Dec-43	29-Jan-44	26-Jun-44
Rudderow	DE-684	De Long	BethQ	19-Oct-43	23-Nov-43	31-Dec-43
Rudderow	DE-685	Coates	BethQ	8-Nov-43	12-Dec-43	24-Jan-44
Rudderow	DE-686	Eugene E. Elmore	BethQ	27-Nov-43	23-Dec-43	4-Feb-44
Rudderow	DE-706	Holt	Defoe	28-Nov-43	15-Feb-44	9-Jun-44
Rudderow	DE-707	Jobb	Defoe	20-Dec-43	4-Mar-44	4-Jul-44
Rudderow	DE-708	Parle	Defoe	8-Jan-44	25-Mar-44	29-Jul-44
Rudderow	DE-709	Bray	Defoe	27-Jan-44	15-Apr-44	4-Sep-44
John C. Butler	DE-339	John C. Butler	Orange	5-Oct-43	12-Nov-43	31-Mar-44
John C. Butler	DE-340	O'Flaherty	Orange	4-Oct-43	14-Dec-43	8-Apr-44
John C. Butler	DE-341	Raymond	Orange	3-Nov-43	8-Jan-44	15-Apr-44
John C. Butler	DE-342	Richard W. Suesens	Orange	1-Nov-43	11-Jan-44	26-Apr-44
John C. Butler	DE-343	Abercrombie	Orange	8-Nov-43	14-Jan-44	1-May-44
John C. Butler	DE-344	Oberrender	Orange	8-Nov-43	18-Jan-44	11-May-44
John C. Butler	DE-345	Robert Brazier	Orange	16-Nov-43	22-Jan-44	18-May-44
John C. Butler	DE-346	Edwin A. Howard	Orange	15-Nov-43	25-Jan-44	25-May-44
John C. Butler	DE-347	Jesse Rutherford	Orange	22-Nov-43	20-Jan-44	31-May-44
John C. Butler	DE-348	Key	Orange	14-Dec-43	12-Feb-44	5-Jun-44
John C. Butler	DE-349	Gentry	Orange	13-Dec-43	15-Feb-44	14-Jun-44
John C. Butler	DE-350	Traw	Orange	19-Dec-43	12-Feb-44	20-Jun-44
John C. Butler	DE-351	Maurice J. Manuel	Orange	22-Dec-43	19-Feb-44	30-Jun-44
John C. Butler	DE-352	Naifeh	Orange	29-Dec-43	29-Feb-44	4-Jul-44
John C. Butler	DE-353	Doyle C. Barnes	Orange	11-Jan-44	4-Mar-44	13-Jul-44
John C. Butler	DE-354	Kenneth M. Willett	Orange	10-Jan-44	7-Mar-44	19-Jul-44
John C. Butler	DE-355	Jaccard	Orange	25-Jan-44	18-Mar-44	26-Jul-44
John C. Butler	DE-356	Lloyd E. Acree	Orange	24-Jan-44	21-Mar-44	1-Aug-44
John C. Butler	DE-357	George E. Davis	Orange	15-Feb-44	8-Apr-44	11-Aug-44
John C. Butler	DE-358	Mack	Orange	14-Feb-44	11-Apr-44	16-Aug-44
John C. Butler	DE-359	Woodson	Orange	7-Mar-44	29-Apr-44	24-Aug-44
John C. Butler	DE-360	Johnnie Hutchins	Orange	6-Mar-44	2-May-44	28-Aug-44
John C. Butler	DE-361	Walton	Orange	21-Mar-44	20-May-44	4-Sep-44
John C. Butler	DE-362	Rolf	Orange	20-Mar-44	23-May-44	7-Sep-44
John C. Butler	DE-363	Pratt	Orange	11-Apr-44	1-Jun-44	18-Sep-44
John C. Butler	DE-364	Rombach	Orange	10-Apr-44	6-Jun-44	20-Sep-44
John C. Butler	DE-365	McGinty	Orange	3-May-44	5-Aug-44	25-Sep-44
John C. Butler	DE-366	Alvins C. Cockrell	Orange	1-May-44	8-Aug-44	7-Oct-44
John C. Butler	DE-367	French	Orange	1-May-44	17-Jun-44	9-Oct-44
John C. Butler	DE-368	Cecil J. Doyle	Orange	12-May-44	1-Jul-44	16-Oct-44
John C. Butler	DE-369	Thaddeus Parker	Orange	23-May-44	26-Aug-44	25-Oct-44
John C. Butler	DE-370	John L.	Orange	22-May-44	29-Aug-44	31-Oct-44

		Williamson				
John C. Butler	DE-371	Presley	Orange	6-Jun-44	19-Aug-44	7-Nov-44
John C. Butler	DE-372	Williams	Orange	5-Jun-44	22-Aug-44	11-Nov-44
John C. Butler	DE-402	Richard S. Bull	Brown	18-Aug-43	16-Nov-43	26-Feb-44
John C. Butler	DE-403	Richard M. Rowell	Brown	18-Aug-43	17-Nov-43	9-Mar-44
John C. Butler	DE-404	Eversole	Brown	15-Sep-43	3-Dec-43	21-Mar-44
John C. Butler	DE-405	Dennis	Brown	15-Sep-43	4-Dec-43	20-Mar-44
John C. Butler	DE-406	Edmonds	Brown	1-Nov-43	17-Dec-43	3-Apr-44
John C. Butler	DE-407	Shelton	Brown	1-Nov-43	18-Dec-43	4-Apr-44
John C. Butler	DE-408	Straus	Brown	18-Nov-43	30-Dec-43	6-Apr-44
John C. Butler	DE-409	La Prade	Brown	18-Nov-43	31-Dec-43	20-Apr-44
John C. Butler	DE-410	Jack Miller	Brown	29-Nov-43	10-Jan-44	13-Apr-44
John C. Butler	DE-411	Stafford	Brown	29-Nov-43	11-Jan-44	19-Apr-44
John C. Butler	DE-412	Walter C. Wann	Brown	6-Dec-43	19-Jan-44	2-May-44
John C. Butler	DE-413	Samuel B. Roberts	Brown	6-Dec-43	20-Jan-44	28-Apr-44
John C. Butler	DE-414	Le Ray Wilson	Brown	20-Dec-43	28-Jan-44	10-May-44
John C. Butler	DE-415	Lawrence C. Taylor	Brown	20-Dec-43	29-Jan-44	13-May-44
John C. Butler	DE-416	Melvin R. Nawman	Brown	3-Jan-44	16-Feb-44	16-May-44
John C. Butler	DE-417	Oliver Mitchell	Brown	3-Jan-44	8-Feb-44	14-Jun-44
John C. Butler	DE-418	Tabberer	Brown	12-Jan-44	3-Feb-44	23-May-44
John C. Butler	DE-419	Robert F. Keller	Brown	12-Jan-44	19-Feb-44	17-Jun-44
John C. Butler	DE-420	Leland E. Thomas	Brown	21-Jan-44	28-Feb-44	19-Jun-44
John C. Butler	DE-421	Chester T. O'Brien	Brown	21-Jan-44	29-Feb-44	3-Jul-44
John C. Butler	DE-422	Douglas A. Munro	Brown	31-Jan-44	8-Mar-44	11-Jul-44
John C. Butler	DE-423	Dufilho	Brown	31-Jan-44	9-Mar-44	21-Jul-44
John C. Butler	DE-424	Haas	Brown	23-Feb-44	20-Mar-44	2-Aug-44
John C. Butler	DE-438	Corbesier	FedN	4-Nov-43	13-Feb-44	31-Mar-44
John C. Butler	DE-439	Conklin	FedN	4-Nov-43	13-Feb-44	21-Apr-44
John C. Butler	DE-440	McCoy Reynolds	FedN	18-Nov-43	22-Feb-44	2-May-44
John C. Butler	DE-441	William Seiverling	FedN	2-Dec-43	7-Mar-44	1-Jun-44
John C. Butler	DE-442	Ulvert M. Moore	FedN	2-Dec-43	7-Mar-44	18-Jul-44
John C. Butler	DE-443	Kendal C. Campbell	FedN	16-Dec-43	19-Mar-44	31-Jul-44
John C. Butler	DE-444	Goss	FedN	16-Dec-43	19-Mar-44	26-Aug-44
John C. Butler	DE-445	Grady	FedN	3-Jan-44	2-Apr-44	11-Sep-44
John C. Butler	DE-446	Charles E. Brannon	FedN	13-Jan-44	23-Apr-44	1-Nov-44
John C. Butler	DE-447	Albert T. Harris	FedN	13-Jan-44	16-Apr-44	29-Nov-44
John C. Butler	DE-448	Cross	FedN	19-Mar-44	4-Jul-44	8-Jan-45
John C. Butler	DE-449	Hanna	FedN	22-Mar-44	4-Jul-44	27-Jan-45
John C. Butler	DE-450	Joseph E. Connolly	FedN	6-Apr-44	6-Aug-44	28-Feb-45
John C. Butler	DE-508	Gilligan	FedN	18-Nov-43	22-Feb-44	12-May-44

John C. Butler	DE-509	Formoe	FedN	3-Jan-44	2-Apr-44	5-Oct-44
John C. Butler	DE-510	Heyliger	FedN	27-Apr-44	6-Aug-44	24-Mar-45
John C. Butler	DE-531	Edward H. Allen	BosNY	31-Aug-43	7-Oct-43	16-Dec-43
John C. Butler	DE-532	Tweedy	BosNY	31-Aug-43	7-Oct-43	12-Feb-44
John C. Butler	DE-533	Howard F. Clark	BosNY	8-Oct-43	8-Nov-43	25-May-44
John C. Butler	DE-534	Silverstein	BosNY	8-Oct-43	8-Nov-43	14-Jul-44
John C. Butler	DE-535	Lewis	BosNY	3-Nov-43	7-Dec-43	5-Sep-44
John C. Butler	DE-536	Bivin	BosNY	3-Nov-43	7-Dec-43	31-Oct-44
John C. Butler	DE-537	Rizzi	BosNY	3-Nov-43	7-Dec-43	26-Jun-45
John C. Butler	DE-538	Osberg	BosNY	3-Nov-43	7-Dec-43	10-Dec-45
John C. Butler	DE-539	Wagner	BosNY	8-Nov-43	27-Dec-44	22-Nov-55
John C. Butler	DE-540	Vandivier	BosNY	8-Nov-43	27-Dec-43	11-Oct-50

World War II Patrol Frigates

Number	Name	Shipyard	Laid Down	Launched	Commissioned
PF-3	Tacoma	Kaiser	10-Mar-43	7-Jul-43	6-Nov-43
PF-4	Sausalito	Kaiser	7-Apr-43	20-Jul-43	4-Mar-44
PF-5	Holquiam	Kaiser	10-Apr-43	31-Jul-43	8-May-44
PF-6	Pasco	Kaiser	7-Jul-43	17-Aug-43	15-Apr-44
PF-7	Albuquerque	Kaiser	20-Jul-43	14-Sep-43	20-Dec-43
PF-8	Everett	Kaiser	31-Jul-43	29-Sep-43	22-Jan-44
PF-9	Pocatello	Kaiser	17-Aug-43	17-Oct-43	18-Feb-44
PF-10	Brownsville	Kaiser	14-Sep-43	14-Nov-43	6-May-44
PF-11	Grand Forks	Kaiser	29-Sep-43	27-Nov-43	18-Mar-44
PF-12	Casper	Kaiser	17-Oct-43	27-Dec-43	31-Mar-44
PF-13	Pueblo	Kaiser	14-Nov-43	20-Jan-44	27-May-44
PF-14	Grand Island	Kaiser	27-Nov-43	19-Feb-44	27-May-44
PF-15	Annapolis	ASB-L	20-May-43	16-Oct-43	4-Dec-44
PF-16	Bangor	ASB-L	20-May-43	6-Nov-43	22-Nov-44
PF-17	Key West	ASB-L	23-Jun-43	29-Dec-43	7-Nov-44
PF-18	Alexandria	ASB-L	23-Jun-43	15-Jan-44	11-Mar-45
PF-19	Huron	ASB-C	1-Mar-43	3-Jul-43	7-Sep-44
PF-20	Gulfport	ASB-C	5-May-43	21-Aug-43	16-Sep-44
PF-21	Bayonne	ASB-C	6-May-43	11-Sep-43	14-Feb-45
PF-22	Gloucester	Walt-But	4-Mar-43	12-Jul-43	10-Dec-43
PF-23	Shreveport	Walt-But	8-Mar-43	15-Jul-43	24-Apr-44
PF-24	Muskegon	Walt-But	11-May-43	25-Jul-43	19-Feb-44
PF-25	Charlottesville	Walt-But	12-May-43	30-Jul-43	10-Apr-44
PF-26	Poughkeepsie	Walt-But	3-Jun-43	12-Aug-43	6-Sep-44
PF-27	Newport	Walt-But	5-Jun-43	15-Aug-43	8-Sep-44
PF-28	Emporia	Walt-But	14-Jul-43	30-Aug-43	7-Oct-44
PF-29	Groton	Walt-But	15-Jul-43	14-Sep-43	5-Sep-44
PF-30	Hingham	Walt-But	25-Jul-43	27-Aug-43	3-Nov-44
PF-31	Grand Rapids	Walt-But	30-Jul-43	10-Sep-43	10-Oct-44
PF-32	Woonsocket	Walt-But	12-Aug-43	27-Sep-43	27-Sep-43
PF-33	Dearborn	Walt-But	15-Aug-43	27-Sep-43	10-Sep-44
PF-34	Long Beach	Cons-Wil	19-Mar-43	5-May-43	8-Sep-43
PF-35	Belfast	Cons-Wil	26-Mar-43	20-May-43	24-Nov-43
PF-36	Glendale	Cons-Wil	6-Apr-43	28-May-43	1-Oct-43
PF-37	San Pedro	Cons-Wil	17-Apr-43	11-Jun-43	23-Oct-43
PF-38	Coronado	Cons-Wil	6-May-43	17-Jun-43	17-Nov-43
PF-39	Ogden	Cons-Wil	21-May-43	23-Jun-43	20-Dec-43
PF-40	Eugene	Cons-Wil	12-Jun-43	6-Jul-43	15-Jan-44
PF-41	El Paso	Cons-Wil	18-Jun-43	16-Jul-43	1-Dec-43
PF-42	Van Buren	Cons-Wil	24-Jun-43	27-Jul-43	17-Dec-43
PF-43	Orange	Cons-Wil	7-Jul-43	6-Aug-43	1-Jan-44
PF-44	Corpus Christi	Cons-Wil	17-Jul-43	17-Aug-43	29-Jan-44
PF-45	Hutchinson	Cons-Wil	28-Jul-43	27-Aug-43	3-Feb-44
PF-46	Bisbee	Cons-Wil	7-Aug-43	7-Sep-43	15-Feb-44

Number	Name	Shipyard	Laid Down	Launched	Commissioned
PF-47	Gallup	Cons-Wil	18-Aug-43	17-Sep-43	29-Feb-44
PF-48	Rockford	Cons-Wil or LA??	28-Aug-43	27-Sep-43	6-Mar-44
PF-49	Muskogee	Cons-Wil	18-Sep-43	18-Oct-43	16-Mar-44
PF-50	Carson City	Cons-Wil	28-Sep-43	13-Nov-43	24-Mar-44
PF-51	Burlington	Cons-Wil	19-Oct-43	7-Dec-43	3-Apr-44
PF-52	Allentown	Froem	23-Mar-43	3-Jul-43	24-Mar-44
PF-53	Machias	Froem	8-May-43	22-Aug-43	29-Mar-44
PF-54	Sandusky	Froem	8-Jul-43	5-Oct-43	18-Apr-44
PF-55	Bath	Froem	23-Aug-43	14-Nov-43	1-Sep-44
PF-56	Covington	GSB-S	1-Mar-43	15-Jul-43	17-Oct-44
PF-57	Sheyboygan	GSB-S	17-Apr-43	31-Jul-43	14-Oct-44
PF-58	Abilene	GSB-S	6-May-43	21-Aug-43	28-Oct-44
PF-59	Beaufort	GSB-S	21-Jul-43	9-Oct-43	28-Aug-44
PF-60	Charlotte	GSB-S	5-Aug-43	30-Oct-43	9-Oct-44
PF-61	Manitowoc	GSB-D	26-Aug-43	30-Nov-43	5-Dec-44
PF-62	Gladwyne	GSB-D	14-Oct-43	7-Jan-44	21-Nov-44
PF-63	Moberly	GSB-D	3-Nov-43	26-Jan-44	11-Dec-44
PF-64	Knoxville	LDS		10-Jul-43	29-Apr-44
PF-65	Uniontown	LDS	21-Apr-43	7-Aug-43	6-Oct-44
PF-66	Reading	LDS	23-May-43	28-Aug-43	19-Aug-44
PF-67	Peoria	LDS	25-May-43	2-Oct-43	2-Jan-45
PF-68	Brunswick	LDS	16-Jul-43	6-Nov-43	3-Oct-44
PF-69	Davenport	LDS	7-Aug-43	8-Dec-43	15-Feb-45
PF-70	Evansville	LDS	28-Aug-43	27-Nov-43	4-Dec-44
PF-71	New Bedford	LDS	2-Oct-43	29-Dec-43	17-Jul-44
PF-72	Hallowell	Wal-Kais	1-Apr-43	14-Jul-43	15-Oct-43
PF-73	Hammond	Wal-Kais	3-Apr-43	26-Jul-43	4-Nov-43
PF-74	Hargood	Wal-Kais	30-Apr-43	7-Aug-43	24-Nov-43
PF-75	Hotham	Wal-Kais	7-Apr-43	17-Aug-43	6-Dec-43
PF-76	Halstead	Wal-Kais	11-May-43	27-Aug-43	18-Dec-43
PF-77	Hammam	Wal-Kais	23-Apr-43	6-Sep-43	31-Dec-43
PF-78	Harland	Wal-Kais	15-Jul-43	22-Aug-43	20-Jan-44
PF-79	Harman	Wal-Kais	27-Jul-43	14-Sep-43	25-Jan-44
PF-80	Harvey	Wal-Kais	7-Aug-43	21-Sep-43	5-Feb-44
PF-81	Holmes	Wal-Kais	17-Aug-43	27-Sep-43	12-Aug-44
PF-82	Hornby	Wal-Kais	28-Aug-43	27-Sep-43	31-Aug-44
PF-83	Hoste	Wal-Kais	7-Sep-43	6-Oct-43	31-Jul-44
PF-84	Howett	Wal-Kais	7-Sep-43	10-Oct-43	25-Jul-44
PF-85	Pilford	Wal-Kais	14-Sep-43	15-Oct-43	6-Jul-44
PF-86	Pasley	Wal-Kais	22-Sep-43	20-Oct-43	19-Feb-44
PF-87	Patton	Wal-Kais	28-Sep-43	25-Oct-43	18-Jul-44
PF-88	Peard	Wal-Kais	28-Sep-43	30-Oct-43	27-Jun-44
PF-89	Phillmore	Wal-Kais	7-Oct-43	5-Nov-43	16-Mar-44
PF-90	Popham	Wal-Kais	11-Oct-43	11-Nov-43	24-Jun-44
PF-91	Peyton	Wal-Kais	16-Oct-43	16-Nov-43	15-May-44

Number	Name	Shipyard	Laid Down	Launched	Commissioned
PF-92	Prowse	Wal-Kais	20-Oct-43	21-Nov-43	21-Jun-44
PF-93	Lorain	ASB-L	25-Oct-43	18-Mar-44	15-Jan-45
PF-94	Milledgeville	ASB-L	9-Nov-43	5-Apr-44	18-Jan-45
PF-99	Orlando	ASB-C	2-Aug-43	1-Dec-43	11-Nov-44
PF-100	Racine	ASB-C	14-Sep-43	15-Mar-44	22-Jan-45
PF-101	Greensboro	ASB-C	23-Sep-43	9-Mar-44	29-Jan-45
PF-102	Forsyth	ASB-C	6-Dec-43	20-May-44	11-Feb-45

APPENDIX C METHOD FOR DETERMINING NUMBER OF BUILDING WAYS

Determining the number of building ways at each yard that was used for the respective building programs was accomplished by comparing each ship's keel laying and launch dates. This method was used because sources listing the number of ways at a given shipyard during World War One and/or World War Two cannot be relied upon. This is because shipyards often built other ship types besides those in the scope of this report. For instance, during World War Two many yards built both destroyer escorts and landing craft. Furthermore, the construction priority that the Navy assigned to a given ship type varied during the war. To continue with the example above, in mid-1942, the Navy assigned the highest construction priority to landing craft. Shipyards that had been building destroyer escorts halted keel laying of additional destroyer escorts and switched to laying down landing craft as building ways became available. As a result, all building ways at many shipyards were not always available solely for destroyer escorts. Therefore, to determine the number of building ways used at each ship yard for the 1,345 ships in this report, the date of keel laying and date of launching are compared. This was accomplished by sorting all ships by their builder (see Table C-1) and plotting the two dates for each ship on a timeline (see Table C-2). This plot then reveals the maximum number of ships on the ways at any given time. This method assumes that a building way is occupied when a keel of a ship is laid down and not available for another keel until that ship is launched. The World War Two record of Bethlehem Steel Corp., San Pedro (BethSP) is listed below as an example. BethSP built 26 destroyers during the war. Only the data for the first six are shown in Table C-1 as a representative sample. The plot of this data in Table C-2 reveals the total number of ways in use at BethSP for a given date. As can be seen, the launch dates for DD-612 and DD 613 are the same as the keel laying dates for DD-544 and DD-545, respectively. Thus, it can be assumed that both are using the same building way and should only be counted once for those dates (see Table C-2). (This assumption is borne out by the cover photo of this report).

Table C-1: SAMPLE - Data used to determine number of building ways

Class	Number	Name	Laid Down	Launched
Bristol	DD-612	Kendrick	1-May-41	2-Apr-42
Bristol	DD-613	Laub	1-May-41	28-Apr-42
Bristol	DD-614	Mackenzie	29-May-41	27-Jun-42
Bristol	DD-615	McLanahan	29-May-41	2-Sep-42
Fletcher	DD-544	Boyd	2-Apr-42	29-Oct-42
Fletcher	DD-545	Bradford	28-Apr-42	12-Dec-42

Table C-2: SAMPLE – Plot of Data to determine number of building ways

Date	Total Ways In Use	DD-612	DD-613	DD-614	DD-615	DD-544	DD-545
1-May-41	2	1	1				
↓	↓	↓	↓	↓	↓	↓	↓
28-May-41	2	1	1				
29-May-41	4	1	1	1	1		
↓	↓	↓	↓	↓	↓	↓	↓
2-Apr-42	4	1	1	1	1	X	
3-Apr-42	4		1	1	1	1	
↓	↓	↓	↓	↓	↓	↓	↓
28-Apr-42	4		1	1	1	1	X
29-Apr-42	4			1	1	1	1

These plots can then be used to determine the fluctuation in the number of building ways in use for the war emergency building programs examined in this report. The effort taken to plot all 1,345 ships, by shipyard, was necessary because the number of building ways dedicated to the building programs is a significant limiting factor in the speed with which the ships could be built.

APPENDIX D REFERENCES AND SOURCES CONSULTED BY TOPIC

Reference 1: Navy-After-Next, *Contingency-Producible Corvette (CPC) Feasibility Study*, S&FAC Report No. 9050-03-C5.

Key Dates for Ships' History (Laid Down, Launched, Commissioned, etc.)

Dictionary of American Naval Fighting Ships (DANFS), James L. Mooney, editor. Washington : Naval Historical Center, Dept. of the Navy, G.P.O., Volumes I-VIII.

Shipyards

An Administrative History of the Bureau of Ships during World War II. First draft narrative prepared by the Historical Section of the Bureau of Ships. Washington: Bureau of Ships, 1952.

http://www.coltoncompany.com/shipbldg/usshipbldrs.htm

Destroyers

Alden, John D. *Flush Decks and Four Pipes*. Annapolis, Maryland: United States Naval Institute, 1965.

Friedman, Norman. *U.S. Destroyers : an illustrated design history*. Annapolis, Maryland: United States Naval Institute Press, 1982.

The National Association of Destroyer Veterans: http://www.destroyers.org

Raven, Alan. *Fletcher-Class Destroyers*. Annapolis, Maryland: United States Naval Institute Press, 1986.

Reilly, John C. Jr. *United States Navy Destroyers of World War II*, Poole, England: Blandford Press, 1983.

Sims, Phillip. Lightweight, High-speed, Modular Multi-mission Warships (1919-1945). Unpublished paper.

Sumrall, Robert F. *Sumner-Gearing-class destroyers : their design, weapons, and equipment*. Annapolis, Maryland: United States Naval Institute Press, 1995.

Williams, William J. "Josephus Daniels and the U.S. Navy's Shipbuilding Program During World War I." *The Journal of Military History*, 60 (January 1996) : 7-38.

Destroyer Escorts

Andrews, Lewis M. *Tempest, fire and foe : destroyer escorts in World War II and the men who manned them.* Charleston: Narwhal Press, 1999.

Destroyer Escort Sailors Association: http://desausa.org/index.htm

Franklin, Bruce Hampton. *The Buckley-Class Destroyer Escorts.* Annapolis, Maryland: United States Naval Institute Press, 1999.

Eagle Boats

Cianflone, Frank A. "The *Eagle* Boats of World War I." *U.S. Naval Institute Proceedings* 844 (June 1973) : 76-80.

Dictionary of American Naval Fighting Ships, Volume VI, Appendix II, *Eagle*-Class Patrol Craft (PE), page 744-747.

Friedman, Norman. *U.S. Small Combatants: An Illustrated Design History.* Annapolis, Maryland: United States Naval Institute Press, 1987.

Furer, J.A. "The 110-Foot Submarine Chasers and *Eagle* Boats" *U.S. Naval Institute Proceedings* 192 (1919) : 743-752.

History of The Bureau of Engineering Navy Department During the World War, Publication Number 5. Washington: Government Printing Office, 1922.

Hounshell, David A. "Ford *Eagle* Boats and Mass Production during World War I." *Military Enterprise and Technological Change: Perspectives on the American Experience*, Merritt Roe Smith, ed. Cambridge, Massachusetts: The MIT Press, 1985.

Lacey, Robert. *Ford: The Men and the Machine.* Boston: Little, Brown and Company, 1986.

"Professional Notes – Engineering" *U.S. Naval Institute Proceedings* 45 (February 1919) : 281-283.

Patrol Frigates

Lane, Frederick C., Ships for Victory; *A History of Shipbuilding Under the U.S. Maritime Commission in World War II.* Baltimore: The Johns Hopkins Press, 1951.

APPENDIX E   ENDNOTES

[1] Reilly, John C. Jr. *United States Navy Destroyers of World War II*. Poole, England: Blandford Press, 1983, p. 11

[2] *History of The Bureau of Engineering, Navy Department During the World War*, Publication Number 5. Washington: Government Printing Office, 1922, p. 24-25.

[3] *History of BuEng*, p. 24-25.

[4] United States Navy Historical Center, Photographic Section, Photo # NH 69499.

[5] *Dictionary of American Naval Fighting Ships (DANFS)*, James L. Mooney, Editor. Washington: United States Government Printing Office.

[6] Williams, William J. "Josephus Daniels and the U.S. Navy's Shipbuilding Program During World War I." *The Journal of Military History*, 60 (January 1996) : p. 24-26.

[7] Pratt Board, as quoted in Williams, p. 24.

[8] Friedman, *U.S. Destroyers*.

[9] As quoted in Williams, p. 25.

[10] As quoted in Williams, p. 26.

[11] United States Navy Historical Center, Photographic Section, Photo # NH 98154.

[12] *DANFS*

[13] Williams, p. 15.

[14] Williams, p. 15.

[15] United States Navy Historical Center, Photographic Section, Photo #NH 43019

[16] *History of BuEng*.

[17] Alden, p.1-3.

[18] United States Navy Historical Center, Photographic Section, Photo #NH 78706

[19] *History of BuEng*, p. 24-25.

[20] United States Navy Historical Center, Photographic Section, Photo #NH 68734

[21] United States Navy Historical Center, Photographic Section, Photo #19-N-6071

[22] Alden, p. 3-5.

[23] United States Navy Historical Center, Photographic Section, Photo #NH 43151

[24] United States Navy Historical Center, Photographic Section, Photo #NH 43163

[25] United States Navy Historical Center, Photographic Section, Photo #NH 43162

[26] United States Navy Historical Center, Photographic Section, Photo #NH 43167

[27] Alden, p. 3-5.

[28] Alden, p. 3.

[29] Alden, p. 3.

[30] Alden, p. 3.

[31] Alden, p. 3.

[32] Alden, p. 9.

[33] United States Navy Historical Center, Photographic Section, Photo #19-LC-38-L-3

[34] *History of BuEng*, p. 24-25.

[35] Hounshell, David A. "Ford Eagle Boats and Mass Production during World War I." *Military Enterprise and Technological Change: Perspectives on the American Experience*, Merritt Roe Smith, ed. Cambridge, Massachusetts: The MIT Press, 1985, p. 182.

[36] DANFS, p. 744-747.

[37] Cianflone, Frank A, "The *Eagle* Boats of World War I," *U.S. Naval Institute Proceedings* 844 (June 1973) : 76-80.

[38] *History of BuEng*, p. 38.

[39] Cianflone, 76-80.

[40] Friedman, p. 37.

[41] Goodall, Stanley, RCNC, "Technical Assessment of Eagle Boats" as quoted in "A's & A's", *Warship XII*, p. 58.
[42] "Professional Notes – Engineering" *U.S. Naval Institute Proceedings* 192 (February 1919) : 281.
[43] United States Navy Historical Center, Photographic Section, Photo
[44] United States Navy Historical Center, Photographic Section, Photo
[45] United States Navy Historical Center, Photographic Section, Photo
[46] United States Navy Historical Center, Photographic Section, Photo
[47] Cianflone, 76-80.
[48] United States Navy Historical Center, Photographic Section, Photo
[49] Cianflone, p. 78.
[50] Hounshell, p. 184.
[51] Lacey, Robert. *Ford: The Men and the Machine*. Boston: Little, Brown and Company, 1986, p. 156-157.
[52] Lacey, p. 157-158.
[53] Hounshell, p. 188.
[54] DANFS, p. 744-747.
[55] United States Navy Historical Center, Photographic Section, Photo
[56] United States Navy Historical Center, Photographic Section, Photo
[57] United States Navy Historical Center, Photographic Section, Photo
[58] United States Navy Historical Center, Photographic Section, Photo
[59] *Proceedings* (February 1919) : 281.
[60] *History of BuEng*, p. 40.
[61] Hounshell, p. 195.
[62] United States Navy Historical Center, Photographic Section, Photo
[63] Hounshell, p. 195-197.
[64] Hounshell, p. 193.
[65] United States Navy Historical Center, Photographic Section, Photo
[66] Hounshell, p. 199.
[67] *History of BuEng*, p. 40.
[68] Hounshell, p. 198-199.
[69] Hounshell, p. 198.
[70] Davis, Commander James H. USN (Ret.) Comments and Discussion on "The Eagle Boats of World War I," *U.S. Naval Institute Proceedings* 844 (November 1973) : 89.
[71] Hounshell, p. 200.
[72] Raven, Alan. *Fletcher-class destroyers*. Annapolis, Maryland: United States Naval Institute Press, 1986, p. 8.
[73] NavSource, Naval History, Photographic History of the U.S. Navy: www.navsource.org
[74] Raven, p. 8.
[75] Raven, p. 9.
[76] NavSource, Naval History, Photographic History of the U.S. Navy: www.navsource.org
[77] Sumrall, Robert F. *Sumner-Gearing-class destroyers: their design, weapons, and equipment*. Annapolis, Maryland: United States Naval Institute Press, 1995.
[78] Sumrall.
[79] Reilly.
[80] NavSource, Naval History, Photographic History of the U.S. Navy: www.navsource.org
[81] NavSource, Naval History, Photographic History of the U.S. Navy: www.navsource.org
[82] *An Administrative History of the Bureau of Ships during World War II*. First draft narrative prepared by the Historical Section of the Bureau of Ships. Bureau of Ships, 1952.
[83] United States Navy Historical Center, Photographic Section, Photo #19-N-30822
[84] *History of BuShips*.
[85] *History of BuShips*.

[86] *History of BuShips.*
[87] Raven, p. 10.
[88] Raven, p. 9.
[89] Raven, p. 9.
[90] Raven, p. 10.
[91] United States Navy Historical Center, Photographic Section, Photo#19-N-50812
[92] Raven, p. 9.
[93] Raven, p. 10.
[94] NavSource, Naval History, Photographic History of the U.S. Navy: www.navsource.org
[95] Franklin, *Buckley Class Destroyers.*
[96] Franklin, *Buckley Class Destroyers.*
[97] NavSource, Naval History, Photographic History of the U.S. Navy: www.navsource.org
[98] Franklin, *Buckley Class Destroyers*, p. 8.
[99] Friedman, *Small Combatants.*
[100] Lane, Frederick C., Ships for Victory; *A History of Shipbuilding Under the U.S. Maritime Commission in World War II.* Baltimore: The Johns Hopkins Press, 1951.
[101] DANFS.
[102] Friedman, *Small Combatants.*